THE RHETORIC OF PRAISE
PRAYER AND PERSUASION IN THE PSALMS

THE RHETORIC OF PRAISE
PRAYER AND PERSUASION IN THE PSALMS

Ryan J. Cook

GLOSSAHOUSE DISSERTATION SERIES 6
GDS 6

GlossaHouse
Wilmore, KY
www.glossahouse.com

THE RHETORIC OF PRAISE

PRAYER AND PERSUASION IN THE PSALMS

GlossaHouse, LLC
110 Callis Circle
Wilmore, KY 40309
www.GlossaHouse.com

Cook, Ryan J. (Ryan Joseph)
 The rhetoric of praise : prayer and persuasion in the Psalms / Ryan J. Cook. – Wilmore, KY: GlossaHouse, ©2018.

   xii, 283 pages 22.86 cm. — (GlossaHouse dissertation series; volume 6)
   A revision of the author's thesis (doctoral)–Asbury Theological Seminary, 2014.

Includes bibliographical references and indexes.

Library of Congress Control Number: 2018943318
ISBN 978-1942697541 (paperback)
ISBN 978-1942697589 (hardback)

   1.   Bible. Psalms—Socio-rhetorical criticism. 2. Praise of God. 3. Jewish way of life. I. Title. II. Series.

BS1430.52.C664 2018   232/.206

The English and Greek fonts used to create this work are available from www.linguistsoftware.com/lgku.htm

Interior design by Fredrick J. Long
Cover design by T. Michael W. Halcomb

For my parents
for instilling and modeling
a curiosity about and a love of Scripture.

For Ashley
who made it possible.

GlossaHouse
GlossaHouse Dissertations Series

Series Editors

Fredrick J. Long
T. Michael W. Halcomb
Carl S. Sweatman

Volume Editors

Fredrick J. Long
Shawn I. Craigmiles

GLOSSAHOUSE DISSERTATION SERIES

The goal of the GlossaHouse Dissertation Series to facilitate the creation and publication of innovative, affordable, and accessible scholarly resources, whether print or digital, that advance research in the areas of both ancient and modern texts and languages.

TABLE OF CONTENTS

INTRODUCTION

The Psalter has been chanted, sung, and prayed by Christians and Jews for millennia. Its theology and imagery have shaped the imagination and piety of generations of the faithful. One profound example of the Psalter's influence can be found in Augustine. In addition to authoring a massive commentary on the book, Augustine quoted from the Psalter over ten thousand times in his other writings.[1] He was saturated in its language and imagery, and the Psalter provided the theological framework in which he could reason and interpret his own circumstances. Augustine read the Psalms within the context of his own Greco-Roman and Christian heritage, which significantly impacted how he interpreted the book. Nevertheless, the question of how the Psalms function in a formative way was and is an important one and one of the foci of this study.

The Psalms grew out of the cultic and religious practices of ancient Israel and early Judaism. Its language, imagery, and theology would have been part of the primary means by which Israel understood the nature of God and their relationship to him. Yet, the question of how the Psalms achieve this function of shaping the belief and piety of ancient Israel is one that has not often been addressed directly. Scholars have been more engaged with questions of dating, compositional history, setting, form, syntax, lexicography, ANE context, and canoni-

---

[1] Augustine, *Expositions of the Psalms*, ed. John E. Rotelle, trans. Maria Boulding, 6 vols., (Hyde Park, NY: New City Press, 2000–2004). This is the largest of any of Augustine's works, on which he labored for thirty years. The figure of ten thousand citations from the Psalms in Augustine's other writing comes from, E. Bouvy, "Saint Augustin. Les Énarrationes sur les Psaumes," *Revue Augustinienne* 3 (1903): 418–36, esp. 419.

cal shaping of the Psalms. These are all important areas of study, but *additional* focus should be given as to how individual psalms functioned to shape the beliefs and practice of ancient Israel.

The ability of a text to shape and influence its audience is one of the primary domains of rhetorical theory, and this study will focus specifically on how praise psalms achieve this function. The goal of this study is to apply rhetorical theory to the interpretation of praise psalms.[2] The first two chapters of this work will provide the background, rationale, and theoretical framework to achieve this goal. In the first chapter, I will outline a selected history of the interpretation of praise psalms with an eye toward the methodologies used and gaps or problems in the study of these psalms. In the second chapter, I will propose and develop a rhetorical approach to the interpretation of the praise psalms. This chapter will deal with several fundamental questions, including: What is meant by "rhetorical criticism"? How is a rhetorical approach different from form criticism or from many literary methods (e.g., reader-response, post-structuralism, etc.)? Is not rhetoric a Western phenomenon? Is it justified to use rhetoric to analyze an ANE document? Since the psalms are both prayers and poetry, is rhetoric an appropriate method to analyze those types of discourse?

Once the theoretical foundation has been laid, I will then apply the rhetorical approach proposed to four praise psalms in four successive chapters (19, 103, 46, and 116). These psalms were chosen based on the form analysis of Claus Westermann.[3] Westermann has apportioned praise psalms in to two major groups: declarative and descriptive praise.

Declarative praise psalms fall into two sub-groups, individual and corporate. Descriptive praise psalms are always corporate. Additionally, he discusses one other major category of descriptive praise psalm,

---

[2] By "praise psalm," I intend psalms that have their primary purpose to give praise to the Deity. This would include the traditional form categories of hymn, individual and corporate thanksgiving song, the victory song, and many of the royal psalms. This understanding has been influenced by the work of Claus Westermann, *Praise and Lament in the* Psalms, trans. Keith Crim (Atlanta: John Knox, 1981).
[3] Ibid.

"creation psalms." Creation psalms are, he states, "the only group of Psalms of praise in the Psalter in which one motif developed into an independent Psalm…. This group shows that where one motif is expanded to form a whole Psalm there is no longer any rigid form."[4] Thus for this study I will analyze one psalm from each of these categories. The final chapter will summarize and synthesize the results of the study.

[4] Ibid., 139.

CHAPTER 1
Praise Psalms: History of Interpretation

1.1 INTRODUCTION

The Psalter has benefited from close scholarly engagement in the last two hundred years. The story of the history of its interpretation has been told often and need not be repeated in detail here.[1]

---

[1] For pre-Enlightenment interpretation see Susan Gillingham, *Psalms through the Centuries*, BBC (Oxford: Blackwell, 2008); William Holladay, *The Psalms through Three Thousand Years: Prayerbook of a Cloud of Witnesses* (Minneapolis: Fortress, 1993); Magne Saebø, ed. *Hebrew Bible/Old Testament: The History of Its Interpretation: Volume I: From the Beginning to the Middle Ages. Part I. Antiquity* (Göttingen: Vandenhoeck & Ruprecht, 1996); Magne Saebø, ed. *Hebrew Bible/Old Testament: The History of Its Interpretation: Volume I: From the Beginning to the Middle Ages. Part II: The Middle Ages* (Göttingen: Vandenhoeck & Ruprecht, 2000); Magne Saebø, ed. *Hebrew Bible/Old Testament: The History of Its Interpretation: Volume II: From the Renaissance to the Enlightenment* (Göttingen: Vandenhoeck & Ruprecht, 2008). For modern interpretation see M. Haller, "Ein Jahrzehnt Psalmenforschung," *ThR* 1 (1929): 377–402; J. A. Montgomery, "Recent Developments in the Study of the Psalms," *AThR* 16 (1934): 185–98; A. R. Johnson, "The Psalms," in *The Old Testament and Modern Study*, ed. H. H. Rowley (Oxford: Oxford, 1951), 162–209; J. J. Stamm, "Ein Vierteljahrhundert Psalmenforschung," *ThR* 26 (1955): 1–68; Sigmund Mowinckel, "Psalm Criticism between 1900 and 1935 (Ugarit and Psalm Exegesis)," *VT* 5 (1955): 13–33; A. S. Kapelrud, "Scandinavian Research in the Psalms after Mowinckel," *ASTI* 4 (1965): 148–62; D. J. A. Clines, "Psalm Research Since 1955: I. The Psalms and the Cult," *TynBul* 18 (1967): 103–26; D. J. A. Clines, "Psalm Research Since 1955: II. The Literary Genres," *TynBul* 20 (1969): 105–25; Erhard Gerstenberger, "Literatur zu den Psalmen," *VF* 17 (1972): 82–99; B. S. Childs, "Reflections on the Modern Study of the Psalms," in *Magnalia Dei: The Mighty Acts of God: Essays on the Bible and Archaeology: In Memoriam G. E. Wright,* ed. F. M. Cross (Garden City: Doubleday, 1976), 377–88; Ronald Clements, "Interpreting the Psalms," in *One Hundred Years of Old Testament Interpretation* (Philadelphia: Westminster, 1976), 76–98; Bernd Feininger, "A Decade of German Psalm-Criticism," *JSOT* 20 (1981): 91–103; Erhard Gerstenberger, "The Lyrical Literature," in *The Hebrew Bible and Its Modern Interpreters,*

The focus of this review of scholarship is on how praise psalms were interpreted since the time of Robert Lowth (1710–1787). The reason for this starting place is two-fold. One reason is simply that Lowth's work on Hebrew poetry is seminal.[2] In many ways, it is with his work that one enters into the modern area of Psalms interpretation. A second reason is that most surveys of Psalms research begin with the advent of form criticism. The result of this is that Psalm scholars who wrote pre-1900s receive far less attention than in other areas of the Hebrew Bible. This is unfortunate in view of the quality work done in that era. This survey is not intended to be exhaustive, but representative. The goal is to clarify the main problems and issues related to the interpretation of praise psalms. As one looks at the last two-hundred years as a whole, it becomes clear that the questions interpreters asked to a large extant determined the methods used, the answers obtained, and the problems encountered in the study of the Psalter.

1.2   PRAISE PSALMS IN THE LATE EIGHTEENTH CENTURY: ROBERT LOWTH

Bishop Robert Lowth towers above other eighteenth century scholars of Hebrew poetry when one considers the deep and pervasive influence his scholarship has had on the field.[3] His series of lectures published in 1753, *De Sacra Poesi Hebraeorum*, was translated into Eng-

---

ed. D. A. Knight and G. M. Tucker (Chico, CA: Scholars Press, 1985), 409–44; James Luther Mays, "Past, Present, and Prospect in Psalms Study," in *Old Testament Interpretation: Past, Present, and Future: Essays in Honor of Gene M. Tucker,* eds. James Luther Mays, David L. Petersen, and Kent Richards (Nashville: Abingdon, 1995), 147–56; David M. Howard, Jr. "Recent Trends in Psalm Study," in *The Face of Old Testament Studies: A Survey of Contemporary Approaches,* ed. David W. Baker and Bill T. Arnold (Grand Rapids: Baker, 1999), 329–68.

[2] Susan Gillingham, *Psalms through the Centuries,* 215–16; David Petersen and Kent Richards, *Interpreting Hebrew Poetry* (Minneapolis: Fortress, 1992), 21–22.

[3] His recognition of Hebrew poetry in the prophetic books was a major breakthrough. Also, his division of parallelism into the categories of synonymous, antithetical, and synthetic held the field virtually unchallenged until the publication of James Kugel's, *The Idea of Biblical Poetry: Parallelism and Its History* (New Haven, CT: Yale University Press, 1981).

lish and continually reprinted down through the twentieth century. During Lowth's career, British scholarship was primarily concerned with issues of lower criticism.[4] Into this scholarly climate, Lowth brought a sensitive and literary interpretation of poetry, which anticipated later scholarship.[5] He famously defined parallelism as the primary characteristic of Hebrew poetry. Additionally, he categorized parallel lines of poetry into the now-familiar groups of synthetic, synonymous, and antithetical.[6]

As he approached the Psalms, Lowth was interested in the historical question of how they were actually performed. In his Lecture XIX, he argues, "the sacred hymns were alternately sung by opposite choirs, and that the one choir usually performed the hymn itself, while the other sung a particular distich ... either in the nature of the proasm or epode of the Greeks."[7] He supports this argument through an analysis of Miraim's response to the song of Moses (Exod 15). Indeed, he avers that it was the antiphonal nature of Hebrew worship which led to the parallel form of poetry. He states, "Now if this were the ancient and primitive mode of chanting their hymns ... the proximate cause will be easily explained, why poems of this kind are disposed in equal stanzas, indeed in equal distichs ... and why these distichs should in some measure consist of versicles or parallelisms corresponding to each other."[8] By arguing that the form of parallelism developed because of its antiphonal use in the cult, Lowth was more akin to later cultic interpretations than to the strictly historical interpretations one finds in the eighteenth and nineteenth centuries.

While Lowth does not discuss psalms in form critical categories, he does discuss a number of praise psalms in his general discus-

---

[4] John Rogerson, "Lowth, Robert," in *Dictionary of Major Biblical Interpreters*, ed. Donald McKim (Downers Grove: IVP Academic, 2007), 680.

[5] Rogerson notes how this aspect of Lowth's work had a profound influence on later scholars like F. W. K. Umbreit and Hermann Gunkel ("Lowth," 681).

[6] Robert Lowth, *Lectures on the Sacred Poetry of the Hebrews*, trans. G. Gregory (Andover: Crocker & Brewster, 1829), 154–66.

[7] Lowth, *Lectures on the Sacred Poetry of the Hebrews*, 154.

[8] Ibid., 156.

sion of lyric poetry. This gives us a window into the kinds of questions he asked and methods he utilized in his interpretation of Israel's praise.

Lowth divided lyric poetry into three classes. The first class is characterized by "sweetness and elegance."[9] The second, or intermediate class, by a "union of sweetness and sublimity;"[10] and the third by the sublime.[11] One can discern by his class divisions that Lowth highlighted the affective and aesthetic aspects of the poetry. Additionally, in his discussion of each class of poetry, after analyzing appropriate psalms, he compared the psalms of that class with Greek and Latin poets, pointing out their similarities and differences. For example, in Lecture XXVI, Lowth compares Ps 91 and 81 with the poetry of Pindar.[12] One can only imagine the work he would have done had the comparative material from the ANE been available. In many ways, his concern for the affective domain of poetry and his comparison of it with the poetry of other cultures serves as kind of forerunner to Gunkel.

In sum, his approach to psalms, including praise psalms, focused on the literary quality of the text as it stands. He was concerned to demonstrate how the language and imagery of the poem serve to create aesthetic effects on the reader. This is a concern that fades into the background for nineteenth century interpreters. C. Bultmann summarizes Lowth's contribution well:

> Mit seinen Poetikvorlesungen hat Lowth den Weg dahin geebnet, Texte des Alten Testaments nicht als lehrhafte Offenbarung, sondern als poetischen Ausdruck einer religiösen Einsicht zu verstehen, die ihre menschlichen Autoren durch die ursprüngliche Bewunderung der Schöpfung, durch die geschichtliche Erfahrung innerhalb eines bestimmten Traditionsraumes oder durch die prophetische Inspiration gewinnen. Die ästhetische Kritik befreit insofern das Verständnis der Bibel von einer engen Orientierung an der Dogmatik.

---

[9] Ibid., 210.

[10] Ibid., 217.

[11] Ibid., 225.

[12] Lowth, *Lectures on the Sacred Poetry of the Hebrews*, 217–22.

Lowth opened the way for texts of the Old Testament to be understood not as didactic revelation, but as the poetic expression of a religious insight which their human authors gained through amazement when first confronted with the creation, and through historical experience in the context of a particular tradition or prophetic inspiration. To this extent he freed the interpretation of the Bible from a narrow concentration upon dogmatics.[13]

1.3 PRAISE PSALMS IN THE NINETEENTH AND EARLY TWENTIETH CENTURIES

Scholarship in the nineteenth century embraced historicist and critical approaches to the Psalter. Indeed, with the general concern for history and the source composition of most of the books of the Old Testament, the Psalter suffered from some neglect.[14] The main sources for Psalms study in this period are introductions and commentaries. It is evident that within a historical paradigm of scholarship, there was room for a variety of methods and approaches to the Psalter. This review will discuss four major figures who serve as representatives of different approaches: Wilhelm de Wette, Franz Delitzsch, Heinrich Ewald, and Charles and Emilie Briggs.[15]

---

[13] C. Bultmann, *Die biblische Urgeschichte in der Aufklärung* (Tübingen: Mohr Siebeck, 1999), 81. This reference was cited and translated by Rogerson, "Lowth, Robert," 681.

[14] Howard states, "For many years, the Book of Psalms occupied a marginal place in biblical studies. The major emphases in the nineteenth and early twentieth centuries were on historical-critical approaches (dominated by the search for hypothetical sources behind—and radical reconstructions of—the text), and on reconstructions of Israel's history and the history of its religion" ("Recent Trends in Psalms Study, 330).

[15] Some important works, which will not be discussed are, E. W. Hengstenberg, *Commentar über die Psalmen,* 3 vols. (Berlin: Ludwig Oehmigke, 1842–1849); Thomas Kelly Cheyne, *The Book of Psalms or the Praises of Israel: A New Translation with Commentary* (New York: Thomas Whittaker, 1895); W. T. Davison, *The Praises of Israel: An Introduction to the Study of Psalms* (London: Charles H. Kelly); Bernhard Duhm, *Die Psalmen,* KHAT 14 (Freiburg: J. C. B. Mohr, 1899); A.

1.3.1   WILHELM DE WETTE

De Wette is a towering figure among the many brilliant scholars of this era. His work arguably, "inaugurated a new era in critical Old Testament scholarship."[16] Even though he is not generally remembered as a Psalms scholar, his work on the Psalter set new directions in the study of the Psalms. He discussed his views on the Psalms in two major works: an Old Testament introduction and a commentary devoted to the book.[17]

In his Introduction, de Wette argued that there were four major types of psalms: individual laments, national laments, meditations on the success of evil in the world, and theodicy psalms.[18] In his commentary, he expanded the list of types to the following: hymns, national psalms concerned with the history of Israel, Zion and temple psalms, royal psalms, laments, and a general class of religious psalms.[19] Although he based his categories mainly on content, his work did in some ways foreshadow form criticism. His approach to exegesis was historicist. He attempted to discover the original setting for each psalm.[20] However, his honesty as a historian led him to be deeply skeptical about the possibility of finding it in many cases.[21] He was more certain about his ability to date the psalms generally, most of which he put in

---

F. Kirkpatrick, *The Book of Psalms* (Cambridge: Cambridge University Press, 1902); J. J. S. Perowne, *The Book of Psalms*, 7th ed., 2 vols. (Andover: Draper, 1890); J. Wellhausen, *The Book of Psalms*, trans. H. H. Furness et al., Polychrome Bible (London: Clarke, 1898).

[16] John Rogerson, *Old Testament Criticism in the Nineteenth Century: England and Germany* (Minneapolis: Fortress, 1984), 28.

[17] Wilhelm de Wette, *Beiträge zur Einleitung in das Alte Testament*, 2 vols. (Halle, 1806–1807); Wilhelm de Wette, *Commentar über die Psalmen* (Heidelberg, 1811, 1823, 1829).

[18] See the summary in Rogerson, *Old Testament Criticism*, 45.

[19] Ibid., 45.

[20] Ibid.

[21] Rogerson comments, "the Psalms commentary appears to be negative because time and again, de Wette argues for the uncertainty of the historical interpretations advanced in the contemporary scholarly literature" (Ibid., 46).

the post-exilic period.[22] De Wette did retain a concern to comment on the aesthetic features of the psalms as a whole.[23] His main contribution to the study of the Psalter is his division of psalm types and his attempt to historically place the psalm in a particular setting.

1.3.2 FRANZ DELITZSCH

Franz Delitzsch is remembered by some as a "significant opponent of the historical-critical method" who "did not...contribute materially to the critical method."[24] Nevertheless, his Psalms commentary was widely influential and used by both conservative and critical scholars.[25] He sought to combine the critical methods under development in his day with a conservative theological viewpoint. The result is a masterful two-volume commentary which retains value even today for its detailed discussion of the language and syntax of the Psalter.[26]

Delitzsch recognized the significant advances critical methodologies contributed to the study of the Psalter. He praised de Wette's commentary for "open[ing] up a new epoch so far as it has first of all set in order the hitherto existing chaos of psalms-exposition, and introduced into it taste and grammatical accuracy."[27] At the same time he criticized de Wette and other critical commentators because, "None of these expositors are truly in spiritual rapport with the spirit of the psalmists."[28] Of particular concern for Delitzsch is the lack of regard

---

[22] John Rogerson, "De Wette, Wilhelm Martin Leberecht," in *Dictionary of Major Biblical Interpreters*, 357.

[23] Although his poetic sensibilities were at times lacking, Rogerson states, "his detailed comments on individual verses often do not succeed in conveying the mood or aesthetic quality of the psalm under discussion" (*Old Testament Criticism*, 46).

[24] Ibid., 112.

[25] S. R. Driver recommends Delitzsch's commentary in his influential introduction (*An Introduction to the Literature of the Old Testament* [New York: Charles Scribner's Sons, 1892], 337).

[26] Franz Delitzsch, *Biblischer Commentar über den Psalter*, 2 vols. (Leipzig: Döbffling and Franke, 1843–49); ET Franz Delitzsch, *Biblical Commentary on the Psalms*, trans. Francis Bolton; 2 vols. (Edinburgh: T&T Clark, 1871).

[27] Ibid., 62.

[28] Ibid., 63.

for the psalm titles. He understood the titles as providing a normative context in which to understand a psalm. Yet, he recognized that psalms take on a life of their own after they are written. He states, "The expositor of the Psalms can place himself on the standpoint of the poet, or the standpoint of the Old Testament church, or the standpoint of the church of the present dispensation – a primary condition of exegetical progress is the keeping of these three standpoints distinct."[29] Thus, Delitzsch sees value in interpreting the psalm from multiple perspectives, each of which could contribute to the overall interpretation of the psalm. Perhaps the best way to understand his method of interpreting praise psalms is to analyze his treatment of a particular psalm.

In his discussion of Psalm 30, Delitzsch begins by comparing it with Ps 29. He states, "The summons to praise God which is addressed to the angels above in Ps. xxix, is directed in Ps. xxx to the pious here below."[30] This type of canonical concern, evident throughout Delitzsch's commentary, was unusual in his day, but serves as a kind of forerunner to some modern scholarly methods.

Delitzsch then turned to consider the historical context of the psalm. Taking his cue from the psalm title, Delitzsch argued that David wrote the psalm.[31] Based on the content of the psalm, he believed the situation which prompted the psalm was as follows:

> David ... having in the midst of the stability of his power come to the verge of the grave, and now being roused from all carnal security, as one who has been rescued, praises the Lord, whom he has made his refuge, and calls upon the pious to join with him in his song.[32]

Regarding the title of the psalm, Delitzsch argues that since the psalm does not contain any obvious references to a sanctuary, the "house" in question must have been the palace.[33] Thus, the full context would be

---

[29] Ibid., 64.
[30] Ibid., 374.
[31] Ibid., 375.
[32] Ibid., 375.
[33] Ibid., 375.

that David, who had been sick and so unable to take possession of his new house, wrote this psalm as a thanksgiving of recovery from illness and as a dedication of his new dwelling.[34]

Although it is easy to be a bit incredulous at Delitzsch's reconstruction of the specific context of the psalm, this type of work was common among scholars of his era. Most other scholars reconstructed contexts from the post-exilic period and their work was at least as speculative as Delitzsch's. Following his historical introduction, Delitzsch then comments on the psalm itself. He breaks the psalm up into 2–3 verse units. Throughout his commentary, he discusses lexical, syntactical, and theological issues.[35] The level of detail and careful attention to the grammar of the text is commendable. However, in his focus on the details, the overall picture, or flow, of the psalm can be lost.

The closest he comes to commenting on the psalm as a whole is where he notes the change of mood in the psalm beginning in v. 12. He states, "The designed result of such a speedy and radical change in his affliction, after it had had the salutary effect of humbling him, was the praise of Jahve; in order that my glory may sing Thy praises without ceasing. And the praise of Jahve forever is moreover his resolve, just as he vows, and at the same time carries it out, in this Psalm."[36]

1.3.3 HEINRICH EWALD

Heinrich Ewald has been described as "one of the greatest critical Old Testament scholars of all time."[37] He is remembered more for his work on the history of Israel and Hebrew grammar than for his work on the Psalms. Nevertheless, his Psalms commentary was highly influential in

---

[34] Ibid., 375.

[35] For example, in v. 5 Delitzsch wonders why the poet used the noun זכר instead of שם. His reasoning is that, "the history of redemption is ... an unfolding of the Name of Jave and at the same time a setting up of a monument, an establishment of a memorial" (*Biblical Commentary on the Psalms*, 377) He also discusses the *qere* and *katib* readings in v. 4; textual difficulties in v. 7; the use of the sequence of perfects in v. 8; the use of the imperfects in v. 9; the absence of the *waw* in v. 12; etc.... (377–79).

[36] Ibid., 379.

[37] Rogerson, *Old Testament Criticism in the Nineteenth Century*, 91.

his time and serves as a contemporary foil to the work of Delitzsch.[38]

Ewald argued that the poems in the Psalter were primarily designed for public temple worship, rather than as expressions of individual piety.[39] Even the few psalms that were originally written by an
individual, he states, "in the intention of the collector, certainly [the
psalm was] to be used by every individual in the community."[40] Ewald
understood the forensic nature of the psalms better than most interpreters of his day. Rather than divide psalms up by forms, or types, Ewald
grouped them by date of composition.[41] He divided them into the following categories: the psalms of David and his times;[42] psalms after
the division of the Davidic kingdom until its end;[43] songs of the Dis-
persion;[44] songs of the restored Jerusalem;[45] and last songs.[46] After describing in detail his method for assigning particular psalms to each
period, he confidently states, "On the age of a song in general a strong
doubt can now hardly exist."[47] Thus he was able to construct a historical context without recourse to the psalm titles.

In his commentary on Ps 30, the title of the psalm plays no role
in his interpretation. Indeed, the title is not mentioned at all in the
commentary proper.[48] Historically, he groups this psalm with "psalms

---

[38] His Psalms commentary is a part of a larger work, Heinrich Ewald, *Die
Dichter des Alten Bundes*, 2 vols. (Göttingen: Vandenhoeck und Ruprecht, 1835–
39); ET Heinrich Ewald, *Commentary on the Psalms*, 2 vols., trans. E. Johnson
(London: Williams and Norgate, 1880).

[39] Ewald, *Commentary on the Psalms*, 1.3.

[40] Ibid., 3.

[41] Ibid., 63.

[42] Ibid., 64.

[43] Ibid., 157.

[44] Ewald, *Commentary on the Psalms*, 2.1.

[45] Ibid., 155.

[46] Ibid., 267.

[47] Ewald, *Commentary on the Psalms*, 1.63.

[48] Ewald discusses the title in the introduction to the commentary as follows, "The words 'song of the dedication of a house,' which, according to p. 40,
were introduced at a late period into the superscription of Ps. xxx., probably do not
denote that this song was sung at the dedication of the house of David, as the LXX
take them, or that the psalm was to be sung at the dedication of any house; for it is

after the division of the Davidic Kingdom until its end."[49] Ewald understands the psalm as a "thanksgiving song."[50] He describes this type of psalm as follows,

> Thanksgiving songs, like this fine song, were presented by the individual,—whether he would thereby fulfil a definite vow or not,—in the temple, with rich sacrifices, music and dancing, and along with the public assistance of a great sacrificial assembly. Hence they are naturally the most attractive and perfect poetry.[51]

The terms he uses and the *Sitz im Leben* he describes are very close to later form critical interpretations. He argues that the specific situation of the poem was that the poet was mortally sick and then recovered. Having recovered, the psalmist looks back on his suffering and discovers that "he has come out of it rather stronger and more courageous, nearer to God, and with the resolve ever to praise him."[52] The poet also realizes that he had been too confident in his security, but now recognizes his dependence on Yhwh.[53] The poet now comes to the temple to give a sacrifice of thanksgiving and sings this poem as part of that celebration. Ewald's commentary on the whole is shorter than Delitzsch's and does not comment at the same level of detail; nevertheless, he had a grasp of the whole. Despite his claim in the introduction that the psalms are not primarily written out of individual experience, his interpretation of Ps 30 was based on reconstructing the experience of the psalmist.

---

self-intelligible that the Hebrews in such cases sung (Deut. xx. 5) merry popular songs, while this cheerful song has no reference at all to such an occasion; and, according to the whole spirit of the Psalter, so commonplace a popular reference would hardly have found place in the superscription. Probably this thank-song had been sung at the dedication of the second Temple (although the song itself may be older) and it was hence so named, because it was appointed to be sung at every yearly memorial celebration of this day" (*Commentary on the Psalms*, 1.55–56).

[49] Ibid., 187.
[50] Ibid., 188.
[51] Ibid., 191.
[52] Ibid., 188–89.
[53] Ibid., 189.

1.3.4   Charles Briggs with Emilie Briggs

Charles Briggs was arguably the most highly regarded American Old Testament scholar of his generation. His work on Psalms stands along-side his work on lexicography and biblical theology as one of his main contributions to the field.[54] His two volume Psalms commentary was the product of forty years of scholarly labor finally completed with the help of his daughter, Emilie.[55] Methodologically he shares the historical concerns of Ewald, Delitzsch, and de Wette. However, he differs with Ewald and Delitzsch in his dating of the psalms. Briggs dates most of the psalms to the Persian and Greek periods, however, a few psalms he assigns to the Davidic, early monarchic, and late monarchic periods.[56]

In his commentary on Ps 30, one is immediately struck by a couple of features in his translation of the poem: he does not include the psalm title and he omits vv. 3, 5, 7 which he regards as later glosses.[57] These verses were added, he avers, to "help adapt the psalm to more general use."[58] In his commentary, he discusses these verses separately. It is instructive to examine his rationale for omitting them. On v. 3, he states, "it mars the beauty of the parall[elism] as stated above. It adds a line to a Str[ophe] already complete without it. It interrupts the harmony of the thanksgiving and is doubtless a gloss."[59] Briggs here demonstrates a difference with the scholars discussed earlier. His goal is to interpret the earliest, original form of the poem, not the poem as it stands in the biblical text. Both Ewald and Delitzsch engage in textual criticism, but Briggs does so more boldly in that he reconstructs the original form of the poem based entirely on internal evidence.

On the historical context of the psalm, Briggs argues that the title cannot refer to either the first or the second temple. Rather, "it is a

---

[54] T. H. Olbricht, "Briggs, Charles," in *Dictionary of Major Biblical Interpreters*, 221.

[55] Ibid., 222.

[56] Charles Augustus Briggs and Emilie Grace Briggs, *The Book of Psalms: Vol. 1*, ICC (Edinburgh: T&T Clark, 1906), xc.

[57] Ibid., 257.

[58] Ibid., 257.

[59] Ibid., 259.

liturgical assignment to the Feast of Dedication instituted by Judas Maccabaeus 165 B.C. To commemorate the purification of the temple."[60]

Purged of its glosses, Briggs analyzes the psalm as comprised of four strophes, he summarizes the content of each strophe thus: 1) vv. 2–4: exalt Yhwh for raising up the nation from death; 2) vv. 6–8: contrast the momentary anger of Yhwh with the lifetime of his favor; 3) vv. 9–11: give the plea that had been made for deliverance; and 4) vv. 12–13: contrast of the previous mourning with the present gladness.[61] As Ewald, Briggs also categorizes this psalm as a thanksgiving poem. However, in contrast to Ewald, Briggs argues that it is not an individual thanksgiving. Rather, it is a national psalm of thanksgiving.[62] Briggs' interpretation of this as a corporate thanksgiving psalm embodies one side of a long-standing debate over the identity of the "I" in the psalms.[63]

His corporate interpretation affects his understanding of many of the images in the psalm. For example, in v. 4, he interprets the phrase, "out of Sheol you have brought me up," as referring to God bringing the nation out of a real corporate death (exile).[64] Sheol, then, is not the realm where individuals go when they die. Rather, it is "the abode of the nations destroyed by their conquerors."[65] Similarly, "those who go down to the pit" (v. 4), refer to conquered nations.[66] Additionally, on the question posed by the psalmist, "Can dust praise you?" (v. 10), Briggs states, "this is not an absolute denial of the possibility of the dead praising God. The nation is meant here and not the individual. It is the national ritual worship that would cease if the na-

---

[60] Ibid., 257.

[61] Ibid., 257.

[62] Ibid., 258.

[63] See e.g., Rudolph Smend, "Über das Ich der Psalmen," *ZAW* 18 (1888): 49–147; A. Rahlfs, *'Ani und 'Anau in den Psalmen* (Göttingen: Vandenhoeck & Ruprecht, 1892); Emile Balla. *Das Ich der Psalmen*, FRLANT 16 (Göttingen: Vandenhoeck & Ruprecht, 1912).

[64] Briggs and Briggs, *Book of Psalms*, vol. 1, 258.

[65] Ibid., 258.

[66] Ibid., 258.

tion perished."[67] Briggs closes his commentary on this psalm by arguing that the psalmist intended to lead the people to a place of worship
and thanksgiving for the nation's restoration. "The psalmist probably
had in mind that great prophecy of the Restoration of Zion, Je. 30–31,
and esp. 31:13."[68]

1.3.5   SUMMARY OF NINETEENTH AND EARLY TWENTIETH CENTURY INTERPRETATION

These four scholars well represent the depth, care, and scope of Psalms
study in this fecund era of Old Testament scholarship. While all these
scholars agree that a historical-critical perspective is necessary, they
all contribute unique methodologies and understandings. Indeed, many
of the main questions in psalms interpretation were raised in this era:
1) the date of the psalms; 2) the identity of the individual in the
psalms; 3) questions about the relationship between the psalm titles
and the psalms themselves; 4) the role of psalms in the worship of pre-
and post-exilic Israel; 5) the plight of the psalmists.[69] However, scholars became increasingly frustrated for two reasons: the content of individual psalms were so general that it was difficult to discern the exact
situation or date behind any give psalm; and Wellhausen's reconstruction of Israel's religious history did not provide a helpful framework
for interpreting the psalms.[70]

While there were some interesting comments on individual
psalms as complete poems (e.g., Ewald), most interpreters in this era
were concerned with the grammar/syntax of individual lines, or with
background issues, and neglected sustained reflection on each psalm as
a whole. New perspectives were needed to move the discussion forward.

---

[67] Ibid., 261.

[68] Ibid., 261.

[69] For example, in Ps 30, Ewald argued that the psalmist had experienced
sickness, while Briggs argued that that the plight was the exile of the nation.

[70] See Clements, "Interpreting the Psalms," 76.

1.4   PRAISE PSALMS IN THE EARLY TWENTIETH CENTURY

In the early twentieth century, two scholars stand apart as providing a new way forward in psalms interpretation, Hermann Gunkel and Sigmund Mowinckel.[71] In the decades leading up to Gunkel, psalms were understood as the product of an individual author giving expression to his/her deeply felt religious beliefs. It is this view that led many scholars to date most psalms late in the post-exilic period. It is not until this period, it was thought, that the kind of individual piety expressed in the Psalms could have been possible. There was some debate about this uneasy consensus. Some scholars argued that the "I" of the psalms was actually not the individual, but a communal identity.[72] Thus, it became easier to argue that some psalms were pre-exilic. Additionally, there were conservative scholars who held to a more traditional date of the psalms.[73] However, this was a minority position.

1.4.1   HERMANN GUNKEL

Hermann Gunkel's influence on Psalms scholarship has been so profound that a close analysis of both his method and his understanding of praise psalms is necessary.[74] Gunkel's method is well known and clearly outlined in the first chapter of his *Introduction*.[75] He argues that

---

[71] Clements, "Interpreting the Psalms," 76–95; Johnson, "The Psalms," in *Old Testament and Modern Study*, 162–207.

[72] Rudolph Smend, "Über das Ich der Psalmen," *ZAW* 18 (1888): 49–147.

[73] E.g., Kirkpatrick, *Psalms*.

[74] Johnson states, "In so far as the study of the Psalter has made any progress during the generation which has passed since the foundation of the Society for Old Testament Study, it is largely due to the influence of one man—Hermann Gunkel" ("The Psalms," 162).

[75] Hermann Gunkel, *Die Religion in Geschicht und Gegenwart*, vol. 1 (Tübingen: Mohr, 1913); ET Hermann Gunkel, *The Psalms: A Form-Critical Introduction*, trans. Thomas Homer (Philadelphia: Fortress, 1967); Hermann Gunkel and Joachim Begrich, *Einleitung in die Psalmen: Die Gattungen der religiösen Lyrik Israels* (Göttingen: Vandenhoeck & Ruprecht, 1933); ET, Hermann Gunkel and Joachim Begrich, *Introduction to the Psalms: The Genres of the Religious Lyric of Israel*, trans. James Nogalski (Atlanta: Mercer University Press, 1998), 1–21; see also, Hermann Gunkel, *Ausgewahlte Psalmen: Ubersetzt und Erklart*, 4th ed. (Göt-

in light of the many difficulties in understanding the Psalter and Hebrew poetry in general, "the particular task of psalm studies should be to rediscover the relationships between the individual songs that did not occur with the transmission, or that occurred only in part."[76] The most effective way to do this is to organize the psalms according to their genre, or form. Each genre grew out of a specific, real-life setting (*Sitz im Leben*).[77] The generic and formulaic language of the Psalter indicate that the original life setting of these poems was the cult.[78]

Gunkel then explored what the cult must have been like based on evidence sprinkled throughout the Hebrew Bible in order to understand the cultic context better.[79] In this discussion, he demonstrated that speech and action belong together in the cult.[80] Thus, the poems in the Psalter would have been tied to particular cultic actions. The most common actions of the cult relate directly to the most common genres in the Psalter: the celebration of sacrifice (hymn), the lamentation of the community (communal complaint), the act of confession and the thanksgiving offering of the pious individual (individual complaint and individual song of thanksgiving).[81]

Gunkel treated most praise psalms under the heading of "hymns."[82] He argued that there are twenty-five true hymns in the Psalter.[83] Additionally, related to the hymn form, are the songs of Zion,[84] the enthronement psalms,[85] and the thanksgiving psalms of Isra-

---

tingen: Vandenhoeck & Ruprecht, 1917); Hermann Gunkel, "Psalmen," in *Die Religion in Geschichte und Gegenwart: Handwörterbuch in gemeinverständlicher Darstellung*, vol. 4, ed. Friedrich Schiele und Leopold Richarnad (Tübingen: J. C. B. Mohr, 1913), 1927–49.

[76] Gunkel and Begrich, *Introduction to the Psalms*, 3.

[77] Ibid., 7.

[78] Ibid., 7.

[79] Ibid., 8–15.

[80] Ibid., 11.

[81] Ibid., 19.

[82] Ibid., 22–65.

[83] Pss 8; 19; 29; 33; 65; 67; 68; 96; 98; 100; 103; 104; 105; 111; 113; 114; 117; 135; 136; 145; 146; 147; 148; 149; 150.

[84] Pss 46; 48; 76; 84; 87; 122.

el.[86] Hymnic elements are also found in numerous other psalms spanning every genre.[87] In regards to form, the hymn is comprised of the following elements: 1) an introduction, comprised of a call to praise; 2) a body, giving the reasons for praise; 3) and a conclusion, a renewed summons to praise.[88] The other genres of praise psalms follow this same pattern with some variation.[89] Additionally, Gunkel painstakingly detailed the various linguistic forms in which each of the three elements of the hymn could appear.[90] This treatment of the linguistic forms has the effect of demonstrating that while hymns do have a number of features in common, there was also a diversity of ways in which a hymn form could be realized.

Following his foundational discussion of the hymn form, Gunkel turned to analyze the original *Sitz im Leben* of the hymn. Through arguments drawn from the Hebrew Bible as well as from comparative ANE texts, Gunkel demonstrated that the hymn form is closely connected to cultic sacrifice and to festivals.[91] Thus, Gunkel suggested that we "briefly visualize an Israelite festival in order to understand the festival hymn."[92] He imaginatively described how an average Israelite would have experienced the festival. Hymns, he averred, were sung at various occasions during the festival: in the early morning; at the entry of the community through the gates into the sanctuary; when gifts were presented; and especially at the time of the sacrifice.[93] Hymns were also sung during the highpoint of the festival, the procession

---

[85] Pss 47; 93; 97; 99.

[86] Pss 124; 129.

[87] Gunkel and Begrich, *Introduction to the Psalms*, 22.

[88] Ibid., 23–41.

[89] E.g., the songs of Zion lack an introduction; the enthronement psalms often begin with the phrase יהוה מלך.

[90] E.g., the body of a hymn could praise Yhwh in nominal statements, through verbs in the perfect or imperfect celebrating his past actions, or in participles describing his regular and repeated actions (Gunkel and Begrich, *Introduction to the Psalms*, 23–41).

[91] Ibid., 41.

[92] Ibid., 41.

[93] Ibid., 42.

through the sanctuary, which also involved dancing.[94] Hymn singing during festivals, Gunkel argued, was performed by individuals, sanctuary choirs, and the congregation. The instrument playing, singing, and dancing caused the festivals to be noisy affairs, comparable to the din of battle.[95]

Having painted a vivid picture of the festivals, Gunkel warns, "it is not advisable to speak of individual worship occasions into which one would have sung the hymn, with the exception of very specific cases that are particularly clear."[96] There are two reasons for this. The Psalms use generic language, which makes it difficult to place an individual praise psalms at a specific point in a festival. For example, while he argues that the primary context for the hymn was the sacrifice, he admits that there are very few references to the sacrifice in any of the hymns, so it is difficult to know exactly which hymns would have been used in this way.[97] A second reason is that many of the hymns in the Psalter do not have a cultic origin. Later poets utilized the hymn form for their "purely private expression of personal piety and pious artistic exercise."[98]

Gunkel then considers the religion, or view of God, portrayed in the hymns. This is a critical element because "Israel primarily expressed the spiritual content of its festivals using this form of the hymn."[99] That is, the hymns can give us a window into the beliefs of ancient Israel. A comparison of Babylonian and Egyptian with Israelite hymns yields insight. Babylonian and Egyptian hymns almost always have a petition attached to the song of praise. Thus, it seems the hymn was utilized to make the gods look favorably on the petitioner. In contrast, the hymns in the Psalter almost never have a petition attached. Gunkel concludes from this, "in contrast to the foreign religions, one finds a *disinterested piety* here. Israel's hymns meet the deepest and

---

[94] Ibid., 43.
[95] Ibid., 45.
[96] Ibid., 47.
[97] Ibid., 42.
[98] Ibid., 46.
[99] Ibid., 47.

most honorable need of all true religion, to worship in the dust that which is beyond us."[100] Additionally, the Babylonian and Egyptian hymns, "for the most part contain lifeless divine predicates strung together."[101] Israel also has its share of dull praise psalms, but "alongside these, there are more than a few that tower above the majority of the ancient oriental poetry, in that they are distinguished by their inner, personal life and especially by their majestic power."[102] The reason Gunkel can argue this is because he views most of the praise psalms as late compositions when there was a focus on the inner spiritual life of the individual.

Gunkel further remarked that the hymns present a remarkably unified portrait of God. He sketched this portrait in some detail, drawing from all the praise psalms to create a theological mosaic of Israel's deity.[103] Some of the most common theological assertions in the praise psalms are as follows: Yhwh's rule over the earth from heaven;[104] his eternality, majesty, and incomparability;[105] his appearance in storm and weather, fire and earthquake, thunder and lightning;[106] his rule over humanity, including his acts in history;[107] and his role as Creator.[108]

Finally, some hymns not only speak about Yhwh's past (his acts in history) and his present (his attributes), but also about his future.[109] Under the influence of the prophets, several hymns look forward to a future day when all nations will worship the God of Israel and he will reign over all.[110] Included among these eschatological hymns are Pss 68; 98; 149; 9:6–13, 16, 17; 75:2, 5–11; the Zion songs,

---

[100] Ibid., 48.
[101] Ibid., 48.
[102] Ibid., 48.
[103] Ibid., 48–54.
[104] Ibid., 50.
[105] Ibid., 49.
[106] Ibid., 51.
[107] Ibid., 52.
[108] Ibid., 53.
[109] Ibid., 54.
[110] Ibid., 55.

and the Enthronement songs.[111]

In summary, Gunkel did not radically alter the consensus in Psalms scholarship regarding the date of the most psalms. Like other scholars of his era, he dated most of the psalms to the late post-exilic period based on content. What he did achieve was that he relegated the question of the date of the psalms from a primary one to a secondary one. He provided a new perspective and a new set of questions to the study of the Psalter. He demonstrated that despite the diversity of poems in the Psalter, most of them can be related to a few major genres. These genres in turn give evidence of an original *Sitz im Leben*.

Gunkel's method of classifying psalms by genre/type proved grist for the scholarly mill. Scholars could debate how to classify various psalms and could even discover new types. Scholars could also busy themselves with discerning a clearer picture of a *Sitz im Leben*. Instead of trying to figure out the exact historical circumstance that led to the creation of a psalm, scholars could identify the general life-setting of a particular type of psalm.

Gunkel also pioneered studying psalms in relation to other ANE hymns and prayers. Both his form-criticism and his comparative analysis come together in the work of his student, Sigmund Mowinckel.

1.4.2 SIGMUND MOWINCKEL

The Norwegian scholar, Sigmund Mowinckel built on the form critical foundation laid by Gunkel and combined it with anthropological insights drawn from Vilhelm Grønbech.[112] Mowinckel discussed praise psalms under the form-categories of hymns, public thanksgiving psalms, and private thanksgiving psalms.[113] His understanding of the

---

[111] Ibid., 56–57.

[112] Mowinckel wrote prolifically on the Psalms, but for our purposes the focus will be on his most mature work: Sigmund Mowinckel, *Offersang og sangoffer* (Oslo: Aschehoug, 1951); ET, Sigmund Mowinckel, *The Psalms in Israel's Worship*, 2 vols., trans. D. R. Ap-Thomas (Grand Rapids: Eerdmans, 2004). For his earlier work, see Sigmund Mowinckel, *Psalmenstudien I–VI*, SNVAO (Kristiania: Dybwad, 1921–1924).

[113] Mowinckel, *Psalms in Israel's Worship*, I.39.

forms themselves is very similar to Gunkel's and need not be repeated here. Mowinckel made a true advance upon Gunkel in two related ways. First, he argued persuasively that the poems in the Psalter are not later, individualized poems based on a genre which originated in the cult. Rather, in the Psalter, we have the cultic compositions themselves.[114] Secondly, Mowinckel provided a dynamic understanding of the cult and described the function of praise psalms within it.[115]

Under the influence of Grønbech, Mowinckel believed that the cult not only provided regulated access between the deity and the community, but it also had a positive function. He states,

> In the cult something happens.... What the congregation wants to achieve through the cult, and what the 'power' from God is to create, is *life*—in the most comprehensive sense of the word, from the fundamental material need: rain, sun, fertility, and the continuation of the race, the strength and victory of the tribe, and so on, up to the spiritual, religious and ethical values that are the life-blood of society—life for everything that belongs to its 'world'.[116]

So, the praise psalms do not just celebrate what Yhwh has done. Through the congregation singing them, these psalms "increase his [Yhwh's] power and renown."[117] That is, the praise psalms give power to Yhwh in order to secure blessing for the congregation. It is this cultic function that makes stereotyped language of praise psalms so important. They are the words that, when combined with cultic action, obtain blessing for the people. Because the psalms belong to the cult,

---

[114] Mowinckel does believe there are a dozen non-cultic psalms, which he labels, "The Learned Psalmography" (*Psalms in Israel's Worship*, II.104–25).

[115] For an overview of Mowinckel's view of the cult and scholarly reactions to it, see D. J. Clines, "Psalm Research since 1955: I. The Psalms and the Cult," *TynBul* 18 (1967): 103–26. For a recent, positive re-evaluation of Mowinckel, see J. J. M. Roberts, "Mowinckel's Enthronement Festival: A Review," in *The Book of Psalms: Composition and Reception*, VTSup 99, ed. Peter Flint and Patrick Miller (Leiden: Brill, 2005), 97–115.

[116] Mowinckel, *Psalms in Israel's Worship*, I.17.

[117] Ibid., 88.

the language becomes freighted. Mowinckel explains,

> Through all the various experiences and emotions associated
> with them [praise psalms] through generations, they may also
> be able somehow to store the religious experience of the gener-
> ations and become symbols and 'ideograms', 'words saturated
> with experience,' as V. Grønbech calls them, words which only
> need to be mentioned to release a series of associations, of
> thoughts, experiences, and emotions. The words convey more
> than they seemingly contain.[118]

Thus, for Mowinckel the praise psalms not only praise, but they also
contain within them a power to bring about blessing.

A helpful way to clarify the different approaches Gunkel and
Mowinckel take to the praise psalms is to examine how each of them
treat the Enthronement psalms (Pss 47, 93, 96, 97, 98, 99). Mowinckel
utilized these psalms as the cornerstone for his New Year's Festival
hypothesis. He argued that there was a New Year's feast in Israel, similar to the Babylonian *Akitu* festival. The content and significance of
this festival for Mowinckel is well summarized by Johnson:

> [At this festival] Yahweh makes all things new, repeating His
> original triumph over the primeval chaos and His work in crea-
> tion. All this is expressed in a ritual drama in which He tri-
> umphs over the kings and nations of the earth, who are the al-
> lies of the primeval chaos, and in a procession at which the Ark
> as the symbol of His presence is borne in triumph to the sanc-
> tuary, where He is acclaimed afresh as the proven, universal
> King. In this way He vindicates the faith of his chosen people,
> sees that, as we might say, they are put right once again, and,
> renewing his covenant with them and with the house of David
> as represented by their reigning king, shows Himself prepared
> to restore their fortunes for the coming year.[119]

---

[118] Ibid., 15.
[119] Johnson, "Psalms," 191.

These psalms celebrate the fact that Yhwh has become king. For Mowinckel this should not be understood as a reference to a historical event, or a reference to a future time, but rather to the practice that Yhwh continually becomes king. Yhwh's kingship is tied to his work of creation, both of which are annually renewed at this festival.[120] In this festival past, present, and future all meld into one reality.[121] The original referent of the "day of the Lord" is the yearly day when Yhwh was enthroned at the festival.[122] The universal language of Yhwh reigning over other nations, even the world, is typical for this type of festival and not to be understood literally. This festival was a development from the Canaanite festival to the deity in Jerusalem, El Elyon.[123] Israel adapted this festival and altered it in two ways. First, the nations took the place of chaos in the creation myth. In Canaanite belief, El Elyon was crowned king because he defeated chaos. In Israel, Yhwh is king because he has defeated the nations.[124] Secondly, Israel added a historical perspective to the mythical. Israel had real, historical experiences with Yhwh and these shaped Israel's religious practices. Mowinckel states, "the cult has been made into history and history has been drawn into the cult."[125] In sum, Mowinckel's understanding of the cult decisively shapes how one understands the language and imagery of these, and many other, psalms.

Gunkel, in his later writing, agreed with Mowinckel about the original *Sitz im Leben* of the enthronement psalms. He accepts that there was an early, Israelite enthronement festival parallel to the Babylonian festival. However, it is not these psalms that we have in the Psalter. Rather, the enthronement psalms in the Psalter came under the influence of Deutero-Isaiah and should be understood eschatologically. Thus, the imagery of Yhwh defeating the nations and ruling over the

---

[120] Mowinckel, *Psalms in Israel's Worship*, I.108.

[121] Ibid., 113.

[122] Ibid., 116.

[123] Ibid., 114.

[124] Ibid., 151–54.

[125] Ibid., 139.

world are to be understood literally as an event in the future.[126]

Mowinckel's understanding of the Psalter had a pervasive influence on the scholarly world. Although many scholars argued against the specific festival argued for by Mowinckel, they usually did so by arguing for a different festal context.[127] Study of the Psalter became a window into the ancient cult of Israel. The praise psalms were understood within this dynamic view of the cult, which profoundly affected how they were interpreted.

In sum, both Gunkel and Mowinckel used the Psalms in order to answer specific questions they put to the text. Gunkel was primarily interested in delineating the original forms of the psalms in order to posit an original setting for them. Mowinckel was primarily interested in reconstructing the original cultic festival setting from the Psalms. With both scholars, a focus on the interpretation of a psalm as an individual poem/prayer can be lost.

1.5   PRAISE PSALMS IN THE LATTER TWENTIETH CENTURY

1.5.1   CLAUS WESTERMANN

In an era dominated by cultic approaches to the Psalter, Westermann provided a thoughtful critique and a fresh approach to the form-critical problems of the Psalter.[128] Westermann held divergent views regarding the setting, form, and function of the praise psalms.[129]

Regarding setting, Westermann believed that the cult-

---

[126] Gunkel and Begrich, *Introduction to the Psalms*, 66–81.

[127] E.g., Artur Weiser, *The Psalms*, OTL (Philadelphia: Westminster, 1962); Kraus, *Psalms 1–59*; John Eaton, *Kingship and the Psalms*, SBT 32 (London: SCM Press, 1976); A. R. Johnson, "The Role of the King in the Jerusalem Cultus," in *The Labyrinth: Further Studies in the Relation between Myth and Ritual in the Ancient World*, ed. S. H. Hooke (New York: Macmillan, 1935), 71–111.

[128] Claus Westermann, *Lob und Klage in den Psalmen* (Göttingen: Vandenhoeck & Ruprecht, 1977); ET, Claus Westermann, *Praise and Lament in the Psalms*, trans. Richard Soulen (Atlanta: John Knox, 1981).

[129] For a helpful discussion of Westermann in the context of German scholarship, see Bernd Feininger, "A Decade of German Psalm-Criticism," *JSOT* 20 (1981): 91–103.

functional approach was actually a step backward in Psalms interpretation. Scholars busied themselves with reconstructing the cultic background of the text to the detriment of a better understanding of the genres of the Psalms.[130] He laments, "[it] seems to me, in spite of all the effort that has been expended on it in the last thirty years, to have produced meager results for the understanding of individual Psalms."[131] In contrast, Westermann argues that there was "no absolute, timeless entity called 'cult,' but that worship in Israel ... developed gradually in all its various relationships ... and that therefore the categories of the Psalms can be seen only in connection with this history."[132] Thus, for Westermann, the proper *Sitz im Leben* for praise psalms was not the cult, but the historical relationship between God and Israel. He explains, "The *Sitz-im-Leben* of the hymn is: the experience of God's intervention in history. God has acted; he has helped his people. Now praise *must* be sung to him."[133] This relational/theological context takes seriously the dialogical nature of the Psalms. For Westermann, the Psalter is interpreted best as communication between God and the Psalmist not as a cultic ritual.

Westermann simplified the form-critical categories from Gunkel to the two major categories of praise and lament. He noticed that functionally there was no true difference between the hymns and thanksgiving songs.[134] Thus, it is best to think of them under the same category. Westermann then divides praise psalms into two subcategories: declarative and descriptive praise.[135] Declarative praise is the original form of praise psalms. The most ancient form is the declarative psalms of praise of the people.[136] There are only two psalms in this category (Pss 124 and 129). These psalms are best understood

---

[130] Westermann, *Praise and Lament*, 20–21.
[131] Ibid., 21.
[132] Ibid., 21.
[133] Ibid., 22.
[134] Ibid., 18.
[135] Which could be either corporate or individual (ibid., 81–139).
[136] Ibid., 81–90.

as a spontaneous response to an act of God, which had just occurred.[137] This form, "consisted of a simple declarative sentence, to which may be added the shout of praise, '*bārūk yahweh!* '"[138] From this form grew the individual declarative praise psalms, which retained the basic form. However, these individual praise psalms were always intended to be uttered publicly. There is no such thing as a private praise.[139]

The descriptive praise psalms also grew out of declarative praise psalms and have their origin in the acts of God. For example, Ps 113 praises God for his "loyal love" (הסד), which is "a way in which God is related in a community."[140] In other words, God's attributes celebrated in these psalms can only be understood within the context of God's covenantal history with Israel. Thus, the primary context in which to understand these psalms remains the history of God's relationship with his people, not a repeated cultic action.[141]

In many ways, Westermann's work is a return to the path outlined by Gunkel. Where he differs from Gunkel is in his heavy emphasis on the relational context of the psalms. The real *Sitz im Leben* of the Psalms is "an occurrence from man to God."[142] Indeed, "Praise of God ... is a mode of existence, not something which may or may not be present in life."[143] Westermann's social and relational approach to the Psalter set a trajectory for Psalms interpretation that has been followed by many.

1.5.2   Walter Brueggemann

Brueggemann has written prolifically on the Psalms and has raised new questions and perspectives for the interpretation of praise psalms in particular.[144] Throughout Brueggemann's writing, the form and

---

[137] Ibid., 83, 88.

[138] Ibid., 84.

[139] Ibid., 105.

[140] Ibid., 121.

[141] Westermann's anti-cultic stance leads him to interpret the enthronement psalms eschatologically, as Gunkel (*Praise and Lament,* 142–51).

[142] Ibid., 154.

[143] Ibid., 159.

[144] See Walter Brueggemann, "The Psalms and the Life of Faith: A Suggest-

function of Psalms are closely related to the point where it becomes difficult to separate the two.[145] We will first discuss Brueggmann's classification of Psalms and then his understanding of the cult in relation to his categories.

Building on the work of Paul Riceour, Brueggemann functionally classifies psalms into three categories: orientation, disorientation, and new orientation. He agrees with Westermann's form-critical distinction between declarative and descriptive praise psalms. However, while Westermann believed these two forms had a similar function, Brueggemann argued that their functions were quite different. Descriptive praise psalms, he argued, were psalms of orientation. Their function was to celebrate and to maintain the status quo.[146] These psalms are "unimaginative" and "not the most interesting."[147] They are used by those in positions of power (i.e., the temple and royal elite) to maintain their standing. Thus, these psalms are often in need of "the radical criticism of suspicion."[148] In contrast, the declarative praise psalms he classifies as psalms of new orientation. These psalms speak of newness and surprise.[149] They celebrate a new work that Yahweh has wrought and can "scarcely be overinterpreted."[150] Thus, "the psalms

---

ed Typology of Function." *JSOT* 17 (1980): 3–32. This article has been recently reprinted in *Soundings in the Theology of the Psalms: Perspectives and Methods in Contemporary Scholarship*, ed. Rolf Jacobson (Minneapolis: Fortress, 2011): 1–26. Some of Brueggemann's other writings on the Psalms are: *The Message of the Psalms* (Minneapolis: Fortress, 1985); "From Hurt to Joy, from Death to Life," *Int* 28 (1974): 3–19; *Abiding Astonishment: Psalms, Modernity, and the Making of History* (Louisville: Westminster, 1991); *Israel's Praise: Doxology against Idolatry and Ideology* (Philadelphia: Fortress, 1988); *The Psalms and the Life of Faith* (Minneapolis: Fortress, 1995).

[145] In a thoughtful analysis of Brueggemann's work, Harry Nasuti comments, "For Brueggemann, setting has largely become synonymous with function" (*Defining the Sacred Songs: Genre, Tradition and the Post-Critical Interpretation of the Psalms*, JSOTSup 218 [Sheffield: Sheffield Academic, 1999], 48).

[146] Brueggemann, "Psalm and the Life of Faith," 7.

[147] Ibid., 6–7.

[148] Ibid., 11.

[149] Ibid., 9.

[150] Ibid., 15.

Westermann labels as descriptive and declarative stand at the far moments of orientation and reorientation and should not be grouped together in terms of function."[151]

Regarding the cultic setting of the Psalms, Brueggemann builds on the dynamic understanding of the cult proposed by Mowinckel.[152] He argues that the praise sung by the cult has both expressive and creative functions.[153] That is, praise psalms give voice to praise, but they also go beyond that and have a world-making function.[154] For Brueggemann, "*every* psalm creates a world with a particular view of God and social reality."[155] Brueggemann looks to the sociological insights of Peter Berger and Thomas Luckmann[156] for support of his contention that Israel's praise functions in this way. This world-making function is directly tied to his categories of orientation, disorientation, and new orientation. There are different worlds created by each of these types of psalms, which serve different communities. For example, the psalms of orientation create a stable world where the structures of power are supported and sustained and Yhwh is envisioned as ruling over and through all. However, the psalms of disorientation and new orientation destabilize the status quo and call for God to do a new work on behalf of the powerless and marginalized. Thus, not only do these psalms create different worlds, but different social groups would utilize different types of psalms.[157] For example, it is difficult to see the established elite using a psalm which would undercut the status quo.

Brueggemann's program for understanding praise psalms is open to criticism on a number of fronts.[158] However, he is correct to

---

[151] Ibid., 10.

[152] Brueggemann, *Israel's Praise*, 4–6. For a helpful review and critique see Nasuti, *Defining the Sacred Songs*, 82–107.

[153] Brueggemann, *Israel's Praise*, 6–28.

[154] Ibid., 12.

[155] Nasuti, *Defining the Sacred Songs*, 89.

[156] Peter Berger and Thomas Luckman, *The Social Construction of Knowledge* (Garden City, NY: Doubleday, 1966).

[157] Nasuti, *Defining the Sacred Songs*, 93.

[158] See the incisive critiques in Nasuti, *Defining the Sacred Songs*, 93–107.

raise the question of how praise functions sociologically. He rightly states, "the Psalms can only be understood and used rightly if we attend to their social interaction and function, not only in their origin but also in their repeated use."[159] Previous scholarship had focused on the form, theology, and function of praise psalms, but they had largely neglected the social implications of praise. Brueggemann's contention that "praise ... affects the shape and character of human life and human community"[160] is an important one worthy of careful reflection.

1.5.3   ERHARD GERSTENBERGER

Erhard Gerstenberger is a traditional form-critic. He advances the conversation not in his delineation of the various forms of the Psalms, in which he closely follows Gunkel, but in his sophisticated understanding of the setting of the Psalms.[161] Gerstenberger's understanding of the cult is similar to Mowinckel's, however, he differs from Mowinckel in arguing that the public cult is not the foundational setting in which many of the psalm forms were developed[162] Rather, he states, "The theory that the royal cult came first in the ancient Near East, only to be democratized much later, is definitely incorrect...The evidence indicates that even the most royalist countries of the ancient Near East had religious rituals that served the daily needs of common people within their respective small social groups."[163] Thus, the small family and clan groups are the context in which religious lyrics originated. It is from these groups that the large state cults received the forms.

Furthermore, the psalms as they stand in the Psalter need to be understood in the context of Israel's complicated history. Israel grew

---

[159] Brueggemann, *Israel's Praise*, ix.

[160] Ibid., 3.

[161] Erhard Gerstenberger, *Der bittende Mensch: Bittritual und Klagelied des Einzelnen im Alten Testament*, WMANT 51 (Neukirchen: Neukirchener Verlag, 1980); idem, "Lyrical Literature," 409–44; idem, "Psalms," in *Old Testament Form Criticism*, TUMSR 2, ed. J. H. Hayes (San Antonio: Trinity University Press, 1974), 179–233; idem, *Psalms: Part 1*, FOTL 14 (Grand Rapids: Eerdmans, 1988).

[162] Gerstenberger, *Psalms: Part 1*, 5–6.

[163] Ibid., 7.

from a fusion of nomadic Israelites with sedentary Canaanites. As a nation, it went through the stages from tribalism to centralized government, then from conquered exiles to re-settled imperil subjects. Each stage influenced the context and content of the Psalms.[164] Thus, Gerstenberger proposes that two social settings be distinguished in Psalms interpretation. The first is the foundational setting of the "small, organic group of family, neighborhood, or community."[165] The second is the large, state-run cult and administration.[166] The psalms need to be understood, "not as poetry composed by timeless individuals but as songs serving small-group and larger society interests."[167]

Regarding the setting of praise psalms, Gersternberger believes that the hymn form grew out of a large state cult and was related to various national festivals, although some hymn forms were related to rites focused on the individual.[168] Thanksgiving songs, on the other hand, have their primary setting in an individual who had experienced salvation/blessing and now offers thanks publicly, either in a formal cultic context, or through a feast given to friends and neighbors.[169]

These proposed settings for praise psalms relate to the origin of the form. However, Gerstenberger dates most psalms to the post-exilic period.[170] Thus, the hymn form may have originated in the state cult, but in the Psalter, most of the hymns derive from a post-exilic situation where there is no large state edifice. This effects the meaning and setting of a number of psalms. For example, Ps 2, he argues has its setting in the synagogue liturgy and is Messianic in nature.[171] Psalm 32 also was written out of the context of synagogue worship. It is "very close to being a homily on penitence," which utilizes the form of the

---

[164] Ibid., 6–9, 21–22, 28, 31–34.
[165] Ibid., 33.
[166] Ibid., 33.
[167] Ibid., 34.
[168] Ibid., 16–19.
[169] Ibid., 14–15.
[170] Ibid., 22.
[171] Ibid., 49.

individual thanksgiving song.[172] Psalm 33 is "a type of petitionary hymn of the early Jewish community, drawing on ancient mythological traditions as well as historical experiences."[173]

To summarize, Gerstenberger believes that psalm forms originate in small, family and clan worship. These forms were taken over and modified for use by the state cult, while at the same time still being used by smaller, familial groups. Finally, the state cultic forms were modified and used by the post-exilic synagogue community as well as by family units in the post-exilic period. It is from this final period that most of the poems in the Psalter originated.

1.6 CONTEMPORARY METHODOLOGIES

Through the middle of the twentieth century, there were a handful of methodologies that were applied to the Psalms. One could draw a relatively straight line from historical approaches, to form criticism, to cult-functional interpretations. However, the late 1960s saw an explosion of different methodologies applied to the text of the Old Testament in general,[174] and Psalms in particular.

Two reasons for the methodological shift were a frustration with the speculative nature of earlier scholarship and a recognition that earlier scholars had focused more on the background of the text than on the text itself. Thus, many of the newer methodologies had a literary, text-imminent bent.

In concert with these intellectual trends, ideologically-based criticism became an accepted mode of interpretation making room for feminist, liberation, and overtly confessional readings of the Psalms.[175] These include liberationist,[176] sociological,[177] intertextual,[178] literary,[179]

---

[172] Ibid., 143.

[173] Ibid., 146.

[174] See *The Cambridge Companion to Biblical Interpretation*, ed. John Barton (Cambridge: Cambridge University Press, 2000), 1–6. This book lists eleven different approaches to the interpretation of Scripture, which is representative of the diversity in the field.

[175] See *The Cambridge Companion to Biblical Interpretation*, esp. chs. 5–8.

[176] E.g., John Pleins, *The Psalms: Songs of Tragedy, Hope, and Justice*, Bi-

feminist,[180] linguistic,[181] structuralist,[182] deconstructionist,[183] and theological/ethical[184] readings. Space prevents us from examining all of these approaches to the Psalter in detail. We will instead focus briefly on the most influential and prolific recent method to be applied to the study of the Psalms, canonical criticism.

The contemporary occupation with the canonical shape of the Psalter was inaugurated by the work of Brevard Childs and Gerald

---

ble and Liberation (Maryknoll, NY: Orbis, 1993).

[177] E.g., Walter Brueggemann, see fn 148.

[178] E.g., Beth LaNeel Tanner, *The Book of Psalms through the Lens of Intertexuality*, StBiLit 26 (New York: Peter Lang, 2001).

[179] E.g., Robert Alter, *The Art of Biblical Poetry*, 2nd ed. rev. exp. (New York: Basic, 2011); James Kugel, *The Idea of Biblical Poetry: Parallelism and Its History* (New Haven: Yale University Press, 1981); L. Alonso Schökel, *A Manual of Hebrew Poetics*, SubBi 11 (Rome: Pontifical Biblical Institute, 1988); Harold Fisch, *Poetry with a Purpose: Biblical Poetics and Interpretation* (Bloomington: Indiana University Press, 1988).

[180] E.g., Carole Fontaine and Athalya Brenner, eds., *A Feminist Companion to Wisdom and Psalms*, FCB 2 (New York: T&T Clark, 1998); Luise Schottroff and Marie-Theres Wacker, eds., *Feminist Biblical Interpretation: A Compendium of Critical Commentary on the Books of the Bible and Related Literature* (Grand Rapids: Eerdmans, 2012).

[181] E.g., Michael O'Connor, *Hebrew Verse Structure*, 2nd ed. (Winona Lake, IN: Eisenbrauns, 1997); Ernst Wendland, ed. *Discourse Perspectives on Hebrew Poetry in the Scriptures*, UBS 7 (New York: United Bible Society, 1994).

[182] E.g., M. Girard, *Les psaumes redécouverts: De la structure au sens*, 3 vols. (Quebec: Belarmin, 1994–1996); Pieter van der Lugt, *Cantos and Strophes in Biblical Hebrew Poetry: with Special Reference to the First Book of the Psalter*, OtSt 53 (Leiden: Brill, 2006); idem, *Cantos and Strophes in Biblical Hebrew Poetry II: Psalms 42–89*, OtSt 57 (Leiden: Brill, 2010).

[183] E.g., David Jobling, "Deconstruction and the Political Analysis of Biblical Texts: A Jamesonian Reading of Psalm 72," *Semeia* 59 (1992): 95–127; Kirsten Nielsen, "The Variety of Metaphors about God in the Psalter: Deconstruction and Reconstruction?" *SJOT* 16 (2002): 151–59.

[184] E.g., Rolf Jacobson, ed. *Soundings in the Theology of Psalms: Perspectives and Methods in Contemporary Scholarship* (Minneapolis: Fortress, 2010); Gordon Wenham, *Psalms as Torah: Reading Biblical Song Ethically* (Grand Rapids: Baker Academic, 2012).

Wilson.[185] These scholars were focused on understanding the intention of the final editors of the Psalter and how they shaped the book from a particular theological perspective. Since Wilson, canonical interpretation has taken a number of different directions. Some have attempted to discover a narrative flow in the final form of the book.[186] Other scholars have been concerned with smaller groups of psalms within the book and how they were edited.[187] Additionally, scholars have traced key theological themes through the book as a whole.[188] Still other scholars have focused on the complex process of the book growth into its final form.[189]

Canonical methods have helpfully raised new questions and debates concerning the editorial shape of the book as a whole, as well as the relationship of smaller groups of psalms to each other within the book. This method has not been without its criticism, nevertheless it remains the dominate approach to the Psalter.[190] In terms of praise

---

[185] Brevard Childs, *Introduction to the Old Testament as Scripture* (Philadelphia: Fortress, 1979), 504–25; Gerald Wilson, *The Editing of the Hebrew Psalter*, SBLDS 76 (Chico, CA: Scholars Press, 1985). For a comprehensive review of canonical approaches to the Psalms, see David M. Howard, Jr. "Recent Trends in Psalms Study"; Kevin Gary Smith and Bill Domeris, "A Brief History of Psalms Studies," *Conspectus* 6 (2008): 97–119; Kilnam Cha, *Psalm 146–150: The Final Hallelujah Psalms as a Fivefold Doxology to the Hebrew Psalter* (Ph.D. Diss.; Baylor University, 2006), 8–39.

[186] E.g., Nancy deClaissé-Walford, *Reading from the Beginning: The Shaping of the Hebrew Psalter* (Macon, GA: Mercer University Press, 1997).

[187] E.g., David M. Howard, Jr. *The Structure of Psalms 93–100* (Winona Lake, IN; Eisenbrauns, 1996).

[188] E.g., J. F. Creach, *The Choice of Yahweh as Refuge in the Editing of the Psalter*, JSOTSup 217 (Sheffield: Sheffield Academic Press, 1996).

[189] E.g., Erich Zenger, "Der Psalter als Buch: Beobachtungen zu seiner Enstehung, Komposition und Funktion," in *Psalter in Judentum und Christentum*, HBS 18, ed. E. Zenger (Freiburg: Herder, 1998), 1–57; Matthias Millard, *Die Komposition des Psalters: Ein formgeschichtlicher Anstaz*, FAT 9 (Tübingen: Mohr, 1994).

[190] See Norman Whybray, *Reading the Psalms as a Book*, JSOTSupp 222 (Sheffield: Sheffield Academic, 1996); John Barton, *Reading the Old Testament: Method in Biblical Study*, rev. and exp. ed. (Louisville: Westminster, 1996), 77–103, 140–56.

psalms, canonical criticism has highlighted the fact that these psalms occur in the context of a book. At times, it is helpful to examine how the placement of the psalm in the book may impact its meaning.

1.7   SUMMARY

The above review of Psalms scholarship is far from comprehensive, yet it is broad enough for us to see some perennial issues in the interpretation of praise Psalms interpretation. The most significant issue in Psalms interpretation has to be the question of setting. Late eighteenth through early twentieth century interpreters assumed that the Psalms were composed by individuals out of the overflow of their religious experience. Thus, these scholars sought diligently to uncover the precise background of the psalmist in order to understand the poem. As this type of scholarship reached the point of diminishing returns, Hermann Gunkel breathed new life into the discipline. He argued that the original setting of the forms of the psalms was cultic and communal, not individualistic. This quickly led to scholars describing and debating the exact cultic background of the Psalms in order to provide a setting in which to understand them. This cult-functional approach, while providing significant insights, seemed more interested in reconstructing Israel's cultic history than in interpreting the Psalms. Or, to put it another way, these scholars mainly used the Psalms to reconstruct cultic history. The various settings provided by these scholars suffered from the same speculative nature that plagued earlier scholarship. Canonical critics sought to provide a different setting to interpret Psalms, the book itself. This has the advantage of being an objectively verifiable setting. The book does exist.[191] These scholars have helped us to understand better how the book has a whole provides a setting in

---

[191] Although which version of the book is most important and discerning the time period when the final form was established continues to be an ongoing debate, see Peter Flint, *The Dead Sea Psalms Scrolls and the Book of Psalms*, STDJ 17 (Leiden: Brill, 1997); Peter Flint, "The Contribution of Gerald Wilson toward Understanding the Book of Psalms in Light of the Psalms Scrolls," in *The Shape and Shaping of the Book of Psalms: The Current State of Scholarship*, AIL 20, ed. Nancy deClaissé-Walford (Atlanta: SBL Press, 2014), 209–30.

which to interpret individual psalms. However, what is lost in this method is the fact that Psalms were originally speech in real life settings. They were spoken between people and between individuals and God. The dialogical nature of Psalms is in danger of being lost in a method that looks to the book level only for an interpretative setting.

The problem of setting has actually bogged down traditional Psalms interpretation to the point where Psalms are primarily being used as evidence to answer background questions.[192] Many of these are important and interesting questions, but in all of this the interpretation of individual psalms as unique poetic compositions can be lost. Specifically, an analysis of how these psalms would have functioned to shape the audience has not been adequately addressed.

Rhetoric, with its detailed attention to both the social context and the language of discourse, provides the interpreter with many conceptual tools to address questions of setting, function and language in order to read the praise psalms well. The purpose of this study is to argue that a rhetorical analysis of praise psalms will foster a clearer understanding of how praise functioned to shape the beliefs and piety of ancient Israel so that the reader will better appreciate the social, psychological, and theological contribution of the praise psalms to Israel's religious life. In the following chapter, our goal is to develop a rhetorical approach that will help us to achieve this goal.

---

[192] E.g., What were the original forms of the Psalms? What was a cultic festival like? What is the overall theme of the Psalter (redactional setting)?

CHAPTER 2
A Rhetorical Approach

2.1   INTRODUCTION

In a 2008 review of scholarship on Hebrew Poetry, Jamie Grant discussed canonical approaches to interpretation as well as linguistic and literary debates concerning parallelism.[1] A glaring omission in this review was any discussion of the interpretation of the poem as a whole. The reason for this, Grant states, is "[i]n terms of the study of the poem as a unit there has not been the same sort of dynamic movement or radical change in recent years. The key ideas have remained largely the same in recent ideas."[2] This omission in scholarship is problematic. Interpretation involves the ancient text, ancient hearers/readers, and modern readers. Each new era necessarily produces new readings of texts since interpreters ask different questions of the text from different contexts. In the current era, there is a heightened concern with the power of language to shape the values, beliefs, and world-view of a community. These concerns are central to a rhetorical approach.

The previous chapter stated that the purpose of this study is to argue that a rhetorical analysis of praise psalms will foster a clearer understanding of how praise functioned to shape the beliefs and piety of ancient Israel so that the reader will better appreciate the social, psychological, and theological contribution of the praise psalms to Israel's religious life. This goal raises a number of questions: What is meant by "rhetorical criticism"? How is a rhetorical approach different from form criticism or from many literary methods (e.g., reader-response, post-structuralism, etc.)? Is it appropriate to use rhetoric, a discipline that was birthed and nurtured in the western world, to ana-

---

[1] Jaime Grant, "Poetics," in *Words & the Word: Explorations in Biblical Interpretation & Literary Theory*, ed. David Firth and Jamie Grant (Downers Grove, IL: InterVarsity Press, 2008), 187–225.

[2] Grant, "Poetics," 222.

lyze an ANE text? Is it an appropriate method to study texts that are both poems and prayers?

These are important and necessary questions. Our task in this chapter will be to define what is meant by rhetoric, to discuss several challenges facing a rhetorical approach to the Psalter, and, finally, to outline a rhetorical approach appropriate to praise psalms.

2.2   DEFINITION OF RHETORIC

Many rhetorical theorists lament the ambiguity associated with the term "rhetoric." The word itself has been defined and re-defined through the millennia to the point where it becomes difficult to use at all without a paragraph of qualification. Wayne Booth colorfully describes this dilemma along with a defense for why the term is still relevant.

> My first problem lies of course in the very word 'rhetoric.' I was tempted ... to define that slippery term once and for all, but I have resisted.... Just how much time should a lecturer spend claiming that, like Humpty Dumpty, he is to be the boss of definitions?... Ted Shultz has recently advised me to abandon the sleazy term altogether and substitute something like 'philosophy of discourse,' or 'theory of communication.' But to abandon the term 'rhetoric,' with its long honorable history, just because it often suggests shoddy practices, would be like abandoning the term 'philosophy,' just because people talk about 'the philosophy of tennis coaching.'[3]

The plight of 'rhetoric' is not quite as bad as Professor Booth describes. The term is most often defined in one of three ways. For some, rhetoric denotes manipulative speech designed to deceive people into thinking a weak argument is actually strong, or into thinking a lie is the truth. This understanding of rhetoric goes back to the earliest sur-

---

[3] Wayne Booth, *The Vocation of a Teacher: Rhetorical Occasions* (Chicago: University of Chicago Press, 1988), 309.

viving discussion of the discipline, Plato's *Gorgias*.[4] Rhetoric also has been defined as the art of persuasion. This understanding was given by Gorgias in Plato's work. A more mature statement of this view of rhetoric is found in Aristotle's *Rhetoric*.[5] Others, however, have understood the word to refer to ornamental speech. That is, rhetoric has to do with the artistic composition of literary or oral works. This view of rhetoric is often associated with the later Roman Empire, that is, the Second Sophistic.[6]

The first definition has always cast a shadow over the term in popular understanding. However, among theorists and practitioners, the second and third definitions have been the most widely used. Rhetoric as the "art of persuasion" is the foundational meaning of the term.[7] The discipline was born from a desire to understand how to influence and shape beliefs and actions. In Socrates's discussion with Gorgias, Gorgias defines the discipline thus:

> I call it the ability to persuade with speeches either judges in the law courts or statesmen in the council-chamber or the commons in the Assembly or an audience at any other meeting that may be held on public affairs. And I tell you that by virtue of this power you will have the doctor as your slave, and the trainer as your slave; your money-getter will turn out to be making money not for himself, but for another,—in fact for

---

[4] Plato, *Lysis. Symposium. Gorgias*, trans. W. M. Lamb, LCL 166 (Cambridge: Harvard University Press, 1925). For a helpful discussion of and incisive critique of Plato's view, see Brian Vickers, *In Defense of Rhetoric* (Oxford: Clarendon, 1989), 83–147.

[5] Aristotle, *Art of Rhetoric*, trans. J. H. Freese, LCL 22 (Cambridge: Harvard University Press, 1926).

[6] Patricia Bizzell and Bruce Herzberg, *The Rhetorical Tradition*, 2nd ed. (New York: Bedford/St. Martin's, 2001), 38; James Herrick, *The History and Theory of Rhetoric*, 4th ed. (Boston: Pearson, 2009), 120–21.

[7] This is such a widespread belief that in a major monograph on the history of rhetoric, Brian Vickers states without qualification, "Rhetoric, the art of persuasive communication, has long been recognized as the systematization of natural eloquence" (*In Defense of Rhetoric*, 1).

you, who are able to speak and persuade the multitude.[8]

This is the understanding of the discipline Aristotle inherited and developed. With this functional goal in mind rhetorical theorists developed handbooks classifying various rhetorical devices, which gave the discipline a more literary bent. From the late Roman period through the Medieval era, rhetoric was a part of standard education. However, "the disappearance of the face-to-face, persuasive context of rhetoric meant that rhetoric theorists lost sight of the audience."[9] That is, with no context in which to use rhetoric practically, it was turned into a literary discipline with the result that many influential medieval writers thought of it as "polishing, decorating, especially dilating, what has been already expressed."[10]

The process of redefining rhetoric from persuasion to style continued in the Renaissance through to the 19th century.[11] However, in the 20th century there was a return to recognizing rhetoric as more than simply verbal ornamentation. This can be seen clearly in the writings of I. A. Richards,[12] Kenneth Burke,[13] Chaim Perelman,[14] Richard McKeon,[15] and Ernesto Grassi[16] among many others. This recent trend

---

[8] Plato, *Lysis. Symposium. Gorgias*, 279.

[9] Vickers, *In Defence of Rhetoric*, 227.

[10] C. S. Baldwin, *Medieval Rhetoric and Poetic (to 1400)* (New York: Macmillan, 1928), 181–82.

[11] Bizzell and Herzberg, *Rhetorical Tradition*, 8–14. For a detailed analysis of this history, see Heinrich Plett, *Literary Rhetoric: Concepts-Structure-Analyses*, ISHR 2 (Leiden: Brill, 2010), 3–32.

[12] I. H. Richards, *The Philosophy of Rhetoric* (Oxford: Oxford University Press, 1936)

[13] Kenneth Burke, *A Rhetoric of Motives* (Berkeley: University of California Press, 1969); idem, *Language as Symbolic Action: Essays on Life, Literature, and Method* (Berkeley: University of California Press, 1968); idem, *Rhetoric of Religion: Studies in Logology* (Berkeley: University of California Press, 1970).

[14] Chaim Perelman and L. Olbrechts-Tyteca, *The New Rhetoric: A Treatise on Argumentation*, trans. John Wilkinson and Purcell Weaver (Notre Dame: University of Notre Dame Press, 1969).

[15] Richard McKeon, *Rhetoric: Essays in Invention and Discovery*, ed. Mark Backman (Woodbridge, CT: Ox Bow, 1987).

toward a functional understanding of rhetoric is broader than simply persuasion, though. This is part of what makes the term "rhetoric" ambiguous today.[17]

Rhetorician Edward P. J. Corbett summarizes these broader concerns in contemporary rhetorical criticism in this way, "rhetorical criticism is that mode of internal criticism which considers the interactions between the work, the author, and the audience. As such, it is interested in the *product*, the *process*, and the *effect* of linguistic activity, whether of the imaginative kind or the utilitarian kind."[18] Thus, rhetorical criticism can focus on the text itself, the intention of the author in shaping the text, and the effect the text would likely have had on an "audience of near contemporaries."[19]

This broader understanding of rhetoric can be seen in the following recent definitions of the discipline. In a standard introductory work, James Herrick defines rhetoric in this way, "I will define the art of rhetoric as the systematic study and intentional practice of effective symbolic expression. *Effective* here will mean achieving the purposes of the symbol-user, whether that purpose is persuasion, clarity, beauty, or mutual understanding."[20] George Kennedy, in an influential work, also broadens the domain of rhetorical studies through this definition:

Rhetoric is not, I think, just a convenient concept existing only in the mind of speakers, audiences, writers, critics, and teachers. It has an essence or reality that has not been appreciated. I shall argue in this book that rhetoric, in essence, is a form of

[16] Ernesto Grassi, *Rhetoric as Philosophy: The Humanist Tradition* (University Park: Pennsylvania State University Press, 1980).

[17] See James Murphy, "The Four Faces of Rhetoric: A Progress Report," *College Composition and Communication* 17 (1966): 55–59.

[18] Edward P. J. Corbett, *Rhetorical Analyses of Literary Works* (New York: Oxford University Press, 1969), xxii.

[19] This phrase is used by George Kennedy, *New Testament Interpretation through Rhetorical Criticism* (Chapel Hill: University of North Carolina Press, 1984), 4. This footnote acknowledges my debt to Kennedy for all subsequent uses of the phrase in this work.

[20] Herrick, *History and Theory of Rhetoric*, 7.

mental and emotional energy. This is most clearly seen when an individual, animal or human, is faced with some serious threat or opportunity that may be affected by utterance.... Rhetoric is thus a 'conservative' faculty.[21]

Taken together these two definitions highlight several important features of rhetoric: rhetoric appeals to both emotion and reason;[22] rhetoric is an intentional use of language; rhetoric is contextual, that is, there was a situation that elicited a piece of rhetoric;[23] and rhetoric is concerned with achieving a goal(s). Bizzell and Herzberg summarize the current state of rhetorical studies this way, "The history of rhetoric is the story of a long struggle to understand the relationships between discourse and knowledge, communication and its effects, language and experience. Thus, the latest theories of rhetoric recover its earliest and most abiding concerns and build on a long tradition that is now, more than ever, worthy of close attention."[24] It is this functional, suasive understanding of rhetoric that this study will utilize. However, before we can build a rhetorical approach to the praise psalms, a discussion of how rhetorical analysis has been practiced in Old Testament studies is necessary in order to situate with study within the world of biblical scholarship.

2.3   RHETORIC IN OLD TESTAMENT STUDIES

Rhetorical criticism has been a fecund area of work in Old Testament studies for the last thirty years.[25] The main lines of rhetorical criticism

---

[21] George Kennedy, *Comparative Rhetoric: An Historical and Cross-Cultural Introduction* (Oxford: Oxford University Press, 1997), 3–4.

[22] Interestingly, Robert Lowth argued that one of the unique features of poetry was that it appealed to reason *and* emotion (*Lectures on the Sacred Poetry of the Hebrews*, 2nd ed. [London: Ogles, Duncan, and Cochran, 1816], 12).

[23] See Lloyd Bitzer, "The Rhetorical Situation," *Philosophy and Rhetoric* 1 (1968): 1–14.

[24] Bizzell and Herzberg, *Rhetorical Tradition*, 16.

[25] For a full discussion of rhetorical criticism in biblical studies through 1994, see Duane Watson and Alan Hauser, *Rhetorical Criticism of the Bible: A*

of the Old Testament, how it has been practiced on the Psalms, and a discussion of how it is similar to and different from other related methods is vital in order to assess how the approach advocated here can advance upon already existing methods and approaches.

Rhetorical criticism has been practiced in a variety of ways in OT studies. One helpful way of categorizing the different types is by examining where the center of attention is for the interpreter. M. H. Abrams presented a helpful model with which to analyze the elements of a literary artifact. Figure 1 is a variation on the triangle he created:[26]

Fig. 1   4. Contemporary Reader
                                      |
                               1. Work
                              /   \
                             /   \
                  2. Artist   3. Original Audience

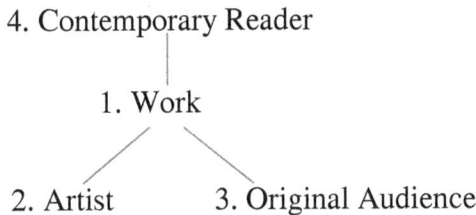

This chart provides us with a helpful paradigm with which to categorize different strands of rhetorical criticism.

Rhetorical criticism's ascent in Old Testament scholarship can be dated to the celebrated SBL Presidential Address by James Muilenburg in 1968.[27] In this address, he challenged students of the Hebrew Bible to supplement their concern for form criticism with what he called rhetorical criticism. He argued that form criticism, while essential, had caused scholars to focus too exclusively on the "typical and representative" features of the text to the neglect of what was unique

---

Comprehensive Bibliography with Notes on History and Method (Leiden: Brill, 1994); David M. Howard, Jr. "Rhetorical Criticism in Old Testament Studies," *BBR* 4 (1994): 87–104; Phyllis Trible, *Rhetorical Criticism: Context, Method, and the Book of Jonah* (Minneapolis: Fortress, 1994); and The Bible and Culture Collective, "Rhetorical Criticism" in *The Postmodern Bible*, ed. Elizabeth Castelli, Stephen Moore, et al. (New Haven: Yale University Press, 1995).

[26] M. H. Abrams, *The Mirror and the Lamp: Romantic Theory and the Critical Tradition* (London: Oxford University Press, 1953), 3–29. Abrams had "universe" at the top of the triangle instead of "contemporary reader."

[27] James Muilenburg, "Form Criticism and Beyond," *JBL* 88 (1969): 1–18.

or particular.[28] He called the scholar, "to supplement his form-critical analysis with a careful inspection of the literary unit in its precise and unique formulation."[29] He called this emphasis on the "unique formulation" of each text "rhetorical criticism." Muilenburg's address was a needed call for scholars to once again examine each text on its own merit. As Phyllis Trible highlights, Muilenburg's address lifted up the words "artistry," "aesthetics," and "stylistics" to explain what he meant by rhetorical criticism.[30] Thus, Muilenburg argued that the work/text itself should be the main locus of rhetorical interpretation (area 1 in the chart above). He called the biblical scholar to two tasks. The first is "to define the limits or scope of the literary unit ... how it begins and where and how it ends."[31] The second major task he explains is as follows:

> to recognize the structure of a composition and to discern the configuration of its component parts, to delineate the warp and woof out of which the literary fabric is woven, and to note the various rhetorical devices that are employed for marking, on the one hand, the sequence and movement of the pericope, and on the other, the shifts or breaks in the development of the writer's thought.[32]

Muilenburg illustrates this concern through an analysis of parallelism, chiasmus, and anaphora in Old Testament texts.[33] His overarching belief was that "a proper articulation of form yields a proper articulation of meaning."[34]

Muilenburg's influence has been profound.[35] Many studies un-

---

[28] Ibid., 5.

[29] Ibid., 7.

[30] Trible, *Rhetorical Criticism*, 26.

[31] Muilenburg, "Form Criticism and Beyond," 8–9.

[32] Ibid., 10.

[33] Ibid., 10–11.

[34] A frequent classroom remark cited by Trible, *Rhetorical Criticism*, 27.

[35] T. B. Dozeman referred to a "Muilenburg School" ("Old Testament Rhetorical Criticism," *ABD* 5.712–15).

der the rubric "rhetorical criticism" practice this type of literary analysis.[36] Additionally, as John Barton pointed out, this method has attract-
ed many conservative interpreters who utilize literary structures to argue for a unified text.[37] However, Muilenburg's program is not without
its critics. Wilhelm Wuellner in an important article took this type of
rhetorical criticism to task.[38] What Muilenburg's program was lacking,
according to Wuellner, was a clear methodology. This led to a failure
among rhetorical interpreters, "to realize how much the prevailing theories of rhetoric were the victims of that 'rhetoric restrained,' i.e., victims of the fateful reduction of rhetoric to stylistics, and of stylistics in
turn to the rhetorical tropes or figures."[39] At the time of Wuellner's
essay, he could rightly say that, "rhetorical criticism has become indis-
tinguishable from literary criticism, as is evident in the works of two
leading literary critics: L. Alonso Schokel and R. Alter."[40] That is not
to say that the "Muilenburg School" has not produced insightful studies. Much of the work done by Muilenburg and his disciples has been
extremely helpful in understanding the biblical text. It is, however, a
rather narrow understanding of rhetoric.[41] Among scholars who apply
rhetorical criticism to the Psalms, it is this type of rhetorical criticism

---

[36] E.g., Jack Lundbom, *Jeremiah: A Study in Ancient Hebrew Rhetoric*,
SBLDS 18 (Missoula, MT: Scholars Press, 1975); Toni Craven, *Artistry and Faith in
the Book of Judith* (Chico, CA: Scholars Press, 1983); Anthony Ceresko, "A Rhetorical Analysis of David's 'Boast' (1 Samuel 17:34–37): Some Reflections on Method," *CBQ* 47 (1985): 58–74; J. J. Jackson and M. Kessler, eds. *Rhetorical Criticism:
Essays in Honor of James Muilenburg* (Pittsburgh: Pickwick, 1974); the essays by
Charles Isbell, J. Cheryl Exum, J. Kenneth Kuntz, and John Kselman in *Art and
Meaning: Rhetoric in Biblical Literature*, JSOTSup 19, ed. Alan Hauser et al. (Sheffield: Sheffield Academic, 1982).

[37] John Barton, *Reading the Old Testament: Method in Biblical Study*, 2nd
ed. (London: Darton, Longman & Todd, 1996), 204.

[38] Wilhelm Wuellner, "Where is Rhetorical Criticism Taking Us?" *CBQ* 49
(1987): 448–63.

[39] Ibid., 451.

[40] Ibid., 452; see also Howard, "Rhetorical Criticism in Old Testament Studies," 88–91.

[41] See also ibid.,104.

that has been the most widely practiced.[42]

The other two types of rhetorical criticism prevalent in OT studies fall under the traditional understanding of rhetoric as the art of persuasion. The first type highlights the relationship between the text and the contemporary reader (areas 1 and 4). Under the influence of contemporary theorists like Stanley Fish,[43] a reader-response type of rhetorical criticism has flourished.[44] This theory argues that all discourse is persuasive and that the reader (or reading community) creates meaning based on the text. This is a direction that Wuellner began to go down in his programmatic essay. He states, "Rhetorical criticism changes the long-established perception of authors as active and readers as passive or receptive by showing the rationale for readers as active, creative, productive."[45] Additionally, Dale Patrick and Allen Scult argue that "the rhetorical perspective bids us to locate the normative text somehow in the exchange between it and the exegete."[46]

This understanding of rhetorical criticism is attractive for two reasons. First, it acknowledges the role the interpreter has in reading the text. Clearly, no one approaches the biblical text as a blank slate. A reader-response approach highlights this fact and embraces it. Secondly, these critics are concerned with contemporary appropriation of the

---

[42] E.g., K. Kuntz, "Psalm 18: A Rhetorical Critical Analysis," *JSOT* 26 (1983): 3–31; Graham Ogden, "Psalm 60: Its Rhetoric, Form, and Function," *JSOT* 31 (1985): 83–94; Leslie Allen, "The Value of Rhetorical Criticism in Psalm 69," *JBL* 105 (1986): 577–98; K. Kuntz, "King Triumphant: A Rhetorical Study of Psalms 20–21," *HAR* 10 (1987): 157–76; Mark S. Smith, "Setting and Rhetoric in Psalm 23," *JSOT* 41 (1988): 61–66; see also most of the studies listed under "Psalms" in Watson and Hauser, *Rhetorical Criticism of the Bible*, 71–77.

[43] Stanley Fish, *Surprised by Sin: The Reader in "Paradise Lost"*, 2nd ed. (Cambridge: Harvard University Press, 2003); idem, *Is there a Text in this Class? The Authority of Interpretive Communities* (Cambridge: Harvard University Press, 1982).

[44] E.g., Beverly Stratton, *Out of Eden: Reading, Rhetoric, and Ideology in Genesis 2–3*, JSOTSup 208 (Sheffield: Sheffield, 1995). For a full discussion of reader-response criticism in biblical studies, see The Bible and Culture Collective, *The Postmodern Bible*, 20–69.

[45] Wuellner, "Where is Rhetorical Criticism Taking Us?," 461.

[46] Patrick and Scult, *Rhetoric and Biblical Interpretation*, 21.

text, which is also a laudable goal. However, this approach is also marked by a belief in the indeterminacy of the text and in the freedom of the interpreter to deal with the text as he or she pleases.[47] Northrop Frye famously quipped, "It has been said of Boehme that his books are like a picnic to which the author brings the words and the reader the meaning. The remark may have been intended as a sneer at Boehme, but it is an exact description of all works of literary art without exception."[48] This well summarizes the reader-response approach to the text. Umberto Eco, who originally argued for the unlimited interpretive potential of any text,[49] later in life expended much effort to demonstrate that there are constraints on interpretation.[50] He argued that many reader-response critics *use* the text rather than interpret it.[51] Although it has produced many helpful readings, reader-response rhetorical criticism suffers from a narrowness of focus as does Muilenburg's program.

Among Psalms scholars, a reader-response oriented rhetorical criticism has been widely used. In some ways, a reader-response approach to the Psalms is in line with the reason for which Psalms were composed. They are designed for the reader to put themselves in the place of the "I" or "we" of the psalmist.[52]

---

[47] For a full and incisive critique of reader-response criticism, see Anthony Thiselton, *New Horizons in Hermeneutics: The Theory and Practice of Transforming Biblical Reading* (Grand Rapids: Zondervan, 1992), chs. 3 & 14.

[48] Quoted by E. D. Hirsch, Jr. *Validity in Interpretation* (New Haven: Yale University Press, 1967), 1.

[49] Umberto Eco, *The Open Work*, trans. A. Cancogni (London: Hutchinson Radius, 1989).

[50] Umberto Eco, "Interpretation and History," in *Interpretation and Overinterpretation*, ed. S. Collini (Cambridge: Cambridge University Press, 1992), 23–43.

[51] Umberto Eco, "*Intentio Lectoris*: The State of the Art," in *The Limits of Interpretation* (Bloomington: Indiana University Press, 1994), 44–64.

[52] E.g., David J. Clines, "A World Established on Water (Psalm 24): Reader-Response, Deconstruction and Bespoke Interpretation," in *New Literary Criticism and the Hebrew Bible*, JSOTSup 143, ed. David J. Clines & J. Cheryl Exum (Sheffield: Sheffield, 1993), 79–90; Yeol Kim and Herrie van Rooy, "Reading Psalm 78 Multidimensionally: the Dimension of the Reader," *Scriptura* 88 (2005): 101–17; William Brown, "The Psalms and 'I': The Dialogical Self and the Disappearing Psalmist," in *Diachronic and Synchronic: Reading the Psalms in Real Time*,

A final way in which rhetorical criticism has been practiced in Old Testament studies could be labeled a "traditional perspective."[53] This type of rhetorical analysis focuses on the relationship between the author/speaker, text/speech, and original audience (areas 1, 2, and 3).[54] This type of rhetorical criticism often utilizes Aristotelian categories.[55] It is frequently associated with the "New Rhetoric" espoused by Chaim Perelman, Kenneth Burke, and I. A. Richards.[56] The "new" part of this rhetoric is that the domain of rhetorical analysis has expanded. Rhetoric has shifted "from its traditional focus on oral rhetoric or letter writing to include all texts as 'signs' through which text-sign producers and their products interact with text-sign receivers and validators."[57] George Kennedy helped to renew rhetorical criticism in New

---

LHB/OTS 488, ed. W. H. Bellinger et al. (New York: T&T Clark, 2007), 26–44; A. Wieringen, "Psalm 122: Syntax and the Position of the I-Figure and the Text-Immanent Reader," in *Composition of the Book of Psalms*, ed. Erich Zenger; BETL 238 (Leuven: Paris, 2010), 745–54.

[53] This phrase is used by Trible, *Rhetorical Criticism*, 57.

[54] Some examples of this method are, Michael Fox, "The Rhetoric of Ezekiel's Vision of the Valley of the Bones," *HUCA* 51 (1980): 1–15; Margaret Zulick, "The Active Force of Hearing: the Ancient Hebrew Language of Persuasion," *Rhetorica* 10 (1992): 367–80; idem, "The Agon of Jeremiah: On the Dialogic Invention of Prophetic Ethos," *Quarterly Journal of Speech* 78 (1992): 125–48; Karl Möller, *Prophet in Debate: The Rhetoric of Persuasion in the Book of Amos*, JSOTSup 372 (Sheffield: Sheffield, 2003); Alison Lo, *Job 28 as Rhetoric: An Analysis of Job 28 in the Context of Job 22–31*, VTSup 97 (Leiden: Brill, 2003). Methodologically this approach has been called for by David M. Howard, Jr. "Rhetorical Criticism in Old Testament Studies," 102–4; Y. Gitay, "Rhetorical Criticism," in *To Each Its Own Meaning: An Introduction to Biblical Criticisms and Their Application*, ed. Steven L. McKenzie and Stephen R. Haynes (Louisville: Westminster/John Knox, 1993), 135–52; and Peter Phillips, "Rhetoric," in *Words & the Word: Explorations in Biblical Interpretation and Literary Theory*, ed. David Firth and Jaime Grant (Downers Grove, IL: IVP Academic, 2009), 226–65.

[55] E.g., Yehoshua Gitay, *Prophecy and Persuasion: A Study of Isaiah 40–48* (Bonn: Linguistica Biblica, 1981).

[56] Perelman and Olbrechts-Tyteca, *New Rhetoric*; Kenneth Burke, *A Rhetoric of Motives* (Berkeley: University of California Press, 1950); I. A. Richards, *The Philosophy of Rhetoric* (Oxford: Oxford University Press, 1936.

[57] The Bible and Culture Collective, *The Postmodern Bible*, 158.

Testament studies. In his book *New Testament Interpretation through Rhetorical Criticism*, he outlined a method that serves as a good example of this type of rhetorical criticism and is one that many Old Testament scholars have cited as influencing their work.[58]

Kennedy's first stage is to determine "the *rhetorical unit* to be studied."[59] The unit should have a wholeness about it, containing "a beginning, a middle, and an end."[60] For example, in the study of Psalms, a rhetorical unit would be delineated the same way one would a "Hymn" or "Lament" in form criticism. The form would define the unit to be studied.

The second stage is to "define the *rhetorical situation* of the unit. This roughly corresponds to the *Sitz im Leben* of form criticism," although there are important differences as seen below.[61] Rhetorician Lloyd Blitzer defines the rhetorical situation this way, "a complex of persons, events, objects, and relations presenting an actual or potential exigence which can be completely or partially removed if discourse, introduced into the situation, can so constrain human decision or action as to bring about the significant modification of the exigence."[62] In other words, the critic attempts to answer the questions, "what was the situation which elicited this discourse?" and "How was the author attempting to change the situation through his/her discourse?" This stage is intensely concerned with defining the audience, the author, and the relationship between them.

The third stage is the "identification of the *rhetorical disposition* or *arrangement*,"[63] and is concerned with demonstrating how a discourse achieves its goals through its structure and content. The interpreter should consider, "what subdivisions it [the text] falls into, what

---

[58] E.g., Karl Möller, *Prophet in Debate*, 37–43.

[59] Kennedy, *New Testament Interpretation*, 33.

[60] Ibid., 33.

[61] Ibid., 33.

[62] Bitzer, "Rhetorical Situation," 4–6. For a critique of Bitzer's work, see Richard Vatz, "The Myth of the Rhetorical Situation," *Philosophy and Rhetoric* 6 (1973): 154–61.

[63] Wuellner, "Where is Rhetorical Criticism Taking Us?" 456.

the persuasive effect of these parts seems to be, and how they work together—or fail to do so—to some unified purpose in meeting the rhetorical situation."[64] The interpreter should examine the text at every level,
and, at the level of the entire discourse, notice how larger sections fit
together to achieve suasive effects. At the micro level, one should examine figures of speech, metaphor, emotive and deductive language to discern how the parts of a discourse fit into the larger scheme.

It is this latter type of rhetorical criticism that this study seeks to
situate itself within. Treating the Psalms as persuasive rhetoric is a
growing area of interest among interpreters.[65] However, applying this
type of rhetorical criticism to praise psalms is not without its difficulties.
The following main section will deal with challenges to a rhetorical approach to the psalms in which these difficulties will be addressed.

2.4   CHALLENGES TO A RHETORICAL APPROACH

2.4.1   RHETORIC AND POETRY: IS POETRY RHETORICAL?

Analyzing the Psalms as specimens of suasive discourse is a growing,
but still not common, approach the Psalter.[66] Perhaps one reason why
rhetorical study of Psalms has not been pursued earlier is the underlying belief that Psalms are poetry and poetry and rhetoric incompatible

---

[64] Kennedy, *New Testament Interpretation*, 37.

[65] Some examples of this type of rhetoric applied to the Psalms include: Patrick Miller, "Prayer as Persuasion: The Rhetoric and Intention of Prayer," *Word &
World* 4 (1993): 356–62; W. H. Bellinger, Jr., "Psalm 61: A Rhetorical Analysis,"
PRSt 26 (1999): 379–88; Johan Coetzee, "Politeness Strategies in the So Called 'Enemy Psalms': An Inquiry into Israelite Prayer Rhetoric," in *Rhetorical Criticism and
the Bible*, JSNTSup 195, ed. Stanley Porter & Dennis Stamps (Sheffield: Continuum,
2002), 209–36; Robert Foster and David M. Howard, Jr., eds., *My Words are Lovely:
Studies in the Rhetoric of the Psalms*, LHB/OTS 467 (New York: T&T Clark, 2008);
Davida Charney, "Keeping the Faithful: Persuasive Strategies in Psalms 4 and 62,"
JHS 12 (2012): 1–13; Ryan Cook, "Prayers that Form Us: Rhetoric and Psalms Interpretation," *JSOT* 39 (2015), 451-67; idem. "'They were Born There': The Nations
in Psalmic Rhetoric," *HBT* 39 (2017), 16-30.

[66] Howard and Foster, *My Words are Lovely*, vii–viii; See also Davida
Charney, *Persuading God: Rhetorical Studies of First-Person Psalms*, HBM 73
(Sheffield: Sheffield Phoenix, 2015).

modes of discourse. Some understand poetry as verbal art, thus non-utilitarian in purpose ("art for art's sake"). Whereas rhetoric, as defined above, is utilitarian speech. However, the belief that rhetoric and poetry are antithetical is a remnant of the Romantic era and most literary theorists today recognize the value of rhetorical criticism in the interpretation of poetry.[67]

The objection against using rhetorical theory to analyze poetry mostly comes down to a definition of poetry. During the Romantic era, Longinus' *On the Sublime* was rediscovered and became widely influential in how poetry was understood.[68] Poetry was defined as both verbal artistry and as an expression of the artist's soul. Thus, "In the course of the 18th c. there was a growing tendency to treat poetry ... as primarily an emotional use of language."[69] This led to definitions of poetry like that of John Stuart Mill, "Poetry is feeling, confessing itself to itself in moments of solitude ... [when the speech is] not itself the end, but a means to an end ... of making an impression upon another mind, then it ceases to be poetry, and becomes eloquence."[70] Thus, any speech with a pragmatic goal in mind was not considered poetry. This

---

[67] See Terry Eagleton, *How to Read a Poem* (Oxford: Blackwell, 2007): 8–16, 89–90; T. V. F. Brogen, "Rhetoric and Poetry," in *The New Princeton Encyclopedia of Poetry and Poetics*, ed. Alex Preminger and T. V. F. Brogen (New York: MJF Books, 1993): 1045–52. Indeed, Kenneth Burke's collection of essays written eighty years ago still serves as a powerful call to understand art rhetorically. He argued against then contemporary conceptions of "art for art's sake" that, "all competent art is a means of communication, however vague the artist's conception of his audience may be..." Indeed, artists were involved in the process of "analysis, discovery, observation, diction, revision, tactics in presentation, which are anything but 'day-dreaming'." The artist, he avers, "must master ways of exerting influence upon the minds and emotions of others," (*Counter-Statement* [Berkeley: University of California Press, 1931], 73–74).

[68] Longinus, *On the Sublime*, trans. W. H. Fyfe, LCL 23 (Cambridge: Harvard University Press, 1995).

[69] M. H. Abrams, "Poetry, Theories of," *The New Princeton Encyclopedia of Poetry and Poetics*, ed. Alex Preminger and T. V. F. Brogan (Princeton: Princeton University Press, 1993), 945.

[70] John Stuart Mill, "What is Poetry?" in *John Stuart Mill: Literary Essays*, ed. Edward Alexander (Indianapolis: Bobbs-Merrill, 1967), 56.

understanding of poetry has continued to influence theorists and interpreters today through critics like Roman Jakobson.[71] However, it is a
rather narrow view of poetry. T. S. Eliot has pointed out that almost all
ancient poetry had pragmatic ends.[72] Originally poetry was intended to
instruct and instill morals as well as delight.[73] Contemporary literary
theorist Terry Eagleton describes the breadth of poetry in this way,

> ... there are forms of poetry which are written with the explicit
> intention of praising, cursing, consoling, inspiring, blessing,
> commemorating, denouncing, offering moral counsel and so on.
> Because the modern age is neurotically suspicious of the di-
> dactic, with its curious assumption that to be taught must be in-
> variably unpleasant, it tends to imagine that poems which seek
> to do this must be inferior modes of writing. They are to be rele-
> gated to the lowly status of the pragmatic, along with bus tickets
> and 'No Entry' signs. But the didactic, a word which simply
> means 'teaching' and originally carried no pejorative overtones,
> is the purpose of one of the finest of all traditional literary gen-
> res, the sermon. Virgil's *Georgics* ... includes technical advice to
> farmers.... Many an accomplished poem has been written with
> an immediate end in view.... Most modern critics revolt at the
> word 'dogma', too, but a great many traditional poems are dog-
> matic, in the original, non-derogatory sense of adhering to a sys-
> tem of belief. Dante and Milton, for example.[74]

Once it is understood that poetry, especially ancient poetry,
was written to achieve goals, then rhetorical analysis becomes a helpful means with which to analyze it. T. V. F. Brogen helpfully describes

---

[71] Roman Jakobson, *Language in Literature* (London: Belknap, 1987), 372.

[72] T. S. Eliot, "The Social Function of Poetry," in *On Poetry and Poets* (London: Faber and Faber, 1962), 16.

[73] See the cogent discussion in Craig Bartholomew and Ryan O'Dowd, "The Poetry of Wisdom and the Wisdom of Poetry," in *Old Testament Wisdom Literature: A Theological Introduction* (Downers Grove, IL: InterVarsity Press, 2011), 47–72.

[74] Eagleton, *How to Read a Poem*, 89.

a rhetorical interpretation of poetry as an interpretation that understands the poem "as if it were a public address."[75] This type of interpretation attempts to identify the causes of audience effects and is
therefore, "necessarily historicist and contextual. They [rhetorical in-
terpreters] conceive of *all* poetry as a kind of social act or perfor-
mance...."[76] This understanding of poetic interpretation fits well with
the Psalms, which primarily functioned as public speech in social settings.[77] Rhetorical criticism, as it has developed since ancient times,
has provided us with conceptual tools to be able to analyze how a text
affects its audience, thus it is potentially helpful to bring those tools
into the study of the Psalter.

2.4.2   RHETORIC AS A WESTERN PHENOMENON

Another objection frequently raised with utilizing rhetorical theory to
interpret the Psalms, or the Hebrew Bible in general, is that rhetoric is
a Western phenomenon. Rhetoric was birthed and developed by the
Greeks and is uniquely suited to Western culture. Thus, it is argued,
using rhetorical categories or terms from the Western tradition of rhetoric is inappropriate to the Hebrew Bible. Some scholars go even further, stating that there was no rhetoric in ANE cultures. Rhetorician
James Murphy et al. state, "There is no evidence of an interest in rhetoric in the ancient civilizations of Babylon or Egypt, for instance, neither Africa nor Asia has to this day produced a rhetoric."[78] This objection comes from an overly narrow understanding of rhetoric and has
been convincingly refuted. Utilizing the definition of rhetoric developed above, it clearly operates in every human culture. Every human

---

[75] Brogen, "Rhetoric and Poetry," 1046.

[76] Ibid., 1046

[77] There is a long-standing debate about whether or not the psalms were
written by individuals out of their personal experience with God, or if they were
written for general use by the congregation (see Ch. 1). No matter how you answer
that question though, the Psalms clearly were used as public documents from early
on in their history. Indeed, the general language of the Psalms would point to the fact
that they were probably written with that end in mind. But even if some were not, the
Psalms have been primarily used as public documents throughout their history.

[78] Murphy et al., *Synoptic History of Classical Rhetoric*, 3.

society seeks to move and persuade with speech. As early as the 1980s, rhetorical scholars have called for analyses of non-Western rhetoric.[79] This has led to numerous studies of non-Western rhetoric, ancient and modern.[80] George Kennedy, in a groundbreaking study of comparative rhetoric, pointed out that rhetoric existed in Greece long before it was codified and conceptualized by Plato and Aristotle. He reminds the reader that Aristotle "constantly cited examples of rhetorical usages from the Homeric poems, Greek drama, and earlier prose writers."[81] Kennedy also argues for utilizing Western terminology in analyzing non-Western rhetoric because it is the only fully developed system of terminology available.[82] Xing Lu in an important monograph on Chinese rhetoric argues for a slightly different approach. She examines similarities and differences between ancient Chinese rhetoric and Greek rhetoric.[83] This allows the reader to clearly see how the culture being studied differs from traditional Greek rhetoric. She also argues that one can begin a rhetorical analysis using terminology from the Western tradition, but then it is important to discover and define rhetorical terms that are native to the culture being studied.[84] This will be an important issue to wrestle with as we approach the praise psalms.

2.5   A RHETORICAL APPROACH TO THE PRAISE PSALMS

Many scholars have outlined steps for a rhetorical approach to interpretation. In addition to George Kennedy's outlined above, Wilhelm Wuellner provides the following steps to a rhetorical approach:

---

[79] Vickers, *In Defence of Rhetoric*, 471–74; Vernon Jensen, "Rhetorical Emphasis of Taoism," *Rhetorica* 5 (1987): 219.

[80] E.g., Carol Lipson and Roberta Binkley, eds. *Rhetoric Before and Beyond the Greeks* (Albany, N.Y.: State University of New York Press, 2004); ibid. *Ancient Non-Greek Rhetorics* (West Lafayette, IN: Parlor, 2009); Mary Garrett, "Classical Chinese Conceptions of Argumentation and Persuasion," *Argumentation and Advocacy* 29 (1993): 105–15.

[81] Kennedy, *Comparative Rhetoric*, 3.

[82] Kennedy, *Comparative Rhetoric*, 6.

[83] Lu, *Rhetoric in Ancient China*, 288–311.

[84] Ibid., 3–4.

Define the rhetorical unit

Identify the rhetorical situation

Identify the rhetorical disposition or arrangement

Identify the rhetorical techniques or style

Identify rhetorical criticism as a synchronic whole.[85]

These steps retain more of a focus on stylistics than Kennedy's approach, but the two are still quite similar. Also, lacking in this approach is an explicit concern with the effect the discourse would have on an audience. Phillip Kern outlined a different approach in his work on Galatians.[86] He described different levels of rhetoric which operate in any society:

Level 1: strategic communication

Level 2: painting, *oratory*, statuary, etc.

Level 3: classical Ch'an rhetoric, Graeco-Roman rhetoric, etc.

Level 4: diatribe, market language, classroom language, handbook rhetoric, etc.

Level 5: species of handbook rhetoric: judicial, deliberative, epideictic[87]

These levels were nuanced and translated into the language of strategic communication and enculturated rhetoric by Peter Phillips:

Level 1: strategic communication

Level 2: rhetorical expression

Level 3: enculturated expressions of primary rhetoric

Level 4: enculturated expressions of secondary rhetoric

Level 5: subordinate divisions of secondary rhetoric and processes of *letteraturizzazione*[88]

---

[85] Wuellner, "Where is Rhetorical Criticism Taking Us?," 455–58.

[86] Phillip Kern, *Rhetoric and Galatians: Assessing an Approach to Paul's Epistle*, SNTSMS 101 (Cambridge: Cambridge University Press, 1998).

[87] Kern, *Rhetoric and Galatians*, 9.

[88] Phillips, "Rhetoric," 237.

It is worth explaining the first three levels since the final two levels would be considered stylistics. By "Level 1," Phillips indicates that a rhetorical analysis examines a discourse as a piece of strategic communication. That is, the author had definite goals in mind he or she was attempting to achieve through words.[89] For too long, he argues, biblical scholars have attempted to bypass authorial intention through form, redaction, and literary criticism. Of course, authorial intention is difficult to determine in the case of anonymous texts, an issue we will consider below.

Level 2, for Phillips, is examining the means by which one person attempts to "mould another person's view of the world" through strategic communication.[90] This communication could be verbal or non-verbal. Thus, in addition to words, one could mold another through architecture, coinage, and statuary – all of which could be subjected to a rhetorical interpretation.[91]

Level 3 examines the specific cultural expressions of a type of rhetoric. For example, it would be concerned not just with how words are used to persuade, but specifically how ancient Israel, or Greco-Roman culture, used words in specific situations for suasive purposes. For praise psalms, this would mean developing an approach that takes into account several factors that influence how these psalms are used rhetorically: The fact that they are poetry, that they are written in an ancient Israelite environment, and that they are religious speech written for communal use. These points will be flushed out below.

The goal of this section is to present a rhetorical approach to the praise psalms. This is not a methodology in the classic sense. The goal is not to create a few steps which, when followed properly, will produce a "rhetorical" reading of the Psalms. Rather, the goal is to de-

---

[89] Ibid., 237–41.

[90] Ibid., 241.

[91] This is a debated point by rhetorical critics. Perelman and Olbrechts-Tyteca has argued only verbal communication can be called rhetorical *(New Rhetoric)*. However, E. Corbett has argued that all human constructed artifacts have a rhetorical potential ("The Rhetoric of the Open Hand and the Rhetoric of the Closed Fist," *College Composition and Communication* 20 [1969]: 288–96).

velop an approach, or a mind-set, in reading the text that is sensitive to rhetorical concerns. Dale Patrick describes the difference between a "method" and an "approach" in this way: "Rather than devise a method, it was our object to chart a way of reading that was sensitive to how the text under study exercises power, communicates its truth claims, and achieves an effect."[92]

This approach understands "rhetoric" in its classic sense with a focus on persuasion and the function of a discourse. This understanding of rhetoric is in line with the Western tradition of rhetoric since Aristotle, which has been updated and nuanced by many modern theorists.[93] However, the Psalms are unique in several ways as well. The western rhetorical tradition was not developed to analyze Semitic praise poetry. Thus, this section will first discuss three unique features of this type of literature that need to be understood when applying a rhetorical perspective to the psalms. Psalms are to be read: as unified compositions, as poetry, and as prayers. Following this, I will outline a rhetorical approach to psalms.

2.5.1 PRAISE PSALMS ARE READ AS UNIFIED DISCOURSE

Rhetorical interpretation of Psalms will have as its goal to analyze how the poem as a whole functions suasively. This is a difference from traditional form criticism on the one hand, which had as its goal to discover the original pre-written forms. On the other hand, it is a different focus from canonical criticism, which has as its goal interpreting an individual psalm in the context of the final form of the book.[94] Thus, the primary focus of this study is not on discerning underlying sources, later additions, original oral forms, or the canonical function of a praise psalm. Not that this perspective denies that there is value in investigating these areas. Rather, it limits itself to understanding each poem as it exists in the Hebrew Bible. Somewhere along the course of

---

[92] Dale Patrick, *The Rhetoric of Revelation in the Bible*, OBT (Minneapolis: Fortress, 1999), 6.

[93] See above, §2.2.

[94] One could study the rhetorical purpose for arranging psalms in a particular sequence, but that is beyond the focus of this study.

Israel's history, each psalm was understood to be a complete whole as it stands. However, this does not deny the value of textual criticism. In each psalm analyzed in this study, the different textual traditions will be examined closely and weighted carefully in discerning what form of the psalm rhetorical analysis should be performed.

2.5.2   PRAISE PSALMS ARE POETRY

Praise psalms are poetic discourse. At this point it will not be helpful to get into the philosophical discussion of "What is poetry?"[95] It is enough for us to recognize that there is a trans-cultural phenomenon of heightened speech. This heightened speech can be helpfully labeled "poetry." What is important is to recognize that poetry falls under the larger umbrella of art. Artistic creations operate on two different levels. Art communicates with an actual audience, but it also creates a world within itself. Rhetoric operates on both of these levels. Howard has labeled these two levels "internal" and "external" rhetorical function.[96]

The external rhetorical function refers to how the praise psalms functioned to shape the beliefs and values of an audience of near contemporaries. That is, praise psalms were not just meant for God's ears. They also were written to educate and shape those who used them and those who heard them. Kenneth Burke gives an example of analyzing the external rhetorical function of a discourse in his article "Antony in

---

[95] E.g., C. L. Stevenson, "On 'What is a Poem?'" *Philosophical Review* 66 (1957): 329–62; Stanley Fish, "How to Recognize a Poem When You See One" in *Is There a Text in This Class?* (Cambridge: Harvard University Press, 1980), 322–38. M. H. Abrams argues that it is not often helpful to create "essential" definitions of key terms like "poetry," which is almost an impossibility. Rather, he argues that "working" definitions are the most helpful. These definitions do not try to define once and for all what "poetry" is, but rather serves to block out an area of inquiry and give the writer some categories with which to organize his work ("What's the Use of Theorizing about the Arts? in *Doing Things with Texts: Essays in Criticism and Critical Theory,* ed. Michael Fischer [New York: Norton, 1991], 40–41).

[96] David M. Howard, Jr. "Psalm 88 and the Rhetoric of Lament," in *My Words are Lovely: Studies in the Rhetoric of the Psalms,* LHB/OTS 467, ed. Robert Foster and David M. Howard, Jr. (New York: T&T Clark, 2008), 132–46.

Behalf of the Play."[97] In this article, Burke examines Antony's "Friends, Romans, Countrymen lend me your ears..." speech from act three of Shakespeare's *Julius Caesar*. He examines this speech not for the rhetorical effect the speech had on the mob audience in the play, but the effect it would have had on the theatre audience, who would have heard the speech from an Elizabethan political context. In the same way, one can examine the effect praise psalms would have had on the audience who heard them and voiced them. Praise psalms were written with an audience in mind. The author(s) assumed that an ancient Israelite, or early Jewish, audience would use these poems for public and private/familial worship.

However, there is also an internal rhetorical function to consider. Artistic works create a world within themselves. Yale philosopher Nicholas Wolterstorff defines art's function this way, "world-projection is perhaps the most pervasive and important of the actions that artists perform by means of their artifacts ... [the artist is] projecting a world for us, presenting to us a world for our consideration. The *world of the work* we may call it."[98] The psalmists achieve their effects, partially at least, through building alternative worlds. They create a world through metaphor, imagery, and hypothetical language and invite the reader to participate in that world.[99] Describing this "world" involves discerning the implied speaker and audience of the psalm itself.[100] For example, the speaker of the psalm could be pictured as a

---

[97] Kenneth Burke, "Antony in Behalf of the Play," in *Philosophy of Literary Form* (Berkeley: University of California Press, 1967), 279–90.

[98] Nicholas Wolterstorff, *Art in Action: Toward a Christian Aesthetic* (Grand Rapids: Eerdmans, 1980): 122–23.

[99] For further reflection on the world-building nature of art, see Martin Heidegger, "The Origin of the Work of Art," in *Poetry, Language, Thought*, trans. Albert Hofstadter (New York: HarperPerennial, 1971), 43–48; Paul Ricoeur, "Naming God," in *Rhetorical Invention and Religious Inquiry*, ed. Walter Jost and Wendy Olmstead (New Haven: Yale University Press, 2000), 166–81; the idea of the world-building nature of psalms has been advocated by Walter Brueggmann, *Israel's Praise: Doxology against Idolatry and Ideology* (Minneapolis: Fortress, 1988), 12–26.

[100] For a theoretical discussion of the implied author, see Wayne Booth, *The Rhetoric of Fiction* (Chicago: University of Chicago Press, 1983), 70–77.

righteous sufferer, as the king, or even as Yhwh. At times, the implied audience of a psalm is God, but almost as often it may be the congregation, the enemy, or the nations.[101] In more dramatic psalms, the identity of the speaker and audience may change in the course of the poem. The essential question at this level is, who is pictured as speaking the psalm to whom and for what purpose? Rhetorical analysis can help us understand this dynamic more clearly. In addition to the implied author and audience, this stage entails describing what type of "world" the implied author and audience inhabit. Umberto Eco has described the alternative worlds created by artists as "small worlds."[102] That is, artists project a world, which highlights particular features and minimize others to achieve their desired effect. For example, one can imagine the different descriptions one could give of the worlds projected in Ps 23 vs. Ps 82; or Ps 1 vs. Ps 74. Thus, this perspective involves describing the speaker, audience, and scenery of the world built by the psalm.

2.5.3   PRAISE PSALMS ARE PRAYERS

Praise psalms are prayers. These affect what type of suasive goals the interpreter should expect to find. Sam Gill has argued that prayers "are often composed for the purpose of edifying, instructing, and influencing people in the matters of dogma, belief, and tradition."[103] That is, prayers do not seek to persuade outsiders to change their perspective on something they strongly disagree with. Rather, they are more concerned with affirming and supporting values that already exist in the community. Prayers have essentially a conservative function.

Chaim Perelman and L. Olbrechts-Tyteca have argued that it is epideictic rhetoric which seeks to affirm and support values embraced

---

[101] For an excellent analysis of the different "voices" and audiences in the Psalter, see Mark J. Boda, "'Varied and Resplendid Riches': Exploring the Breadth and Depth of Worship in the Psalter," in *Rediscovering Worship: Past, Present, Future*, MNTS, ed. Stanley E. Porter (Eugene, OR: Wipf & Stock, forthcoming).

[102] Eco, *Limits of Interpretation*, 64–82.

[103] Sam Gill, "Prayer," in *Encyclopedia of Religion*, vol. 11, ed. Lindsay Jones (New York: MacMillan, 2004), 490.

by a community.[104] This type of rhetoric, "forms a central part of the art of persuasion."[105] The way in which a society increases the "intensity of adherence" to communal norms is central to understanding any society.[106] Thus, understanding how Israel sought to increase adherence to communal norms through praise psalms becomes an important window into ancient Israelite society. Praise psalms would have been especially effective in increasing this adherence for two reasons. First, praise psalms, understood as public prayers, "are always spoken in a particular social context, a community, which is implicitly or explicitly under the guidance and ... authority of institutions (e.g., temples) and community leaders."[107] That is, the praise psalms in the Psalter were authorized prayers and, as such, they embodied the norms and beliefs of the community. Additionally, praise psalms increased the adherence to communal norms due to their function as prayers. Prayer has a powerful formative aspect to it. Gordon Wenham points out that "prayer commits the worshiper to particular attitudes and patterns of behavior and ... this must affect our interpretation of the psalms."[108] A rhetorical approach to praise psalms should consider the unique rhetorical function of prayer as a part of its analysis.

2.5.4   DISCERN THE SOCIAL SITUATION OF PRAISE PSALMS

One of the difficulties with applying rhetorical criticism to praise psalms is that rhetorical analysis assumes a setting. Rhetorical theorists from the earliest times onward have recognized the importance of setting in rhetorical discourse. Aristotle famously defined rhetoric, "as the faculty of observing in any given case the available means of persuasion."[109] It is his emphasis on "in any given case" that highlights

---

[104] Perelman and Olbrechts-Tyteca, *New Rhetoric*, 47–51.

[105] Ibid., 49.

[106] Ibid., 49.

[107] Alan Lenzi, ed. *Reading Akkadian Prayers and Hymns: An Introduction.* ANEM 3 (Atlanta: Scholars Press, 2011), 7.

[108] Gordon Wenham, *Psalms as Torah: Reading Biblical Song Ethically* (Grand Rapids: Baker Academic, 2012), 59.

[109] Aristotle, *Rhetoric*, I.2.

the importance of setting in rhetoric.[110] Thus, to analyze a piece of writing as rhetorical, one must have some idea of the setting.

The problem, then, for Psalms interpretation becomes clear. What is the setting for praise psalms? Or, what is the setting for any individual psalm within the Psalter?[111] Rolf Jacobson has poignantly highlighted this as a problem for a rhetorical approach to the psalms.[112] He discusses historical, theological, and canonical attempts to create a setting. Jacobson describes the dilemma facing rhetorical interpreters. On the one hand, a social situation must be imagined to practice a rhetorical analysis. On the other hand, what does an interpreter do when there are "competing historical, theological, and canonical ways of framing the rhetorical situation of any given psalm"?[113] His answer to this question is worth quoting at length:

> Rhetorical analysts of the Psalms should pay attention to their own rhetorical situations and aims and *weigh those when considering how to imagine the rhetorical situation of a psalm.* That is, an essay, or commentary, or conference paper, or critical note, or lecture, or sermon, or discussion in which a psalm is analyzed rhetorically is itself an act of rhetoric. As such, it has its own rhetorical purpose (what it is trying to do) and its own rhetorical situation.... When trying to frame the rhetorical situation of a psalm, the rhetorical situation of the analysis

---

[110] This point was made by Rolf Jacobson, "The Altar of Certitude": Reflections on the 'Setting' and Rhetorical Interpretation of the Psalms" in *My Words are Lovely: Studies in the Rhetoric of the Psalms,* LHB/OTS 467 (New York: T&T Clark, 2008), 4–5.

[111] This is a familiar problem for rhetorical analysis of any poetry. Theorist Terry Eagleton demonstrates that this is not an insurmountable problem, "Poetry is language which comes without these contextual clues, and which therefore has to be reconstructed by the reader in the light of a context which will make sense of it. And such contexts are in embarrassingly plentiful supply. Yet they are not just arbitrary either: on the contrary, they are shaped in turn by the cultural contexts by which the reader makes sense of the world in general" (*How to Read a Poem,* 109).

[112] Jacobson, "Altar of Certitude," 3–18.

[113] Ibid., 17.

should be a part of the conversation.[114]

There is much in this conclusion to commend. It is, of course, important to consider the rhetorical situation of the interpreter as well as the text. I wholeheartedly agree that the "rhetorical situation of the analysis" should be part of the conversation. However, Jacobson implies that the situation of the interpreter should play a decisive role in determining the setting. That is, he seems to be arguing that in the face of diverse possibilities for the rhetorical situation of the psalm, the interpreter should look at his/her situation and let that define which of the possible rhetorical situations of the psalm fits best into his/her context. This becomes very close to a straight reader-response approach to the psalm. I would argue that the text itself can provide the interpreter with more of a boundary for interpretation than Jacobson implies.[115]

The problem of how to interpret a poem when one does not know the original author or situation of the text in question has been helpfully addressed by Umberto Eco. He argues that when one cannot speak of an authorial intent, it is still possible to speak of a "text-immanent intent," which can serve as a boundary in interpretation.[116] Eco indicates that it is possible to discover the "intention of the text" as a way to discern good readings from bad, or better, more plausible readings from less plausible.[117]

Several factors need to be considered when elucidating the textual intent of a discourse. For example, the contemporary reader should be able to determine if a text was written for a single addressee (e.g., a personal letter); or for a community. This would be discerned by examining the content of the text itself. Does it deal with issues of general interest, or is it directed at a single reader? A personal letter will be more difficult for a reader with no knowledge of the author or addressee to interpret. There could be many unique references that the

---

[114] Ibid., 18.

[115] See Phillips, "Rhetoric," 239.

[116] Umberto Eco, "Between Author and Text," in *Interpretation and Overinterpretation*, ed. Stefan Collini (Cambridge: Cambridge University Press, 1992), 67–87.

[117] Ibid., 78.

author would have assumed the addressee knew, but an outside reader would have no knowledge of.

However, the psalms do not function as private communication. They are public documents. They assume that a large community of Yhwh worshippers will be able to understand and use them for their own worship. This makes discovering the textual intent a bit easier. Eco explains, "when a text is produced not for a single addressee but for a community of readers, the author knows that he or she will be interpreted not according to his or her intentions but according to a complex strategy of interactions which also involves the readers, along with their competence in language as a social treasury."[118] That is, when an author knows they are writing for a large group of people, they take into account the knowledge, linguistic competence, and perspectives of the intended audience. They will carefully craft their discourse with a consideration of how their writing will be understood in the community for which they are writing. The knowledge and competence an author will assume not only includes grammatical conventions, but also shared cultural references and values.[119] The challenge for a modern interpreter is to understand and enter the linguistic and cultural context that the original author assumed. This means paying careful attention to cultural norms, linguistic usages, and the larger context of Israelite faith and experience. One can then argue for how an audience of near contemporaries would have understood a psalm as well as which social contexts a psalm would be most appropriately used in, which would be the textual intent.

This discussion, however, does not mean that there is "one" correct interpretation of a given praise psalm. Since the psalms are public documents designed for public worship, the author undoubtedly intended the poems to be utilized in different situations. One could be praising God for different reasons. Thus, the psalm would be concerned to shape the praise of the worshipper in a particular direction. That is, the authorial goals a rhetorical interpretation would be con-

---

[118] Ibid., 67.
[119] Ibid., 68.

cerned about describing are analyzing the ways in which the author wanted to shape the perspectives and beliefs of the audience regardless of the specific reason for the praise. Additionally, it may be difficult to know if a particular psalm is pre- or post- exilic. The different historical contexts would affect the assumed textual intent. Thus, for some psalms it may be helpful, rather than declaring a particular psalm is pre- or post-exilic, to instead present how the different contexts would produce different readings of a psalm.

Thus, the social setting of a particular praise psalm would need to be posited inductively based on the text-imminent intent of the psalm. This is a more interpretively helpful way forward than simply highlighting the situation of the contemporary interpreter and letting that determine the setting posited for the psalm.

2.5.5   ANALYZE THE FORMATIONAL INTENT OF PRAISE PSALMS

From ancient times, the Psalms have been recognized as having an ability to shape the user. Athanasius famously distinguished the Psalms from the rest of scripture because of its unique formative power.[120] He states,

> For in the other books one hears only what one must do and what one must not do.... But in the Book of Psalms, the one who hears, in addition to learning these things, also comprehends and is taught in it the emotions of the soul, and, consequently, on the basis of that which affects him and by which he is constrained, he also is enabled by this book to possess the image deriving from the words...And the one who hears [the Psalms] is deeply moved, as though he himself were speaking, and is affected by the words of the songs, as if they were his own songs.[121]

---

[120] Athanasius, *Letter to Marcellinus*, trans. Robert Gregg (Mahwah, NJ: Paulist, 1980), 108.

[121] Ibid., 108.

The Psalms do not just teach historical truths about God, or command obedience. Rather, they involve the user in having them recite the words of the psalmist as their own. This insight has not been lost on modern scholarship. Harry Nasuti has referred to the formative nature of the Psalms as "sacramental." He states, "the Psalms have what one may call sacramental power in that they are the means of bringing about a reality that would not exist without their use...the Psalms may be seen as the means by which the rest of Scripture is actualized in the believer."[122] A helpful way of understanding this insight is to borrow the language of Speech-Act Theory and view the Psalms as self-involving speech.[123] J. L. Austin opened up this line of research through his analysis of language use that went beyond mere description.[124] Many praise psalms describe God and how he interacts with the world. But they also go beyond description. By involving the worshipper in making these statements their own, they help to bring about a new relationship between the worshipper and God. The worshipper often makes vows or commits him/herself to certain beliefs or practic-

---

[122] Harry Nasuti, "The Sacramental Function of the Psalms in Contemporary Scholarship and Liturgical Practice," in *Psalms and Practice: Worship, Virtue, and Authority*, ed. Stephen Reid (Collegeville, MN: Liturgical Press, 2001), 79, 81. A similar view has been advocated by James Luther Mays, "Means of Grace: The Benefits of Psalmic Prayer," in *The Lord Reigns: A Theological Handbook to the Psalms* (Louisville: Westminster, 1994), 40–46.

[123] Several scholars have applied Speech Act Theory to Psalms interpretation. E.g., Andreas Wagner, *Beten und Bekennen: Über Psalmen* (Newkirchen-Vluyn: Neukirchener Verlag, 2008); Karl Möller, "Reading, Singing and Praying the Law: An Exploration of the Performative, Self-Involving, Commissive Language of Psalm 101," in *Reading the Law: Studies in Honour of Gordon J. Wenham*, LHB/OTS 461, ed. J. G. McConville and Karl Möller (London: T&T Clark, 2007), 111–37; Gordon Wenham, *Psalms as Torah*, 57–76; Herbert Levine, *Sing unto God a New Song: A Contemporary Reading of the Psalms* (Bloomington: Indiana University Press, 1995); Gordon Wenham, "Reflections on Singing the Ethos of God," *EuroJTh* (2009): 115–24; Andy Warren, "Modality, Reference and Speech Acts in the Psalms," *TynBul* 53 (2002): 149–52; Kit Barker, "Divine Illocutions in Psalm 137: A Critique of Nicholas Wolterstorff's 'Second Hermeneutic,'" *TynBul* 60 (2009): 1–14.

[124] J. L. Austin, *How to Do Things with Words*, 2nd ed., ed. J. O. Urmson and M. Sbisa (Oxford: Oxford University Press, 1975).

es in the psalm that profoundly impact the life of the worshipper. While this study will not formally adopt Speech-Act Theory as a part of its methodology, I will occasionally utilize insights from this approach as a part of the rhetorical analysis of the psalms studied.

2.5.6   UTILIZE THE TOOLS AND CATEGORIES OF RHETORICAL
        CRITICISM TO ANALYZE THE ARGUMENT OF PRAISE PSALMS

Central to a rhetorical approach to praise psalms is demonstrating that praise psalms have goals they are attempting to achieve. The way in which they go about achieving these goals could be termed the "argument" of the psalm. Thus, an important part of a rhetorical interpretation of praise psalms will be to analyze both the ultimate goal of the praise psalm and how a particular psalm achieves its goals; in short, to analyze the argument of the psalm.

A question arises at this point of how we should analyze the argument of praise psalms. The Hebrew Bible does not have a conceptual framework, or stated rhetorical theory. In Phillips' words, the Hebrew Bible presents us with "pre-conceptual" rhetoric.[125] Since ancient Israel did not provide us with a theoretical framework or vocabulary to utilize in analyzing its rhetoric, the question then becomes, what kind of terms should we use to analyze Hebrew rhetoric? There is a debate about whether critics should use emic or etic categories to describe a culture's writing/rhetoric.[126] "Emic" is an attempt to utilize indigenous terminology. That is, to find words native to biblical Hebrew with which to describe its rhetoric. "Etic" description is the utilization of vocabulary from one culture and applying it to another.[127]

Those who argue for emic descriptions believe that it is not possible to use Western rhetorical terms without importing and imposing Western culture and values onto the interpretation of these decidedly non-Western texts. This perspective would mean that the inter-

---

[125] Phillips, "Rhetoric," 252.

[126] Lu, *Rhetoric in Ancient China*, 14–43.

[127] See Jeannie Brown, "Genre Criticism," in *Words & the Word: Explorations in Biblical Interpretation & Literary Theory*, ed. David Firth and Jamie Grant (Downers Grove, IL: IVP Academic, 2008), 129.

preter would have to develop a way of analyzing Hebrew rhetoric by creating an indigenous vocabulary of rhetorical terms. The problem with this is that it means introducing dozens of new terms that would make the monograph inaccessible to the uninitiated.

A better way forward is to utilize the sophisticated vocabulary and conceptual framework that has been developed in Western culture and use it in the analysis of Hebrew rhetoric.[128] For example, earlier I discussed how praise psalms could function as epideictic rhetoric. This does not mean that the author, or an audience of near contemporaries, would have used or understood that term. In one sense a praise psalm is not epideictic rhetoric. Rather, it resembles epideictic rhetoric. The term "epideictic" helps the modern interpreter understand one of the ways in which a praise psalm functioned. So, the Western tradition of rhetorical criticism gives the interpreter many terms to use for Hebrew rhetoric in an analogous way to how they are used in Western rhetoric.[129] The terms can then be refined and nuanced in ways particular to Hebrew rhetoric. In this study, I will be using categories and terms from both ancient rhetoricians (e.g., Aristotle) and modern theorists (e.g., Chaim Perelman and George Kennedy). In short, I will be drawing from the main insights of Western rhetorical tradition.[130] The goal is not to simply link Western rhetorical terms to various poetic devices and think something has been accomplished. Rather, the goal is to foster better understanding of individual praise psalms.[131] Deeper under-

---

[128] E.g., Thomas Sloane, ed. *Encyclopedia of Rhetoric* (Oxford: Oxford University Press, 2001).

[129] Roland Meynet has attempted to describe in broad terms some of the differences between Hebrew and Greco-Roman rhetoric: 1) it is more concrete than abstract; 2) it uses parataxis more than syntax; and 3) it is more intuitive than linear (*Rhetorical Analysis: An Introduction to Biblical Rhetoric*, JSOTSup 256 [Sheffield: Sheffield Academic, 1998], 172–77).

[130] For a helpful introduction to the Western rhetorical tradition, see James Herrick, *History and Theory of Rhetoric*; see also Patricia Bizzell and Bruce Herzberg, *Rhetorical Tradition*.

[131] This has been successfully done with poems in literary criticism, for an example, see Thomas Sloan, "Rhetorical Analysis of John Donne's 'The Prohibition,'" in *Rhetorical Analysis of Literary Works*, ed. Edward Corbett (London: Ox-

standing is often achieved through analogy, but in the end it is an analogy, not an identification of Western rhetorical devices in Near Eastern literature. Thus, this study will utilize Western terminology, both
from classic and modern rhetorical theory in analyzing the "argument"
of praise psalms. The usefulness of this approach will be demonstrated
in its application.

2.5.7   OUTLINE FOR THE ANALYSIS OF PRAISE PSALMS

As stated earlier, it is not advisable to create "steps" to rhetorical criticism and view this as the way rhetorical criticism is done. Rhetorical
analysis is more of a mind-set one cultivates to analyze texts, rather
than a wooden system of interpretation. Nevertheless, it is possible and
important to structure our study in a way that highlights the unique
contribution of this approach. So, while not claiming that this is the
only way to engage in rhetorical analysis of the praise psalms, the following outline presents an ordered way in which rhetorical analysis
can be accomplished:

1) Determination of the rhetorical unit;[132]
2) Description of the world of the psalm: its internal argument.
   This stage involved discerning the implied/textual author
   and audience and the rhetorical function of the text within
   the world of the psalm itself;[133]
3) Determination of the possible rhetorical situation(s) of the
   psalm;[134]
4) Analysis of the argument of the psalm: its external argument;

---

ford University Press, 1969), 3–15. Sloan reflects on the utility of a rhetorical analysis in this way, "It would appear that a rhetorical analysis of this poem is useful in
exploring the connections between structure and meaning" (12). I would go beyond
that and say that a rhetorical analysis is also helpful in clarifying how a poem was
intended to function. That is, how a poem works to shape the emotions, thoughts,
and perspectives of the reader.

[132] Kennedy, *New Testament Interpretation*, 33.

[133] See §2.5.2.2.

[134] See §2.5.4.2.

5) Evaluation of a rhetorical interpretation of the psalm in light of other approaches.

In essence, this final section will highlight how rhetorical analysis can deepen our understanding of these texts.

2.5.8   SCOPE OF THE STUDY

This study seeks to apply rhetorical criticism to praise psalms. In order to achieve this goal, I will analyze four particular praise psalms in the following chapters. These psalms were chosen based on the form analysis of Claus Westermann.[135] Westermann has divided praise psalms into two major groups: declarative and descriptive praise. Declarative praise psalms fall into two sub-groups, individual and corporate. Descriptive praise psalms are always corporate. Additionally, he discusses one other major category of descriptive praise psalm, "creation psalms." Creation psalms are, he states, "the only group of Psalms of praise in the Psalter in which one motif developed into an independent Psalm.... This group shows that where one motif is expanded to form a whole Psalm there is no longer any rigid form."[136]

Thus, for this study I will analyze one psalm from each of these categories:

Creation Psalm: Psalm 19
Descriptive Psalm of Praise: Psalm 103
Declarative Praise of the People: Psalm 46
Declarative Praise of the Individual: Psalm 116

While this is not the only way one could categorize praise psalms, Westermann's categories are well known and provide a helpful outline in order to analyze a wide variety of praise psalms.

---

[135] Westermann, *Praise and Lament in the Psalms.*
[136] Ibid., 139.

CHAPTER 3
Rhetorical Analysis of Psalm 19

3.1   INTRODUCTION

C. S. Lewis famously asserted, "I take this [Ps. 19] to be the greatest poem in the Psalter and one of the greatest lyrics in the world."[1] Not all have shared his assessment.[2] Yet, as Bruce Waltke points out, Ps 19 has been one of the most well-known and celebrated psalms having been the subject of poems by Gerard Manley Hopkins and Charles Péguy as well as serving as the inspiration for Haydn's *Creation*.[3] Additionally, the psalm has been served well by intense scholarly attention over the last two-hundred years.[4] Thus, this psalm will serve as a good test case to determine if a rhetorical approach to the psalm as outlined in the previous chapter has anything to contribute to the conversation about this well-known poem.

Psalm 19 is difficult to classify form-critically. Part of the reason for this is related to debates about its unity (see below). Waltke captures the diverse aspects of this poem well when he articulates its unique character as "a psalm of wisdom, thanksgiving, and petition."[5] Claus Westermann classified it among the group of Creation psalms. This is a group of psalms in which one theme has come to dominate to the extent that there is no rigid form.[6] Thus, this psalm will also serve

---

[1] C. S. Lewis, *Reflections on the Psalms* (Orlando, FL: Harcourt, 1958), 54.

[2] See the scathing remarks on the poetry of Psalm 19 in Bernhard Duhm, *Die Psalmen*, KHAT (Leipzig: Mohr Siebeck, 1899), 60–64.

[3] Bruce Waltke and James Houston, *The Psalms as Christian Worship: A Historical Commentary* (Grand Rapids: Eerdmans, 2010), 340.

[4] E.g., see the scholars discussed in John H. Eaton, *Psalms of the Way and the Kingdom: A Conference with the Commentators*, JSOTSup 199 (Sheffield: Sheffield Academic 1995), 14–54.

[5] Waltke and Houston, *Psalms as Christian Worship*, 340.

[6] Westermann understood this as a sub-category of the "Descriptive Psalm of Praise." Other creation psalms include Pss 8, 29, 104, 139, and 148 (*Praise and*

as an exemplar of this type of praise psalm.

In this chapter, I will present a rhetorical approach to Ps 19 in the following way. First, I will present a translation of the psalm and discuss the rhetorical unit. This is where issues concerning the unity and coherence of the psalm will be addressed. Second, I will analyze the internal argument of the psalm. This will be accomplished by describing the world of the psalm. This includes a description of the implied speaker, audience, and world created by the poem. Then, utilizing the tools of rhetorical criticism, I will analyze the internal argument of the psalm. Third, I will discuss possible social situations in which the psalm had its origin. Fourth, I will analyze the external argument of the psalm. This will be accomplished through discussing exegetical difficulties, clarifying the structure, and finally utilizing rhetorical tools to describe its suasive impact.

3.2   TRANSLATION

Title
To the Leader, a Psalm of David.   (1)
Strophe 1
The heavens are reporting the glory of El   (2)
  The work[7] of his hands, the sky is announcing
Day to day gushes forth news   (3)
  And night to night, it declares knowledge
There is no news and there are no words   (4)
  their voice is not heard
In all the earth their voice[8] has gone forth   (5)
  And to the end of the world their words
For the sun he has set a tent in them[9]

Lament in the Psalms, 139).

   [7] The Targums, Symmachus, and the Vulgate indicate that the word here has a masculine plural construct ending. This is not a significant change interpretively. The translations likely shifted to the plural for semantic reasons, God is spoken of as creating more than one "work" (e.g., Pss 107:24; 111:2; 118:17).

   [8] I have emended קַוָּם to קוֹלָם for a defense of this emendation, see §3.6.

   [9] בָּהֶם is a bit awkward here. I assume they refer back to the "heavens." The

And he is like a bridegroom coming forth from his chamber (6)
    He rejoices like a hero to run a path[10]
From the end of the heavens is his entrance (7)
    And his circuit is to[11] their end
    There is nothing hidden from its heat.

Strophe 2

The law of	Yhwh is perfect	(8)

    Restoring life
The testimony of Yhwh is reliable
    Making wise the naïve

The instructions of	Yhwh are right	(9)

    Rejoicing the heart
The command of Yhwh is pure
    Enlightening the eyes
The fear of Yhwh is clean (10)
    Standing continually
The judgments of Yhwh are trustworthy
    They are altogether just.
    They are more desirable than gold (11)
    And more than pure gold
And they are sweeter than honey
    Than honey from a comb

Strophe 3

Indeed, your servant is warned by them (12)
    In keeping them, great reward
Mistakes, who can understand? (13)
    From sins of ignorance, hold me guiltless
Indeed, from presumptuousness hold back your servant (14)
    Let them not rule over me
Then I will be complete

---

phrase is omitted in the LXX.

    [10] אֹרַח does not have an object suffix on it. The suffix is likely assumed from the first half of the verse(מְחֻפָּתוֹ). It is included in the LXX and Syriac.

    [11] עַל here has the sense of "to, toward" as in later Hebrew, see *HALOT*, 825.

and I will be guiltless from great transgression
Let the words of my mouth be pleasing   (15)
And the meditations of my heart before you
O Yhwh, my rock and my redeemer

3.3   DETERMINATION OF THE RHETORICAL UNIT

There has been significant debate concerning the unity of Ps 19. In the
previous chapter, I stated that a rhetorical approach analyzes a psalm as
a unified discourse. Thus, if a psalm is already given a beginning and
ending in the Hebrew Bible why address the debate? Nevertheless, there
are some psalms in the final form of the Psalter that in the course of
transmission have been separated, and thus should be treated as a single
unit.[12] It is also possible that two psalms which were independent compositions became compressed into one unit. Some scholars believe that
is what happened with this psalm. Artur Weiser treats the two parts of
Ps 19 as independent compositions that have been artificially combined
in the canonical Psalter.[13] In fact, outside of a few dissenting opinions,
most scholars believe that Ps 19 is the result of at least two different
hands.[14] The question at issue is not whether the psalm went through
various stages of redaction or addition, but whether the psalm as a
whole was ever artfully intended to be an integrated unit.

---

[12] E.g., Pss 9–10; 42–43

[13] Artur Weiser states, "Psalm 19 consists of two independent songs which in
subject-matter, mood, language, and metre differ from each other so much that they
cannot be composed by the same author" (*The Psalms: A Commentary,* trans. H. H.
Hartwell, OTL [Philadelphia: Westminster, 1962], 197).

[14] Dissenting voices include: Michael A Fishbane, *Text and Texture: Close
Readings of Selected Biblical Texts* (New York: Schocken 1979), 86; Nahum M
Sarna, *Songs of the Heart: an Introduction to the Book of Psalms* (New York:
Schocken, 1993), 74; Alfons Deissler, "Zur Datierung und Situierung der
'Kosmischen Hymnen' Pss 8, 19, 29," in *Lex tua veritas; Festschrift für Hubert
Junker zu Vollendung des siebzigsten Lebensjahres am 8 August 1961* (Trier:
Paulinus-Verlag, 1961), 47–58; Samuel Terrien, *The Psalms: Strophic Structure and
Theological Commentary* (Grand Rapids: Eerdmans 2003), 208–9; Philip Nel,
"Psalm 19: The Unbearable Lightness of Perfection," *JNSL* 30 (2004): 103–17.

Older commentaries tended to treat the two parts of the psalm as two different compositions.[15] However, more recent scholarship has recognized that whatever the origin of Ps 19A and B, the two halves have been intentionally and skillfully crafted together to form a unified whole.[16] These scholars have demonstrated a compelling case that thematic, conceptual, and cultural links bind the two sections of the psalm together so that it can be justifiably understood as a unified whole. These links will be enumerated in the ensuing discussion.

3.4 DESCRIPTION OF THE WORLD OF THE PSALM: ITS INTERNAL ARGUMENT

Describing the world of the psalm involves attention to three parts. First, the implied speaker and implied audience need to be defined. That is, the speaker and audience that interact within the world of the poem itself. For example, if the heavens are commanded to praise Yhwh (e.g., Ps 148:4), then they become a part of the implied audience of the poem.[17] Second, the world of the psalm needs to be described. Umberto Eco described how artists create "small-worlds," which highlight the specific parts of the "real" world they want to highlight to

---

[15] Julian Morgenstern, "Psalms 8 and 19a," *HUCA* 19 (1946): 491–526; Weiser, *Psalms*, 197; Hans-Joachim Kraus treats Psalms 19A and B as originating from different contexts and thus unrelated compositions. Nevertheless, he states that one must think about how the two parts relate since tradition has welded them together (*Psalms 1–59: A Continental Commentary*, trans. Hilton Oswald [Minneapolis: Fortress, 1993], 269).

[16] Rolf P. Knierim, "On the Theology of Psalm 19," in *Ernten, was man sät* (Neukirchen-Vluyn: Neukirchener Verlag, 1991), 322–50; John H. Eaton, *The Psalms: A Historical and Spiritual Commentary* (New York: T&T Clark, 2003), 108; Jonathan T. Glass, "Some Observations on Psalm 19," in *Listening Heart: Essays in Wisdom and the Psalms in Honour of Roland E. Murphy*, JSOTSup 58, ed. K. Hoglund (Sheffield: Sheffield Academic, 1987), 147–48; John Goldingay, *Psalms: Psalms 1–41*, vol. 1, BCOTWP (Grand Rapids: Baker, 2006), 284; J. Ross Wagner, "From the Heavens to the Heart: The Dynamics of Psalm 19 as Prayer," *CBQ* 61 (1999): 245–61; William P. Brown, *Seeing the Psalms: A Theology of Metaphor* (Louisville: Westminster John Knox, 2002), 83.

[17] For a discussion of the implied author, see Booth, *Rhetoric of Fiction*, 70–77.

achieve their intended effect.[18] Thus, the geography and ethos of the world of the psalm will be elucidated. This will necessitate a discussion of how ANE themes and concepts play a role in the psalm. Third, the internal argument of the psalm will be described. That is, how is the implied speaker intending to persuade/shape the implied audience. Often the internal argument of a psalm will be somewhat different than the external argument.

3.4.1   THE IMPLIED AUTHOR

No author, implied or otherwise, is hinted at until v. 12, where the author is identified as עַבְדֶּךָ.[19] While the term, in the context of the title and the placement of the psalm in the Psalter, could connote "king," (cf. Ps 18), it could also describe an ordinary Israelite.[20] While the term was used as a "polite and humble reference to oneself" (e.g., Gen 33:5),[21] it was most often used by someone of lower social status addressing someone of a higher status (e.g., Gen 42:10), or by equals if

---

[18] Eco, *Limits of Interpretation*, 64–82.

[19] This feature of the psalm has been noted by some commentators, e.g., J. Ross Wagner comments on the first half of the psalm, "Significantly, there is no mention of human beings. Not even the psalmist is noticeably present" ("From the Heavens to the Heart," 253). The first place some would look to for clues on authorship is to the psalm title. The role of the psalm title in the interpretation of a psalm has been the subject of much debate among recent interpreters. E.g., see Brevard Childs, "Psalm Titles and Midrashic Exegesis," *JSS* 16 (1971): 137–50; Leslie C. Allen, "David as Exemplar of Spirituality: the Redactional Function of Psalm 19," *Biblica* 67 (1986): 544–46; Wilhelm VanGemeren and Jason Stanghelle, "A Critical-Realistic Reading of the Psalm Titles," in *Do Historical Matters Matter to Faith? A Critical Appraisal of Modern and Post-Modern Approaches to Scripture*, ed. James Hoffmeier et al. (Wheaton, IL: Crossway, 2012), 281–301. The approach of this study is to examine the psalm titles on a case-by-case basis. At times, the title may be helpful in approaching the interpretation of a psalm, other times the title may not have a significant impact on the meaning of the poem. In the case of this psalm, the title does not play a significant role in the interpretation of the psalm.

[20] E.g., Patrick D. Miller, "Kingship, Torah Obedience, and Prayer: the Theology of Psalms 15–24," in *Neue Wege der Psalmenforschung: Für Walter Beyerlin*, ed. E. Zenger (Freiburg: Herder, 1994), 279–97.

[21] *TWOT*, 639.

one wanted to show deference to the other (e.g., Gen 32:4). The use of
עֶבֶד here has its closest parallel to the extensive use of the term in Ps
119, where it clearly does not refer to a king (cf. Ps 119:23, 38, 49, 65,
76, 84, 91, 122, 124, 125, 135, 140, 176).[22]

The author is further pictured as one with a great concern for
moral and ceremonial purity (vv. 13–15).[23] The faults that the psalmist
frets over go beyond outward actions to include inner thoughts as well
(v. 15). This is someone with a high religious sensibility.[24] The servant
of Yhwh believes that he is capable of committing a gross infraction of
God's Torah.[25] Thus, he prays for God to restrain (חשׂך) him from doing so (v. 14). The author has both high sensitivity to moral infractions
and an acute awareness of his own frailty. Additionally, he has a deeply personal and relational connection to Yahweh, calling him *his* rock
and *his* redeemer (v. 15). "Rock" (צוּר) is a familiar term in the
Psalms[26] stressing the psalmist's dependence on God for protection.
The "rock" referred to here could either be the temple, which served in
times of distress as a haven (e.g., Judg 9:46–49), or to a natural geographical feature. Keel describes the geographical reference in this
way, "In some parts of Palestine, in the regions east of the Dead Sea,

---

[22] See also the discussion in Goldingay, *Psalms: Psalms 1-41,* 294. For a
cogent, non-royal *Sitz im Leben* for Psalm 119, see Frank Lothar Hossfeld and Eric
Zenger, *Psalms 3: A Commentary on Psalms 101–150,* Hermeneia (Minneapolis:
Fortress, 2011), 262–63.

[23] Note the use of נקה in vv. 13 and 14.

[24] E.g., see Terrien's description of the psalmist, "Friend of the sages, the
poet was deeply concerned with cosmology. As a strict Yahwist, he is thrilled by the
marvel of nature, but he does not confuse the world with the deities of oriental religions. He was profoundly offended by the invasion of solar cults in the Jerusalem
temple. He served Yahweh, his maker, and he applied himself with an almost obses-
sive fervor to his search for perfection. The terror of an ultimate transgression implies a danger as grave as that of cultic and cultural syncretism. His spirituality led
him to the concluding intuition of a theologian. He is tormented by the very satisfac-
tion that his accomplishments have produced in his mind. He is seduced by the perspective of being equal to God" (*Psalms,* 215).

[25] I am using the masculine singular pronoun "he" because it matches the
grammatical person and gender of עַבְדְּךָ (v. 14).

[26] It is used of God 25x in 15 different psalms.

and in the Arba, wadi beds, cut deep into the soft chalk or sandstone, have isolated, mighty rocks that could serve as natural strongholds. In times of need, the population of the open country and of the smaller towns withdrew to these rocks of refuge (cf. Jer 4:29; 16:16; 49:16; 1 Sam 13:16)."[27] In either case, the psalmist envisions Yhwh as his most secure ally. The term "Redeemer" (גֹּאֵל) is more relational in nature. For ancient Israel, a גֹּאֵל was a close relative responsible to buy back a brother from slavery (Lev 25:47–55). Behind this usage, "stands the strong feeling of tribal solidarity: not only the members of the clan, but also their possessions, form an organic unity, and every disruption of this unity is regarded as intolerable and as something which must be restored or repaired."[28] It is this sense of close, yet dependent relationship that the psalmist articulates with this image for God.

The picture of the psalmist derived from vv. 11–14 can then be read back into the beginning of the psalm as well. It is this close relationship with Yahweh that explains the psalmist's insight into the unheard discourse of the heavens. The psalmist's entire horizon is dominated by the reality of God. He looks to the heavens and sees them chattering away about God. He concerns himself with the Torah as the most important reality on earth (v. 11). This is the perspective of a poet-philosopher—a wise man, one who has spent his life contemplating divine realities. J. Ross Wagner captures the psalmist well when he states,

> The psalmist contemplates the unceasing praise of God's majesty that issues forth from the creation, and he longs to join in with acceptable words of praise. He muses on the beauty and perfection of Torah and prays to be made whole and blameless like that instruction and the One who gives it. As the psalm comes to its climax, this longing and prayer burst forth in a heartfelt plea for forgiveness and aid, a plea that is grounded in

---

[27] Othmar Keel, *The Symbolism of the Biblical World: Ancient Near Eastern Iconography and the Book of Psalms*, trans. T. Hallett (Winona Lake, IN: Eisenbrauns, 1997), 180.

[28] H. Ringgren, "גאל," *TDOT* 2:351.

an intimate understanding of Yhwh's faithfulness and mercy.[29]

3.4.3 THE IMPLIED AUDIENCE

The clearest indication of an implied audience comes in vv. 11–14. Beginning in v. 11, the psalmist uses the 2ms pronoun (עַבְדְּךָ) which indicates that he is addressing God. Yhwh continues as the main textual audience through the end of the poem. However, Yhwh is not indicated as the audience in the first part of the poem. Indeed, vv. 2–10 speak about God in the third person. Thus, another audience must be presumed. This gives a dramatic element to the psalm. The psalmist addresses one audience, then shifts at the appropriate moment to address God directly, all the while keeping the other audience in view. But just who constitutes the former audience? The text is ambiguous at this point, both about the implied author and audience. This is itself rhetorical significant, as will be discussed below. What can be said is that the audience in vv. 2–7 seems to be universal in scope.[30] The heavens (שָׁמַיִם) and the sky (רָקִיעַ) by definition serve as a covering for the entire world.[31] Their message is also said to go out "into all the world" (בְּכָל־הָאָרֶץ) and "to the ends of the earth" (וּבִקְצֵה תֵבֵל). This would imply that their message has relevance for all people. Additionally, the imagery of day and night, of the sun and its circuit, and the more generic noun for God (אֵל) all serve to indicate that the psalmist is speaking to all people. However, two factors mitigate against the view that the implied audience is composed of all people. Verses 8–10 speak specifically about revelation that was unique to Israel. Additionally, the seven-fold repetition of the name Yhwh, gives the overall poem an exclusively Israelite feel. Secondly, when one considers the per-

---

[29] Wagner, "From the Heavens to the Heart," 261.

[30] Goldingay maintains, "[Ps. 19] begins by addressing on one in particular and does so through the first section and on through vv. 7–10 until it comes to address and plead with God in vv. 11–14; there is no address to the congregation, in the usual manner of Israelite Praise" (*Psalms: Psalms 1-41*, 286

[31] See John Walton, *Ancient Near Eastern Thought and the Old Testament: Introducing the Conceptual World of the Hebrew Bible* (Grand Rapids: Baker Academic, 2006), 168–69; Keel, *Symbolism of the Biblical World*, 16–47.

suasive intent of the psalm, the audience narrows even more. The psalmist does not attempt to persuade a universal audience. The poem ends on an inward note. The key to defining the internal audience of the poem comes in v. 15. The psalmist prays that his words (אִמְרֵי־פִי) and thoughts (הֶגְיוֹן לִבִּי) would be acceptable to Yhwh. In the context of the psalm, the words and thoughts mentioned would be equivalent to vv. 2–12. Thus, within the world of the psalm, the entire poem can be viewed as primarily self-speech. But it is not just self-speech. The psalmist intends his meditations to be overheard by Yhwh as part of the motivation for Yhwh's help in maintaining purity (vv. 13–15). In sum, while it seems that there are two audiences in view for the psalm, there is actually only one, Yhwh. The psalmist is rehearsing his meditations concerning truths about creation and the Law as motivation for Yhwh to act on his behalf.

3.4.4   THE WORLD OF PSALM 19

Psalm 19 presents us with an ordered, vibrant world. The cosmos is an animate, speaking, rejoicing, "sound-and-light show"[32] all directed at celebrating the glory of God. The heavens and sky continually speak of El's glory. Keel has demonstrated from ANE iconography that in the ancients understood the world as "composed of earth and sky, with the sky protectively spreading its wings over the earth and ensuring prosperity. The harmonious relation between heaven and earth is represented and guaranteed by the king."[33] In this psalm the unity of creation is found, not in the king, but in the mutual goal of proclaiming the glory of El. Not only do the sky and the heavens speak, but the day bubbles forth (נבע) to the following day and night to night. The sun is envisioned as lounging in his divinely provided tent in the evenings only to burst forth in power and joy each day. Significantly, there is no sense of conflict or chaos here. In Egyptian, Mesopotamian, and Canaanite thought, the Sun (Re/Shamash/Shapshu) traveled through the

---

[32] William Brown, "The Sun of Righteousness: Psalm 19 and the Joy of *Lex*," in *Seeing the Psalms*, 103.

[33] Keel, *Symbolism of the Biblical World*, 29.

netherworld at night where he was assailed by demons and had to fight his way back up for the morning.[34] Rather than being pictured as a warrior battling his way through the night, the sun is pictured as a bridegroom emerging in joy from his chamber.

The idea that the heavens could speak is a familiar one in the ANE. In the Baal Cycle, El's messengers declare to Kothar-wahasis (CAT 1.4, 13–14):[35]

> Word of tree and whisper of stone,
>> The converse of heaven to hell
>> Of deeps to stars
> The word people do not know,
>> Earth's masses do not understand,
> Come and I will reveal it.

Similar to Psalm 19, this passage references the speech of the heavens which people do not really hear (Ps 19:4). However, this speech can be revealed by El. Similarly, while people cannot audibly hear the discourse of the heavens, Yhwh reveals to people everything they really need to know (Ps 19:8–10).[36]

The sense of ordered praise and joy continues in the second

---

[34] The ideas of what exactly the sun did in the netherworld varied somewhat between cultures. In Egypt, Re's travel through the netherworld was the most perilous, in Mesopotamian thought, Shamash dispensed light and food to those in the netherworld, see Walton, *Ancient Near Eastern Thought and the Old Testament*, 171. On Solar imagery in Psalm 19, see Walter Harrelson, "Psalm 19: A Meditation on God's Glory in the Heavens and in God's Law," in *Worship and the Hebrew Bible: Essays in Honour of John T. Willis*, JSOTSup 284, ed. M. P. Graham (Sheffield: Sheffield, 1999), 144–45; and William Brown, "Sun of Righteousness," 81–104.

[35] Translated by Simon B. Parker and Mark S. Smith, *Ugaritic Narrative Poetry* (Atlanta: Scholars Press, 1997), 91.

[36] It is important to note that the context of this text from the Baal Cycle and Ps 19 are quite different. The heavens are not declaring the glory of El in this text. The Baal Cycle text is discussing preparations for making rain. See the discussion of the two texts by H. van Zyl, "Psalm 19," in *Studia biblica et semetica: Festschrift Theodoro Christiano Vriezen*, ed. W. C. Van Unnik and A. S. Van Der Woude (Wangeningen: Veenman, 1966), 146–47.

strophe of the psalm even as the cadence of the poem changes. Stable words like "perfect" (תְּמִימָה) "steadfast" (נֶאֱמָנָה) and "upright" (יְשָׁרִים) give the sense of reliability and sturdiness to human life informed by Yahweh's teaching. The only force of chaos which can interrupt and destabilize the harmonious world painted by the psalmist comes from within the psalmist himself. As the poet contemplates the realities of the cosmos and the Torah, he realizes the potential of his own trans-gression and evil breaking out.[37] Thus, the world of the psalm is one of ordered joy and life under God, which is threatened only by the poten-tial chaos within the psalmist.

3.4.5   THE INTERNAL ARGUMENT OF PSALM 19

As stated earlier, the primary internal audience through the poem is Yhwh. Yet, in vv. 2–11 the psalmist is pictured as speaking to himself, giving his own thoughts and meditations, which Yhwh overhears. The persuasive center of gravity for this psalm comes in the imperative and jussive expressions in vv. 13–15. The psalmist primarily attempts to persuade Yhwh to declare him free from punishment (נִקֵּיתִי, v. 13), to restrain him from presumptuousness, and to not let it rule over him (v. 14). Thus, the internal argument of the poem could be usefully classi-fied as deliberative rhetoric.[38] That is, the psalmist endeavors to con-vince Yhwh to take a particular course of action in the future. Aristotle stated that the *telos* of deliberative rhetoric was the advantageous. That is, the speaker would attempt to demonstrate that a particular course of action leads to the most desirable outcome in a given situation.[39]

In this poem, the persuasive goal is achieved primarily through a lengthy section of self-deliberation. As a reader, we are not sure of this until v. 15. The language of vv. 2–11 has a universal, timeless quality. The mention of the heavens, firmament, day, night, and sun all lend a sense of universality to the poem. Yet, by the time we get to v.

---

[37] Nel states, "This interpretation of Ps 19 establishes this psalm as one of the most individualistic and reflective of the psalms" ("Psalm 19," 103).

[38] See the classic definition in Aristotle, *Rhetoric*, I.iii.10–30.

[39] See the discussion in Murphy et al., *Synoptic History of Classical Rhetoric*, 72–73.

15 we recognize this as self-deliberation. It is this section of the psalm that constitute the "words of my mouth" and the "meditations of my heart." Rhetorical theorists remind us that self-speech, or self-deliberation, is a rhetorical device aimed at bolstering the perceived value of the discourse.[40] Thus, this may give an air of authenticity to the statements the psalmist makes in vv. 2–11.

The self-deliberation is divided into two sections: vv. 2–7 and vv. 8–11. Both of these sections consist of a set of facts and truths.[41] The term "facts" in rhetorical theory is "generally used to designate objects of precise, limited agreement."[42] The term "truths" refers to more complex systems "relating to the connections between facts."[43] The psalmist talks about the structure of the cosmos (heavens, firmament, day, night, and sun) and the relationship of those elements to El (they proclaim his glory). This is a position that is not argued for, but argued from. In rhetorical theory, a fact loses its status as soon as it is questioned. That is, when it can be no longer used as a starting point, but becomes a conclusion of an argument.[44] This move is not made in this psalm. It is nowhere questioned that the heavens declare the glory of El.

These features of argumentation continue into vv. 8–11. The Torah of Yhwh is celebrated for many attributes that are not in question. The psalmist stays in the realm of facts and truths. There is a body of writing and tradition ("facts") variously labeled as law (תּוֹרָה) witness (עֵדוּת), instructions (פִּקּוּדִים), commandment (מִצְוָה), fear (יִרְאָה), and judgments (מִשְׁפָּטִים) of Yhwh. This collection has certain attributes, which are enumerated.

The psalmist's goal in stating these facts and truths is twofold. First, it demonstrates a large area of agreement between the psalmist and Yhwh. Some level of agreement between speaker and audience is foundational for any successful argument.[45] That the psalmist believes that

---

[40] Perelman and Olbrechts-Tyteca, *New Rhetoric*, 41.

[41] As defined in Perelman and Olbrechts-Tyteca, *New Rhetoric*, 67–70.

[42] Ibid., 68–69.

[43] Ibid., 69.

[44] Ibid., 68.

[45] Ibid., 65.

Yhwh will agree with his statements is implied in the final petition (v. 15). Secondly, in choosing the facts and truths that he does, the psalmist creates an orderly, harmonious picture of the world. There is no hint of chaos here. The cosmos is united in its goal of declaring the glory of El. Similarly, the Torah also is a stable resource for humanity. This second point becomes important to set up the petitions in vv. 12–15.

In v. 12, the text gives its first indication that all is not harmonious in the world. Not all people live in accordance with the commands of Yhwh. The psalmist states that he is "warned" by them and rewarded for observing them. Thus, the psalmist presents a carrot-and-stick motivation for keeping the Torah. In this way, he has successfully introduced the fact that chaos can erupt into the world from within himself. He goes on to enumerate the different types of infractions possible: errors (שְׁגִיאוֹת), sins of ignorance (מִנִּסְתָּרוֹת), and presumptuous sins (זֵדִים). This sets up well the psalmist's petition to Yhwh to keep him back from and to declare him innocent of sin. Yhwh should be motivated to do this not only for the sake of the psalmist, but also for the sake of Yhwh, so that the harmonious order of the world will not be disrupted.[46] The psalm then closes with the psalmist's appeal to Yhwh as his "rock" and "redeemer." This is an appeal to the close relationship between the speaker and Yhwh. By referring to Yhwh by these terms, the psalmist is encouraging Yhwh to act as a "rock" and a "redeemer."

In sum, within the world of the poem, the psalmist attempts to convince Yhwh to hold him back from sin/transgression and to declare him innocent, so that he will be whole/complete (תמם, v. 14). To achieve this goal, the psalmist uses the device of self-deliberation wherein he enumerates several facts and truths about the cosmos and the Torah. These demonstrate both the wide areas of agreement between Yhwh and the speaker and they serve to motivate Yhwh to maintain the harmony and order portrayed therein. The psalmist then asks Yhwh to restrain the forces of chaos within him and concludes by appealing to the close relationship between the two parties.

---

[46] Thus, I agree with Wagner that this psalm is primarily a petition ("From the Heavens to the Heart," 245–61).

3.5   THE POSSIBLE HISTORICAL SETTINGS/SITUATIONS OF THE PSALM

It is not surprising given the general nature of the language in Psalm 19 that several potential historical/sociological settings have been proposed.[47] The language of the psalm is general enough that some commentators do not even attempt to provide a historical/sociological setting for the psalm.[48] Of those that do posit a setting, the most common is that the psalm was written to function as a part of an individual's spiritual life.[49] One can understand why, as this setting coheres well with the "internal world" of the poem. Franz Delitzsch describes the setting of the psalm in this way, "It is morning, and the singer rejoices on the one hand in the dawning light of day, and on the other, with a view to the day's work which lies before him, places himself in the light of the Thôra."[50] The picture here is of an individual Israelite utilizing the psalm as a part of personal worship. Similarly, Phillip Nel describes the poem as "one of the most individualistic and reflective of the psalms."[51] Erhard Gerstenberger has a variation on this view. He argues that the psalm was a personal prayer used in communal worship at a Torah oriented synagogue.[52] This is similar to Craigie's view that the setting for vv. 8–15 be understood, "as a creative and literary work, though later it came to be used within the regular worship of Israel."[53]

Others argue that the psalm has its origin in the communal life of Israel. The communal understanding is further nuanced. Kraus ar-

---

[47] For a helpful overview of several commentators' views on this psalm, see Eaton, *Psalms of the Way and the Kingdom.*

[48] Goldingay, *Psalms: Psalms 1–41*, 284–85; Terrien, *Psalms*, 205–16.

[49] Franz Delitzsch, *A Commentary on the Book of Psalms,* vol. 1, trans. D. Eaton (New York: Funk and Wagnalls, 1883), 346; Fishbane, *Text and Texture*, 84; James Luther Mays, "The Place of the Torah-Psalms in the Psalter," *JBL* 106 (1987): 12; Nel, "Psalm 19," 103.

[50] Delitzsch, *Commentary on the Book of Psalms,* 1.346.

[51] Nel, "Psalm 19," 103.

[52] Erhard Gerstenberger, *Psalms: Part 1: With an Introduction to Cultic Poetry*, FOTL 14 (Grand Rapids: Eerdmans 1988), 102–03.

[53] Peter Craigie, *Psalms 1–50*, WBC 19 (Waco, TX: Word, 1983), 180.

gued that the two parts of the psalm both originated in connection with different parts of the autumnal festival.[54] Steven Croft posits a wisdom setting. That is, that the psalm was written by post-exilic sages for a didactic purpose in the temple.[55] Mitchel Dahood agrees that the psalm is didactic in function, but does not argue for the late date.[56] Nahum Sarna has argued for a more religio-political setting. He avers that the poem was written in the wake of the Josianic reform as a polemic against a cult of sun worshippers.[57] This also is a didactic purpose, but a more focused one than Croft has posited.

Still others have argued that the primary setting for this poem is literary. James Mays interprets the poem in light of its role in the canonical book.[58] In this setting, he argues that Ps 19 demonstrates its primary setting as modeling a type of piety which was based on devotion to the law and a faith in the reign of God.[59] William Brown and Patrick Miller discuss its meaning in the context of Pss 15–24.[60] For Brown, Ps 19 functions as a complement and a corrective to the psalms of this group.[61] It nuances the temple entrance liturgies (Pss 15, 24) by subordinating, or even replacing, the temple, by the Torah.[62] Additionally, it highlights personal piety over and against the royal

---

[54] Kraus, *Psalms 1–59*, 269.

[55] Steven Croft, *The Identity of the Individual in the Psalms*, JSOTSup 44 (Sheffield: Sheffield Academic 1987), 166; so also W. Brown, *Seeing the Psalms*, 100; Deissler, "Zur Datierung und Situierung der 'Kosmischen Hymnen' Pss 8, 19, 29," 51.

[56] Mitchell Dahood, *Psalms I: 1–50*, AB 16 (New Haven: Yale University Press, 1965), 121.

[57] Sarna, *Songs of the Heart*, 74.

[58] Mays, "Place of the Torah-Psalms in the Psalter," 1–2.

[59] Ibid., 12.

[60] William Brown, "'Here Comes the Sun!' The Metaphorical Theology of Psalms 15–24," in *Composition of the Book of Psalms*, ed. E. Zenger (Leuven: Uitgeverij Peeters, 2010), 259–77; Miller, "Kingship, Torah Obedience, and Prayer," 127–42.

[61] Brown, "'Here Comes the Sun!'," 275.

[62] Ibid., 275.

focus of Pss 18, 20, 21.[63] In a similar vein, Leslie Allen has looked to the psalm title to provide a setting.[64]

One of the reasons why these different contexts have been postulated is because scholars have failed to distinguish between the internal and external settings of the psalm. For example, it seems clear that Delitzsch, Fishbane, and Terrien focus only on the internal setting of the psalm. That is, the psalm itself envisions an individual praying to God, thus that setting becomes the context in which they interpret the psalm. On the other hand, Gerstenberger, Kraus, Croft, and Sarna focus primarily on the external setting. These scholars are interested in considering how the psalm was intended to function in Israelite society. The canonical interpretations of Mays and Brown go beyond the original external function to consider the function of the psalm once it became part of a canonical book.

When one examines the external settings proposed, there is a remarkable similarity evidenced. The language of the poem, its form and content, support the understanding that Ps 19 had a didactic function in the context of authorized communal worship.[65] This provides us with enough of a social context for a rhetorical analysis.[66] The leader would be using this psalm as a model prayer for the community. It would function to inform and to strengthen the belief of the congregation concerning how they should understand the relationship between the world, God, the Torah, and themselves. Thus, it would function as epideictic rhetoric.[67] In epideictic rhetoric, the speaker is primarily an

---

[63] Ibid., 275–76.

[64] Allen, "David as Exemplar of Spirituality."

[65] One could further speculate about more specific details. It seems reasonable to assume an outdoor setting (v. 1), during morning or evening prayers (v. 2). Perhaps the prayer was written for use before the reading of the Torah in worship (vv. 8–10).

[66] The context of corporate authorized worship can have the effect of adding meaning to the text beyond just the words on the page. See Donald Evans, *The Logic of Self-Involvement: A Philosophical Study of Everyday Language with Special Reference to the Christian Use of Language about God as Creator* (London: SCM Press, 1963), 51.

[67] Perelman and Olbrechts-Tyteca, *New Rhetoric*, 47–51; The ancient Ro-

educator.[68] Thus, psalms like this one played a vital role in Israelite society. As Perelman and Olbrechts-Tyteca state, this type of discourse
enables a community to maintain an identity and to "increase adherence
to values held in common by the audience and the speaker ... without
such common values upon what foundation could deliberative and legal
speeches rest?"[69]

3.6   EXEGETICAL DIFFICULTIES

Strophe 1: vv. 2–7

Verse 2:
This startling opening consists of two perfectly balanced cola:

A   The heavens הַשָּׁמַיִם

  B   are reporting מְסַפְּרִים

    C   the glory of EL כְּבוֹד־אֵל

    C'   the work of his hands וּמַעֲשֵׂה יָדָיו

  B'   is announcing מַגִּיד

A'   the sky הָרָקִיעַ

Every term in the first half of colon is matched by one in the
second. Additionally, the differences in meaning between the two cola
all amount to the second colon sharpening and narrowing the first. The
subjects (A and A') both reference the same reality, the heavens/sky.
The two terms are often used synonymously in poetry, although the second term is more specific than the first.[70] There is also a grammatical

---

man rhetor Menander analyzed hymns to the gods as examples of epideictic rhetoric,
see D. Donald Andrew Russell and Nigel Guy Wilson, *Menander Rhetor* (Oxford:
Oxford University Press, 1981), 7.

[68] Perelman and Olbrechts-Tyteca, *New Rhetoric*, 51.

[69] Ibid., 52–53.

[70] The two terms are equated in Gen 1:8, "And God called the sky (רָקִיעַ)
'heavens' (שָׁמָיִם)." Yet, a few verses later, the author makes a distinction between the
two, the sky is a defined part of the heavens, see Gen 1:14, "And God said, 'Let there
be lights in the sky of the heavens (בִּרְקִיעַ הַשָּׁמַיִם)'" The "sky" refers to the solid
dome, which include the stars, sun, and moon. The "heavens" includes that, but also
includes the storehouses of wind, rain, snow, etc. above the "sky" and the abode of

difference between them (dual vs. singular). The participles (מְסַפְּרִים and מַגִּיד) both are used almost exclusively for human speech. The first term is more general and can refer to a number of types of speech.[71] The second term (מַגִּיד) is almost exclusively used in a formal context. For example, it is used of a soldier reporting to a superior (2 Sam 18:11).[72] The middle term (C and C') also evidences this narrowing. One aspect of God's glory is what he has made.[73] The narrowing and focusing of the second line compared to the first is typical in Hebrew poetry.[74] However, one wonders if more is not going on here. The two cola are so structured and provide a narrowness at each level in a way that parallels the movement of the psalm as a whole. The psalm begins by celebrating the praise of the heavens, which would have been the broadest category in the ANE, the heavens cover everything.[75] The psalm ends with the words and meditations of an individual's heart. This overarching movement of the psalm from general to specific is foreshadowed in the grammatical/semantic movement in the first line of the poem.

The divine name is used with great intention in this poem. Scholars have long pointed out that vv. 1–7 do not mention the name יהוה, but rather reference the more generic אֵל. This has been used as an argument for the separate composition of the two main halves of the psalm.[76] However, El is a more appropriate term to use when one is

---

God. See Keel, *Symbolism of the Biblical World*, 47–57.

[71] For example, it is sued of the conversation Gideon overheard in the Midianite camp when one soldier told his dream to the other (Judg 7:14).

[72] For all uses as a participle: Gen 41:24; 2 Sam 1:5, 6, 13; 4:10; 18:11; Isa 41:26; 42:9; 45:19; 46:10; Jer 4:15; Amos 4:13; Zech 9:12; Ps 147:19.

[73] The work of one's hands reflects their character. Thus, the Deuteronomy encourages people to obedience so that the Lord will bless the work of their hands (14:29). However, it also states that if you make idols with your hands it leads to destruction. Deuteronomy 4:28 talks about how people "serve the work of human hands," that is, idols.

[74] James L Kugel, *The Idea of Biblical Poetry: Parallelism and Its History* (Baltimore: Johns Hopkins University Press, 1998), 51–58.

[75] Keel, *Symbolism of the Biblical World*, 31.

[76] E.g., Briggs and Briggs, *Book of Psalms: Vol. 1*, 163–64.

speaking about the more generic praise of the heavens.[77] Additionally, by the end of the poem it is clear that Yhwh = El. Thus, the high god of the Canaanite pantheon is celebrated as Yhwh. Further, the shift to speak about Yhwh in vv. 8–15 is cogent because the subject matter is focused on the Law, where Yhwh's name is revealed. It is also significant that the divine is referenced seven times in vv. 8–15 compared to one time in vv. 2–7.[78] This fact along with the shift to the more personal name of Yhwh in the second half of the psalm could indicate that the Law provides a clearer, more personal, and more complete revelation about God than the speech of the heavens.

Several commentators have noticed the connections between this verse and Gen 1.[79] Indeed, if we include vv. 3–5 in our search we find the words: heavens, sky, day, night, and sun. In Gen 1, God speaks the heavens and sky into existence. The poet here makes the point that they now speak about God.

Verse 3:

The main interpretive difficulty in this verse regards the subject of the two verbs. Is the subject the "sky" from v. 1?[80] Thus, "day to day" and "night to night" would be adverbial temporal phrases. Or, is the subject "day" and "night"? Thus, the meaning would be that one day communicates to the next. This view makes the best sense both with the imagery used in the psalms as well as syntactically.[81] That is,

---

[77] "El" is both broader than Israelite and connotes the creation deity. See Frank Moore Cross, *Canaanite Myth and Hebrew Epic: Essays in the History of the Religion of Israel* (Cambridge: Harvard University Press, 1973), 1–78.

[78] Heptads and 7 + 1 series were common in ANE culture and the Old Testament. See Arvid S. Kapelrud, "Number Seven in Ugaritic Texts," *VT* 18 (1968): 494-99; J. Hehn, *Siebenzahl und Sabbat bei den Babyloniern und im Alten Testament: eine religionsgschichtliche Studie,* Leipziger semitistische Studien (Leipzig: J. C. Hinrichs, 1907).

[79] Craigie, *Psalms 1–50,* 180; Duhm, *Psalmen,* 59; Fishbane, *Text and Texture,* 86.

[80] Goldingay, *Psalms: Psalms 1–41,* 287–88.

[81] As most commentators have recognized, see Craigie, *Psalms 1–50,* 180; Arnold Albert Anderson, *The Book of Psalms* (Grand Rapids: Eerdmans, 1981), 168; Delitzsch, *Commentary on the Book of Psalms,* 1.347; Fishbane, *Text and Texture,*

it is more probable that the line would have its own subject embedded within it rather than carrying over the subject from the previous verse.

The two verbs are used exclusively with human subjects other than in this passage.[82] Thus, the personification of the cosmos continues in this verse. Knierim points out that there are actually two chains of transmission mentioned in this verse, "one of speech from day to day, and one of knowledge from night to night.... Day belongs to day because each day outpours speech, whereas the disclosure of knowledge belongs to the night."[83] Strictly speaking this is true and helps make sense of why the verbs were chosen for each colon. Yet, the content of their speech/revelation should be understood as identical. Additionally, "day" and "night" from this verse are related to the "heavens" and the "sky" of v. 2. What is the relationship between the two pairs? Verse 3 focuses and gives an example of how the heavens and sky proclaim God's glory. That is, v. 3 sharpens v. 2. It accomplishes this in a very sophisticated matter. Verse 2 indicated that the "heavens" and "sky" proclaimed God's glory continuously (participles). Verse 3 utilizes "day" and "night" to pick up on both the spatial and temporal aspects of v. 2. On the one hand, "day" and "night" refer "to everything visible in the heavens during the day and during the night (so metonymies of subject)."[84] That is, "day" stands for what is visible in the heavens during the day (i.e., the sun) and "night" for what is visible in the night (i.e. moon and stars). On the other hand, the merism of "day" and "night" connote a temporal meaning ("all the time").

Verse 4–5a:

The main interpretive issue in verse 4, which has been felt since the LXX,[85] is the meaning of the second colon. The question is,

---

86; Harrelson, "Psalm 19," 143; Knierim, "On the Theology of Psalm 19," 326–27; Allen Ross, *A Commentary on the Psalms: Vol. 1* (Grand Rapids: Kregel, 2011), 474–75; Wagner, "From the Heavens to the Heart," 250; Weiser, *Psalms*, 198.

[82] For נבע see Ps 59:8; 78:2; 94:4; 119:171; 145:7; Prov 1:23; 15:2, 28; 18:4; Eccl. 10:1. For חוה see Job 15:17; 32:6, 10, 17; 36:2.

[83] Knierim, "On the Theology of Psalm 19," 326–27

[84] Ross, *Commentary on the Psalms: Vol. 1*, 474–75

[85] LXX: οὐκ εἰσὶν λαλιαὶ οὐδὲ λόγοι, ὧν οὐχὶ ἀκούονται αἱ φωναὶ

does the verse mean that the testimony of the heavens is heard by everyone?[86] That is, the second colon is translated "without their voice
being heard" or "where their voice is not heard." Thus, the point of the
verse would be that their voice is heard everywhere. Or, does the verse
mean that the testimony of the heavens is actually not proclaimed in
speech, there is no audible voice?[87]

Evidence overwhelmingly supports the latter position. Of the
fifty-nine uses of בְּלִי in the Hebrew Bible, it functions in all of them as
a simple negative. The first option requires the reader to supply the
meaning "where" at the beginning of the second line. Thus, "there is
no speech, there are no words, *where* their voice is not heard."[88] What
seems to be occurring in this verse is that two negatives (אֵין and בְּלִי),
which are often used together for emphasis,[89] are here distributed to
the two cola. Thus, the point of the verse is that the דַּעַת (19:3), which
the heavens communicate, is paradoxically inaudible.[90]

The meaning of קַו in 5a has generated several different interpretations. Dahood suggests that it comes from the root *qāwāh* II,
meaning "to collect."[91] The noun form would then mean "call." That
is, to collect people through a call. Kraus compares the use of קַו here
with its use in Isa. 28:10, 13 and argues that it denotes a line of written
text.[92] While this explanation is attractive, Goldingay rightly comments that this may be an example of "explaining the unknown by the

---

αὐτῶν ("There are no speeches nor words in which their voices are not heard").

[86] Goldingay, *Psalms: Psalms 1–41*, 288; Delitzsch, *Commentary on the Book of Psalms*, 1.348–49; Terrien, *Psalms*, 206; Weiser, *Psalms*, 199; LXX.

[87] Craigie, *Psalms 1–50*, 177; Dahood, *Psalms I: 1–50*, 120; Eaton, *The Psalms*, 108; Fishbane, *Text and Texture*, 86; Knierim, "On the Theology of Psalm 19," 322; Kraus, *Psalms 1–59*, 277; Jean-Luc Vesco, *Le Psautier de David: Traduit et Commenté*, vol. 1 (Paris: Les Éditions du Cerf, 2006), 208.

[88] For the classic defense of this position, see Delitzsch, *Commentary on the Book of Psalms*, 1.348–49.

[89] E.g., 1 Kgs 1:3, see GKC§152y.

[90] Kraus, *Psalms 1–59*, 271.

[91] Dahood, *Psalms I: 1–50*, 122.

[92] Kraus, *Psalms 1–59*, 268.

unknown."[93] Terrien argues that the word here denotes a musical string (e.g., Sir. 44:5), and thus translates it "melody."[94] Given the obscurity of קָו in this context, Craigie is surely correct that the LXX translation (φθόγγος) gives evidence that the text has been corrupted and should read קוֹלָם.[95] The ל was accidentally dropped from the text.

Verses 5b–7

These verses are relatively free from exegetical debates.[96] The larger question of whether or not the reference to the sun is intended to be polemical will be discussed below.

Strophe 2: vv. 8–11

These lines constitute a carefully structured poetic unit. The pattern is as follows:

Description of the Law	A B C / A' B' C' (v. 8)
	A B C / A' B' C' (v. 9)
	A B C / A' B' D (v. 10)
Value of the Law	A B C / A' B' C' (v. 11)

In vv. 8–10, the ABC elements are all perfectly paralleled: A = noun phrase denoting written revelation; B = adjectival description of the written revelation; C = participial phrase describing the effects of the written revelation.[97] The D element in v. 10 serves as a skillful

---

[93] Goldingay, *Psalms: Psalms 1–41*, 282.

[94] Terrien, *Psalms*, 210.

[95] Craigie, *Psalms 1–50*, 178.

[96] The antecedent of בָּהֶם (v. 5b) is "heavens." This phrase is omitted in the LXX, but should be retained here, see Kraus, *Psalms 1–59*, 268. Additionally, Goldingay translates חַמָּה (v. 7) as "ferocity" instead of "heat" based on the imagery of the sun as a warrior (cf. Judg 5:31). However, this cannot be lexically sustained. He does rightly point out that חַמָּה often denotes the "sun" (cf. Isa 30:26) and not just its "heat." Thus, the phrase "nothing is hidden from its חַמָּה" is not logically difficult. The Isa 30:26 text references the "light of its חַמָּה" thus referring to both the light and heat produced by the sun. See Goldingay, *Psalms: Psalms 1–41*, 290.

[97] Vesco points out that there are five effects of the Law listed here, which could be a subtle allusion to the five books of the law. See Vesco, *Le Psautier de David*, 209. He states, "Chaque aspect de la Loi est décrit en cinq mots (vv: 8–10). Y

transition to v. 11.[98]

There are two main exegetical debates in these verses: the meaning/scope of the term תּוֹרָה, and the meaning of the phrase יְרְאַת יְהוָה. On the scope of תּוֹרָה, some argue that it refers specifically to Yhwh's commands concerning behavior,[99] others understand it as a general reference encompassing the written and oral tradition Israel possessed,[100] still others see it as a reference to some form of the written "Law of Moses."[101] In one sense, the meaning of the poem does not hinge on this question. Yet, it is significant that the poet avoids any specific reference for the תּוֹרָה (e.g., "the Law of Moses"). This allowed the poem to include more of the canon as a referent of תּוֹרָה. This lack of specificity indicates that it should probably be understood as including all of the revelation of Yahweh accepted by the community (written and oral).

The phrase יְרְאַת יְהוָה has generated some debate. The difficulty is that all five other parallel phrases in this section refer to revelation of Yahweh. Nowhere else in the Hebrew Bible does the phrase יְרְאַת יְהוָה refer to a body of revelation.[102] Thus, some commentators have understood the phrase to refer, not to Yhwh's revelation (subjective genitive), but to a reverential attitude toward Yhwh (subjective genitive).[103] However, this breaks the parallelism and flow of the poem. Other scholars solve this difficulty through emendation. Many scholars

---

aurait-il là une discréte évocation des cinq livres de la Loi?" (209).

[98] The last word of v. 10 has consonantal connections (ה and ד) with the first word of v. 11 (הַנֶּחֱמָדִים יַחְדָּו). That in combination with the altered word order of v. 10 (A'B'D) prepares the reader/hearer well for the transition.

[99] E.g., Goldingay, *Psalms: Psalms 1–41*, 290.

[100] E.g., Terrien, *Psalms*, 211.

[101] E.g., Kraus, *Psalms 1–59*, 273; Ross, *Commentary on the Psalms: Vol. 1*, 478.

[102] Although, one could argue that the phrase יְרְאַת יְהוָה refers to the *Torah* in Ps 111:10. "The beginning of wisdom is the fear of Yhwh / good insight to all who do them." The question is, how can you "do" (עשה) the "fear of Yhwh"? Yet, the line makes sense if one understands יְרְאַת יְהוָה as a reference to the *Torah*, which is often the object of the verb עשה. If this is the case, it is another occurrence of יְרְאַת יְהוָה referring to a body of authorized teaching.

[103] Terrien, *Psalms*, 212; Weiser, *Psalms*, 202; Sarna, *Songs of the Heart*, 87.

follow the suggestion in the BHS and emend יִרְאַת to אמרת.[104] Dahood
suggests that we detach, "the *mem* from *'ēnāyim* to read *'ēnāy*, "my
eyes," and join[ed] it to the following word to read *mir'at yhwh*."[105]
This suggestion is based on the Ugaritic root *mr'*. Both of these sug-
gestions maintain the parallelism of the poem, but require significant
alteration of the MT. A better way forward is suggested by Goldingay.
He argues that the term here is another subjective genitive referring to
the revelation from Yhwh. It "denotes reverence that Yhwh lays down,
teaching that indicates what reverence for Yhwh looks like. Verse 9
thus adds another pair of terms referring to Yhwh's teaching as a
whole and in its specificity."[106] Thus, the phrase is synonymous with
the other terms in vv. 8–10.

Strophe 3: vv. 12–15

The main interpretive difficulty in this section has to do with
the three terms: נִסְתָּרוֹת, שְׁגִיאוֹת, and זֵדִים. The precise meaning/referent
of the first and last terms in this series have been debated. Jacob
Milgrom has decisively demonstrated that the term שְׁגִיאוֹת refers to intentional acts which one did not know were sinful.[107] More debated has
been the referent of זֵדִים. Scholars argued that it refers to arrogant people,[108] idols,[109] demons,[110] or intentional sins.[111] The word is used thir-

---

[104] James Durlesser, "A Rhetorical Critical Study of Psalms 19, 42, and 43,"
StudBib 10 (1980): 181–82; Kraus, *Psalms 1–59*, 268

[105] Dahood, *Psalms I: 1–50*, 123–24.

[106] Goldingay, *Psalms: Psalms 1–41*, 291. So also David J. A. Clines, "Tree
of Knowledge and the Law of Yahweh: Psalm 19," *VT* 24 (1974): 12.

[107] Jacob Milgrom, "Cultic שגגה and Its Influence in Psalms and Job," *JQR*
58 (1967): 115–25.

[108] John Goldingay, "The Dynamic Cycle of Praise and Prayer in the
Psalms," *JSOT* 6 (1981): 295; Knierim, "On the Theology of Psalm 19," 334; Kraus,
Psalms 1–59, 268.

[109] Dahood, *Psalms I: 1–50*, 124.

[110] Mowinckel, *The Psalms in Israel's Worship*, vol. 1, 114.

[111] Clines, "Tree of Knowledge and the Law of Yahweh: Psalm 19," 13;
Eaton, *The Psalms*, 111; Milgrom, "Cultic שגגה and Its Influence in Psalms and Job,"
120; Terrien, *Psalms*, 214

teen times in the Hebrew Bible.[112] In all but one other instance it denotes a person who is insolent.[113] However, Jer 43:2 uses it as an adjective modifying הָאֲנָשִׁים. What seems to be happening in this psalm is
that the term זֵדִים, which normally referred to "insolent" people, was
used to refer to "insolent/arrogant" as a character trait. This trait then
gets personified and used as the subject of מָשַׁל. Thus, it should be understood here as sinful attitude that the psalmist is trying to avoid. This
interpretation fits best in context of the psalm.

3.7   STRUCTURE

Strophe 1: vv. 2–7:   **The Speech of the Heavens**
    vv. 2–3:   Announcement:
                    Heavens/sky and day/night glorify El
    vv. 4–5a: Clarification:
                    Not actual speech, yet communicates universally
    vv. 5b–7:   Illustration: The sun

Strophe 2: vv. 8–10   **Description of the Law and its Effects**
    vv. 8–10:   Exposition: The Law and its attributes

Strophe 3: vv. 11–15 Desire of the Psalmist
    v. 11:   Value of the Law and Reason
    vv. 13–14:   Plea of the Psalmist
    v. 15:   Summary: Desire of the Psalmist

3.8   RHETORICAL ANALYSIS: THE EXTERNAL ARGUMENT

The rhetorical center of gravity for this psalm can be found in the final
verse. The goal of the poet is to encourage the auditor to adopt the attitude expressed there.[114] The poet is trying to drive the auditors to the
place where they desire that their words and thoughts are pleasing to

---

[112] Ps 86:14; 119:21, 51, 69, 78, 85, 122; Prov 21:24; Isa 13:11; Mal 3:15; 4:1.

[113] Jer 43:2.

[114] For this analysis, I will use the term "pray-er" to refer to the audience using the prayer as a part of their worship. The term "pray-er" indicates that the audience is involving themselves in this poem, making it their own.

Yhwh. The emphasis is on the "words" and "thoughts," which in the context of the psalm would be the content of vv. 1–14. That is, the poet desires to shape how the auditor views the heavens, the Torah, and their response to the Torah (vv. 12–14). In this way, the psalm could be viewed as didactic in intent. Now, an audience of near contemporaries undoubtedly would have agreed that having one's words and thoughts be pleasing to Yhwh is a worthy goal. Thus, the psalmist is not trying to convince those praying to adopt an attitude they would raise objections against. Rather, the psalmist is attempting to increase the intensity of adherence to this value.[115]

The fact that this is the rhetorical goal of the poem can be demonstrated a couple of different ways. One is the principle of linearity.[116] This is the last line that the audience would hear, which would provide an interpretive framework for how they would understand the entire poem. However, just because a line comes last does not always mean that it is the rhetorical focus of a text. More evidence is necessary. In Ps 19, the final verse is highlighted by the use of apostrophe in v. 12, which brings a sense of climax to the final strophe.[117] Finally, the jussive verb (יִהְיוּ) brings a sense of self-involvement to the line. It also resonates with the repeated use of the jussive in Gen 1 (יְהִי) the sub-text of Ps 19:2–7. All of this serves to give a sense of climax to v. 15 and supports the position that it is the rhetorical goal of the poem. Recognizing this rhetorical goal gives a focus to our analysis of the poem.

3.8.1 STROPHE ONE

Verses 2–3

The psalm opens not by addressing either God or the congregation directly. There is no call to worship and there is no call on the deity. These verses announce a topic, or theme, which gets amplified in

---

[115] Perelman and Olbrechts-Tyteca, *New Rhetoric*, 48–49.

[116] Kennedy, *New Testament Interpretation Through Rhetorical Criticism*, 47.

[117] Richard Lanham, *A Handlist of Rhetorical Terms* (Berkeley, CA: University of California Press, 1991), 20.

vv. 4–7. On the surface, these lines do not attempt to convince or persuade, rather they simply state truths about the created order. Yet, in a
context of organized worship, the report of facts can serve a suasive
purpose.[118] There are several ways in which these verses help the poet
achieve his/her rhetorical goal. The imagery in these verses is of two
dyads (שָׁמַיִם/רָקִיעַ and יוֹם/לַיְלָה) celebrating and expounding the glory of
God.[119] "Heavens" and "sky" are totalizing words. In the ancient world,
the sky was "perceived to be spatially and temporally endless."[120] Thus
they covered everything. "Day" and "night" likewise have important
connotations. On the one hand, they function as metonymies of subject,
standing for what is visible during the day and night (e.g., sun, moon,
and stars).[121] On the other hand, they function as a merism to indicate
"all the time." Thus, the poem personifies these important elements and
indicates that they are proclaiming the glory of El. In the ancient world
the "heavens" (שָׁמַיִם) sun, moon, and stars were all considered major
deities. Both by calling these elements מַעֲשֵׂה יָדָיו and by having them report God's glory, God's honor and status is elevated.[122]

These lines receive additional weight when one considers the
connection of the pairs שָׁמַיִם/רָקִיעַ and יוֹם/לַיְלָה with Gen 1. Genesis 1
utilizes each of these terms. While this is not a direct appeal to authority (*argumentum ad verecundiam*), these allusions do invite the listener
to consider these verses in light of that foundational text. In Gen 1,
God speaks the שָׁמַיִם/רָקִיעַ and יוֹם/לַיְלָה into existence. Here, they fulfill
their created purpose and speak back God's glory.

The worshipping community by voicing the truths proclaimed
in vv. 2–3 would be affirming themselves that proclaiming כְּבוֹד־אֵל is a

---

[118] Evans, *Logic of Self Involvement*, 70.

[119] כְּבוֹד־אֵל should be understood as the referent of דַּעַת and אֹמֶר (v. 3).

[120] Keel, *Symbolism of the Biblical World*, 31.

[121] Ross, *Commentary on the Psalms: Vol. 1*, 474–75.

[122] In a way, the psalmist here is appealing to both the "loci of quality" and
the "loci of quantity." Quantity in that God's glory is proclaimed all the time. Quality in that the "heavens" are doing the proclaiming. The sun, moon, and stars were
revered in the ancient world, thus having them glorify God greatly added to God's
prestige. See Perelman and Olbrechts-Tyteca, *New Rhetoric*, 89–93.

vital activity to be engaged in. Thus, it would function as both commissive and behavitive speech.[123] In fact, proclaiming the glory of God
would be the types of words (אָמַר) and thoughts (הָגָיוֹן) God would find
pleasing (v. 15). In the opening verses of this poem, the audience would
already be encouraged to compare their own speech and thoughts with
that of the heavens, thus supporting the overall rhetorical goal of the
psalmist. Additionally, the truths these verses proclaim function as an *a
fortiori* argument. That is, if the heavens (including sun, moon, and
stars) proclaim God's glory, how much more should they?

Verses 4–5a

Verse 4 strikingly reverses the train of thought initiated by vv.
2–3. What is the reason for this? The poet here accomplishes a couple
of goals with this line. On the one hand, it is a kind of protocatalep-
sis.[124] That is, it answers an objection the worshipping community
might raise. The poet here admits that the heavens do not speak in an
audible way. The poet highlights this point by fronting each cola with
a negative marker—a kind of literal and grammatical anaphora
(בְּלִי...אֵין...אֵין). But, by admitting that the heavens do not really speak
or have a voice, an element of paradox enters the poem. The worshipper now understands that there must be a difference between the אֹמֶר in
v. 3 and the אֹמֶר in v. 4. This is an example of what Perelman and
Olbrechts-Tyteca would call a quasi-logical argument.[125] Paradox is a
particularly powerful rhetorical tool. By not specifying what the words
for "speech" mean in vv. 2–3 (יְחַוֶּה ,אֹמֶר, מַגִּיד, מְסַפְּרִים) except that they
do not mean literal speech, the poet actually deepens the original point
that the heavens communicate the glory of God.[126] In essence you have
two terms here: in v. 4 the terms אֹמֶר and דְּבָרִים denote literal speech. In
vv. 3–4, the terms אֹמֶר, מַגִּיד, מְסַפְּרִים, and יְחַוֶּה must denote something

---

[123] Evans, *Logic of Self Involvement*, 51. Evans states that a worship service
is primarily made up of commissive and behavitive speech. That is, speech that
commits oneself to future actions and emotions/attitudes.

[124] Lanham, *Handlist of Rhetorical Terms*, 120.

[125] Perelman and Olbrechts-Tyteca, *New Rhetoric*, 217.

[126] Ibid., 444.

like "communicating truth about God in a non-verbal way." By not elucidating exactly how the heavens communicate God's glory, the worshipper is driven both to think more deeply about how the heavens do communicate, but they also have the value of proclaiming God's glory deepen for them.[127]

The poet then deepens the paradox by restating the fact that the words of the heavens actually do go out to the entire world (v. 5a). The repetition of the concept of the entire world (בְּכָל־הָאָרֶץ and בְּקָצֵה תֵבֵל) reinforces the universality of the cosmic speech. The use of קוֹל and מִלָּה both deepen the paradox since they denote audible speech.[128]

The flow of the poem thus far has a logic to it. Verse 2 announces a theme, which is elaborated in v. 3. Verse 4 then nuances and reinforces this statement through paradox. The theme is then picked up again in v. 5a stressing the heaven's intelligibility and global reach. This sets up well the shift to vv. 5b–7.

Verses 5b–7

In these verses, the poet narrows the focus from the heavens to the most prominent entity in the heavens, the sun. This focus on the sun serves as an illustration of how the heavens declare God's glory. Rhetoricians since Aristotle have carefully distinguished between an illustration and an example. An example is particular case, or situation, from which one can support an argument for a general rule. An illustration is used to "strengthen adherence to a known and accepted rule, by providing particular instances which clarify the general statement,

---

[127] See the insightful essay by Cleanth Brooks, "The Language of Paradox," in *The Well Wrought Urn: Studies in the Structure of Poetry* (London: Dobson, 1947), 1–20. He argues that the language of paradox is actually what gives poetry its depth and power. The playing off of different definitions of words against one other without being precise engages the intellect, the emotions, and the imagination.

[128] In thirty-eight uses, מִלָּה universally denotes spoken words. The closest connection with the word to a written word is found in Job 19:23, "Oh that my words were written...." Here Job indicates that his desire would be that his spoken speech מִלָּה would become written. The fact that the word is universally used as vocal speech, as opposed to written, supports the emendation of קַו to קוֹל in the first colon, since it would make the terms more adequately parallel.

show applications, and increase its presence to the consciousness."[129]
The poet here clearly uses the sun as an illustration. The audience
would have already agreed that the heavens to celebrate God's glory.
Nevertheless, the illustration serves an important function here. As Perelman and Olbrechts-Tyteca state,

> [An illustration] seeks to increase presence by making an ab-
> stract rule concrete by means of a particular case ... it corrobo-
> rates the rule, it can even ... actually serve to state the rule. Il-
> lustrations are undoubtedly often chosen for their affective im-
> pact ... Very often the purpose of an illustration is to promote
> understanding of a rule ... [Writers often present] the amazing,
> unexpected, and prestigious illustration which depends on its
> startling nature to bring out the significance of a rule.[130]

All of these points are relevant to Ps 19. The discussion of the sun increases presence of the theme (v. 2), corroborates the theme, has an
affective impact, and promotes understanding.

The focus on the sun is indicated through its fronting in the
first colon (לַשֶּׁמֶשׁ). The poet first highlights God's glory in relation to
the sun through indicating that God functions as the sun's provider and
benefactor.[131] Verse 5b discusses the sun at night. Verse 6 indicates the
sun's daytime glory. Then, v. 7 provides an overview of sun's routine
as a whole from dawn to dusk. The sun's nighttime activities are re-
ported as simply residing in a tent. This paves the way for a discussion
of how the sun's daytime activities communicate God's glory. The
sun's daytime routine is presented with two analogies.

Analogies function to "facilitate the development and extension of thought."[132] As has been recognized since ancient times, analogies are made up of four parts: A is to B as C is to D.[133] In the two

---

[129] Perelman and Olbrechts-Tyteca, *New Rhetoric*, 357.

[130] Ibid., 360.

[131] אֵל is the understood subject of the verb שָׂם.

[132] Perelman and Olbrechts-Tyteca, *New Rhetoric*, 384.

[133] The research on analogies is vast and demonstrates its vital role in human
thought, for an overview see the discussion and references in the following: P.

analogies here the "B" portion is missing, yet implied. Thus, A) the sun B) at dawn is like C) a bridegroom D) coming forth from his tent. And A) the sun B) in its daytime circuit is like C) a hero D) running the path. Part of what gives an analogy its power is that it forces the worshipper to tease out the precise connection between the two sets of terms. Thus, the worshipper becomes involved in the creative process. This, in turn, increases the intensity of adherence to the theme being illustrated.[134] Additionally, the image used for the analogy plays an important role. Perelman and Olbrechts-Tyteca, citing an example from John Calvin, illustrate how an analogy can be made to devalue the subject:[135] "That election of Amadeus, duly solemnized by the authority of a general and holy council, went up in smoke, except that the aforesaid Amadeus was appeased by a cardinal's hat as a barking dog by a morsel."[136] The opposite is occurring in Ps 19. Both the images of a bridegroom and a hero are positive in the ancient world. Both of them connote a sense of vitality, joy, and youthful exuberance. It is the display of these very qualities of the sun that communicate God's glory.[137]

Achinstein, "Models, Analogies, and Theories," *Philosophy of Sciece* 31 (1964): 328–49; P. Bartha, *By Parallel Reasoning: The Construction and Evaluation of Analogical Arguments* (New York: Oxford University Press, 2010); C. Eliasmith and P. Thagard, "Integrating Structure and Meaning: A Distributed Model of Analogical Mapping," *Cognitive Science* 25 (2001): 245–86; R. F. Harrod, *Foundations of Inductive Logic* (London: Macmillan, 1956); M. Mitchell, *Analogy-Making as Perception* (Cambridge: Bradford, 1993); C. Sustein, "On Analogical Reasoning," *Harvard Law Review* 106 (1993): 741–91; A. Wylie, "An Analogy by Any Other Name is Just as Analogical," *Journal of Anthropological Archaeology* 1 (1982): 382–401.

[134] H. S. Lee and K. J. Holyoak, "Absence Makes the Thought Grow Stronger: Reducing Structural Overlap Can Increase Inductive Strength," in *Proceedings of the Thirtieth Annual Conference of the Cognitive Science Society*, ed. V. B. L. Sloutsky, and K. McRae (Austin: Cognitive Science Society, 2008), 297–302.

[135] Perelman and Olbrechts-Tyteca, *New Rhetoric*, 378.

[136] John Calvin, *Institutes of the Christian Religion*, trans. F. L. Battles (Philadelphia: Westminster, 1960), 26–27.

[137] The repetition of the root יצא in vv. 5 and 6 support this position. Just as the voice of the heavens "goes out" to all the earth, the sun "goes out" from its tent like a bridegroom. Both of these goings out are the going forth of communication concerning the glory of God.

Verse 7 is a summary statement. Similar to v. 5, the poet once again stresses the universality of the message.[138] From one end of the heavens to the other the sun reaches. This point is reinforced by the negative affirmation וְאֵין נִסְתָּר מֵחַמָּתוֹ (7b).

The illustration serves a didactic function. When the congregation sees the breaking of the dawn, the intense heat of noonday, and the sunset; they are encouraged to recognize that this all communicates כְּבוֹד־אֵל. This truth, which could seem banal if stated prosaically, is deepened through the use of paradox and analogical illustration.[139] The poetry is elliptical, forcing the hearer to meditate on the significance of the imagery and make connections for his/herself.

3.8.2   STROPHE TWO

Verses 8–10

The poet here makes a remarkable shift in tone, cadence, and imagery.[140] Three features of the speech in vv. 8–10 influence one to realize that while the heavens do declare God's glory, the תּוֹרָה is more complete and clearer than its heavenly counterpart. The first feature is the shift from terse, compact poetic lines to the more expansive lines of vv. 8–10.[141] The second is the pervasive, monotonous use of the personal divine name, יהוה.[142] This is striking in contrast to the paltry single occurrence of אֵל in the first strophe (v. 2).[143] Both of these facts

---

[138] Note the double use of קצה (v. 7).

[139] One is reminded of Cleanth Brooks' analysis of Wordsworth's sonnet "Composed upon Westminster Bridge." All Wordsworth is really saying in this poem, Brooks avers, is "the city is beautiful in the morning light and it is awfully still." Yet, it is the use of paradox that gives the poem its power. See Brooks, "The Language of Paradox," 5–6. One can even go further than Brooks by demonstrating that paradox (as also metonymy, metaphor, and analogy) forces the reader to be involved in the meaning-creation process, thus driving the meaning and significance of the poem deeper into the reader/hearer.

[140] See discussion above on the unity of the poem.

[141] Verses 2–7 range from two to four words per colon. Verses 8–10 have five words per colon.

[142] Six uses in these two verses.

[143] This is especially true when one considers there were other opportunities

would encourage the worshipper to understand that the written revelation is more personal and more informative than the speech of the
heavens. Also, vv. 8–10 are highly structured to an unusual degree.[144]
This in comparison to the more loosely structured lines in the first
strophe implies that there is a quality of orderliness and clarity about
this revelation not present in the cosmic speech.

Verses 8–10 do not on the surface attempt to persuade or convince. They are descriptive statements, which amplifying a theme similar in function to v. 2. The variety of terms utilized to refer to תּוֹרָה
elucidates different aspects of the "instruction."[145] Yet, there is something odd about the attributes listed for the תּוֹרָה.[146] As Goldingay
states, "This is a puzzling list of qualities to attribute to God's instructions. It is persons or lives that are whole or have integrity.... It is persons or promises that are reliable or faithful.... It is persons or hearts
that are clean.... It is hearts and promises that are pure."[147] Goldingay
argues that these descriptions involve metonymy and should be seen as
"pregnant expressions."[148] That is, Yhwh's instruction is said to be
תְּמִימָה, נֶאֱמָנָה, יְשָׁרִים, בָּרָה, טְהוֹרָה, and אֱמֶת because it produces "people
and lives of that kind."[149] This is an insightful comment, yet it could be
stated more specifically. With the focus on speech throughout, we can
argue that the connection should be that just as the speech ("instructions") of Yhwh is characterized by integrity, reliability, uprightness,
cleanness, purity, and truth; so also does it produce people whose
speech is characterized thus.

Rhetorically, these verses function similarly to v. 2. By stating
that Yhwh's speech is characterized by these six qualities, they are im-

---

to include the divine name in vv. 2–7 (e.g., 2b, 5b).

[144] See discussion under exegetical observations above.

[145] These nuances have been helpfully discussed by several commentators,
e.g., Goldingay, *Psalms: Psalms 1–41*, 290–91, Kraus, *Psalms 1–59*, 273–75.

[146] תְּמִימָה, נֶאֱמָנָה, יְשָׁרִים, בָּרָה, טְהוֹרָה, אֱמֶת (integrity, reliability, uprightness,
cleanness, purity, and truth).

[147] Goldingay, *Psalms: Psalms 1–41*, 291.

[148] Ibid., 292.

[149] Ibid., 292.

plying that their own speech should be as well. This would be an example of implied commissive and behabitive speech.[150] Also, these statements would function as a type of argument a fortiori. That is, if God's speech is like this, how much more should our speech be. But there is an additional means of persuasion in these verses. The poet lists five benefits or rewards that God's speech provides. D. J. Clines has convincingly demonstrated that a sustained allusion to the Tree of Knowledge (Gen 2–3) lies behind the description of these benefits.[151] Thus, all the benefits that humanity has desired since the garden are available through the instruction of Yhwh. This is one of the oldest and most effective rhetorical devices, an appeal to what is advantageous to the audience.[152]

3.8.3   STROPHE THREE

Verses 11–12

These verses make explicit the value of Yhwh's instruction based on its characteristics and effects (vv. 8–10). The way in which the poet states the value of Yhwh's instruction is through comparison. Comparison can be a very effective means of persuasion because it "seems much more susceptible of proof than a simple statement…or analogy. This impression is due to the concept of measure underlying these statements."[153] The poet here implies that Yhwh's instruction can be classed among "desirable" (חמד) and "sweet" (מָתוֹק) things. Thus, the writer compares Yhwh's instruction with the outstanding examples of both of those classes.

Gold was certainly desirable in the ancient world as today.[154]

---

[150] Evans, *Logic of Self Involvement*, 51.

[151] Clines, "Tree of Knowledge and the Law of Yahweh: Psalm 19," 8–14.

[152] Aristotle, *Rhetoric*, 1.3.5. This is normally a characteristic of a deliberative argument, but Aristotle also points out its application to epideictic rhetoric (*Rhetoric*, 1.3.6).

[153] Perelman and Olbrechts-Tyteca, *New Rhetoric*, 242.

[154] This assertion hardly needs supporting. Gold was an important measurement of the glory of a king (1 Kgs 10:14–25); gold was a common form of offering to a deity (e.g., 1 Sam 6:4; Exod 35:22); and it was used for the construction of many

The poet here utilizes a device of heightening by stating that Yhwh's instruction is more desirable than gold, even more than much fine gold.[155] Both gold and Yhwh's instruction could be classified as desirable objects. The situation is less clear with the next comparison. Upon first impression, Yhwh's instruction would not seem to be literally sweet, thus making the comparison with honey an analogy within the comparison. Yet, the connection between sweetness of taste and sweetness of words is a natural one. Proverb 16:24 states, "Pleasant words are a honeycomb, sweet (מָתוֹק) to the appetite and healing to the bones." Even closer to our passage is Ezek 3:3, "And he said to me, 'Son of man feed your stomach and fill your belly with this scroll which I am giving to you. So I ate and it was in my mouth like honey for sweetness (מָתוֹק)." Thus, the sweetest and most desirable objects which an audience of near contemporaries could likely think of is said to pale in comparison to the sweetness and desirability of Yhwh's instruction.

Verse 12 presents an additional reason why Yhwh's instruction is valuable. On the one hand, it warns the worshipper, thus helping them avoid disaster. On the other hand, through keeping Yhwh's instruction great reward is available. This is clearly an appeal to the advantageous. Yet, there is more going on here. By voicing this truth, the congregation commits themselves to certain attitudes and actions. There is a performative element at work. In stating this line, the congregation does two things:[156] 1) they acknowledge that Yhwh's instructions do in fact warn and provide the opportunity for reward; and 2) they report their own state of mind in relation to this truth (autobiographic element).[157] That is, they affirm they want to keep Yhwh's instruction.

There is one other important element in this verse. The poet

---

of the implements of the temple (e.g., Exod 25:23–40).

[155] פַּז likely indicated gold which was more refined (HALOT, 921).

[156] Evans, Logic of Self Involvement, 43.

[157] They report this through implication. That is, by voicing this line publicly one is implying agreement to it. Of course, they may be implying this disingenuously (i.e. perhaps because they want others to approve of them), but that is another case altogether. See the discussion in Evans, Logic of Self Involvement, 40–43.

here changes the addressee by speaking to Yhwh directly.[158] This brings a personal tone in the poem not present up to this point. As the congregation voiced the self-designation, עַבְדְּךָ, they necessarily imply a particular relationship between themselves and the deity. The personalization at this point sets up well the congregation for the climactic final line.

Verses 13–14

The poet sets up the climactic line (v. 15) through a discussion of sin. Verses 13–14a discuss three categories of sin, which can be distinguished according to intention.[159] Jacob Milgrom has persuasively parsed out the difference between the three terms used here (שְׁגִיאָה, סתר, זֵד). שְׁגִיאָה refers to acts which were consciously performed, but were done in either negligence or ignorance. Milgrom states, "either the offender knows the Law but accidently violates it, or he acts deliberately without knowing he did wrong."[160] סתר refers to "acts of which the doer is unconscious and which are sinful."[161] These two accidental sins are set over against זֵד, which refers to an intentional sin. Once one understands the definitions, then the verbs used with each category of sin are comprehensible.

The sins are highlighted through fronting in all three cola (vv. 13–14a). Additionally, the two imperatives (נַקֵּנִי and חֲשֹׁךְ) bring intensity to the plea. By commanding Yhwh to declare them innocent of unconscious sins and to restrain them from intentional ones, the congregation has the value of avoiding sin emphasized for them. The commands to Yhwh stand in tension with the self-designation of the psalmist in v. 14a (עַבְדְּךָ). Servants do not normally command their master. In one sense, this underlines the intensity of the plea. The two cola of v. 14b summarize the plea. The congregation pleads that sin not be allowed to rule over them so that they will be "perfect" (תמם) and innocent (נקה) of great transgression.

---

[158] Indicated by the self-referential עַבְדְּךָ. This is an example of apostrophe.

[159] Milgrom, "Cultic שגגה and Its Influence in Psalms and Job," 120.

[160] Ibid., 118.

[161] Ibid., 120.

The overall effect of these verses is to instill in the worshipper a sense of humility. They have been reminded of the speech of the heavens concerning God. They have celebrated the value and wonder of the Torah. Now, they affirm that they can live up to neither standard even if they try. They are dependent upon Yhwh to declare them innocent and to keep them from intentional sins. This skillfully leads the worshipper to affirm the final plea of the psalm (v. 15) and adopt the attitude toward Yhwh the poet intended to create.

Verse 15

The entire poem up to this point has been leading the prayer up to this point. The poet has skillfully prepared the prayer to adopt the attitude articulated here as their own. The prayer affirms their desire to have their words and thoughts be acceptable before Yhwh. The word "acceptable" (רָצוֹן) connotes pleasing sacrificial acts.[162] Thus, the words and thoughts of the prayer are put on par with, or viewed as analogous to animal sacrifice. This final plea also highlights the reality that Yhwh knows the speech and thoughts of the prayer, thus bringing a higher level of accountability and humility. Finally, the poem ends by listing two titles for Yhwh. Yhwh is the prayer's "rock" and "redeemer."

3.9   CONCLUSION

Most previous scholarship on Ps 19 has focused either on its prehistory, ANE background, structure, or canonical placement. The rhetorical approach offered here builds on insights from all of those areas, but focuses its interpretive energy on the poem as a whole. It is concerned with analyzing the poem both as a work of art (its internal argument) and as socially embedded suasive discourse (its external argument). Distinguishing between these two levels is an important feature of this analysis. This chapter demonstrated that one of the reasons why commentators have posited such diverse settings for this poem was through a failure to recognize these two different levels of discourse.

Through our analysis of the internal argument of the psalm

---

[162] E.g., Lev 22:19–29.

concluded the following: The psalmist attempted to convince Yhwh to hold him back from sin/transgression and to declare him innocent, so that he will be whole/complete (תמם, v. 14). To achieve this goal, the psalmist uses the device of self-deliberation wherein he enumerates several facts and truths about the cosmos and the Torah. These demonstrate both the wide areas of agreement between Yhwh and the speaker and they serve to motivate Yhwh to maintain the harmony and order portrayed therein. The psalmist then asks Yhwh to restrain the forces of chaos within him and concludes by appealing to the close relationship between the two parties. Thus, the poem functions as deliberative rhetoric at this level.

My analysis of the external argument of the psalm demonstrated that the poet had particular attitudes and beliefs he was attempting to instill within the worshipping community. Thus, the poem could be classified as epideictic rhetoric. The type of attitude the poet most wanted to instill is clearly stated in v. 15. Recognizing this gives a focus and intentionality to the psalm as a whole. I was able to outline the various devices with which the poet worked to instill and support his rhetorical goal.

CHAPTER 4

Rhetorical Analysis of Psalm 103

4.1 INTRODUCTION

Psalm 103 provides us with a prime example of a descriptive psalm of praise. Robert L. Foster has compiled a list of the most common *topoi* in the praise psalms, almost half of which appear in this psalm.[1] Thus, this psalm represents well the diversity and richness of Israelite praise. Additionally, this psalm demonstrates how praise poetry can function to interpret Scripture.[2] As will be discussed below, Ps 103 is a liturgical appropriation of the Exod 32–34 narrative in general and Exod 34:6–7 in particular. The utilization of language and imagery from the exodus tradition functions in two different ways. On the one hand, it lends weight and authority to the psalm. It places the psalm firmly within Mosaic orthodoxy. On the other hand, it provides the worshipper with a lens through which to interpret the source text (Exod 32–34). One of the main rhetorical goals of this psalm is to shape the worshipper's view of God. For a historically oriented community like Israel, there is almost no more effective way to accomplish this than to ruminate on and explicate one of its foundational narrations of Yhwh's character.

This chapter will present a rhetorical approach to Ps 103 in the following way: first, I will present a translation of the psalm. Following that, I will discuss the rhetorical unit. That is, I will discuss unity and coherence of the psalm with particular attention to how form crit-

---

[1] Robert L. Foster, "*Topoi* of Praise in the Call to Praise Psalms: Toward a Theology of the Book of Psalms," in *My Words are Lovely: Studies in the Rhetoric of the Psalms*, LHBOTS 467, ed. R. Foster and David M. Howard, Jr. (New York: T&T Clark, 2008), 86. He lists thirteen different *topoi* of praise, five of which he lists as being represented in Ps 103.

[2] As J. Clinton McCann helpfully put it, the psalms provide us with "instruction for profession and profession for instruction," (*A Theological Introduction to the Book of Psalms: The Psalms as Torah* [Nashville: Abingdon 1993], 125–45).

ics have understood it. Third, I will describe the world of the psalm. Fourth, I will discuss possible social situations for the psalm. Finally, I will analyze the external argument of the psalm utilizing rhetorical tools to describe its suasive impact.

4.2   TRANSLATION

Of David   (1)

Strophe 1

Bless Yhwh, my soul

And all my inward parts,[3] his holy name

Bless, my soul, Yhwh   (2)

And do not forget all his benefits[4]

The forgiver of all your sins[5]   (3)

The healer of all your diseases[6]

The redeemer of your life from the pit   (4)

The one who crowns you with loyal love and compassions

The one who satisfies with the beauty of your jewelry[7]   (5)

---

[3] The BHS apparatus as well as several commentators argue that the plural form here קְרָבַי, should be vocalized as a singular, קִרְבִּי. Kraus gives the main argument for revocalization: the word does not appear in the plural anywhere else in the Hebrew Bible (*Psalms 60–150*, 289). In contrast, Frank Lothar Hossfeld and Eric Zenger call the emendation "superfluous" (*Psalms 3* [Hermeneia; trans. L. Maloney; Minneapolis: Fortress, 2011], 31). Indeed, it is difficult to understand why scribes would change the vocalization to make the word a *hapax legomenon* unless that was the tradition handed down to them.

[4] A Hebrew fragment from Cairo gives evidence for this word as a singular. However, the plural makes good sense in the context and is attested in the MT tradition as well as the LXX.

[5] The long suffix יְכִ- is likely included because of the assonance with בָּרֲכִי (vv. 1, 2); cf. Leslie C. Allen, *Psalms 101–150*, WBC 21 (Waco, TX: Word, 1983), 18; Goldingay, *Psalms: Psalms 90–150*, 163. The suffix likely betrays an Aramaizing influence, less likely an Ugaritic influence. For the latter, see Mitchell Dahood, *Psalms III: 101–150*, AB 17A (New Haven: Yale University Press, 1970), 25. 4QPs[b] has ךְ- as the suffix.

[6] See note 10 on the suffix, so also vv. 4 and 5.

[7] The form עֶדְיֵךְ ("your jewelry") has proved difficult. The LXX translates the word with ἐπιθυμία, probably trying to make sense of the MT text. Most com-

Your youth is renewed like an eagle

Yhwh does righteousness   (6)

    And justice for all the oppressed

He has made known[8] his ways to Moses   (7)

    To the children of Israel, his deeds

Compassionate and merciful is Yhwh   (8)

    Slow to anger and abounding in loyal love

Strophe 2

He will not always accuse   (9)

He has not done to us according to our sins   (10)

    And he has not repaid us according to our guilt

For as the heavens are high over the earth   (11)

    His loyal love is strong[9] over those who fear him

As distant as the east is from the west   (12)

    He has made distant our transgressions from us

As a father has compassion on children   (13)

---

mentators resort to emendation. The most common emendation of the text is to re-place the word with עֹדְכִי ("your days/continuing") following one of the BHS sugges-tions. This is often supported by reference to Pss 104:33; 146:2 (e.g., Kraus, *Psalms 60–150*, 289; Allen, *Psalms 101–150*, 18; Dahood, *Psalms III: 101–150*, 26; Paul-Eugène Dion, "Psalm 103: A Meditation on the 'Ways' of the Lord," *Église et théologie* 21 [1990]: 16; Hossfeld and Zenger, *Psalms 3*, 31). One argument for keeping the MT as it stands ("your jewelry") is that the word is used in Exod 33:4, which is the sub-text of this entire psalm, which states: When the people heard this bad news, they mourned and didn't put on their jewelry (עֶדְיוֹ). For the Yhwh said to Moses: "Tell the Israelites: You are a stiff-necked people.... If I went with you for a single moment, I would destroy you. Now take off your jewelry (עֶדְיְךָ) and I will de-cide what to do with you." So the Israelites remained stripped of their jewelry (עֶדְיָם) from Mount Horeb onward (vv. 4–6). The word jewelry is used here 3x in 3 verses. Given the deep connection between this psalm and the Exod 32–34 narrative, the use of this wording is surely intentional. The satisfying with jewelry is a reversal of the punishment for sin in Exod 32.

[8] This is a preterit use of the prefix form sometimes found in poetic texts re-counting history; see *IBHS*, 498 and also David Robertson, *Linguistic Evidence in Dating Early Hebrew Poetry*, SBLDS 3 (Missoula: Scholars Press, 1972), 17–55.

[9] Kraus, following the BHS, emends גָּבַר here to גָבַה without textual support (*Psalms 60–150*, 289). This is unnecessary; see Hossfeld and Zenger, *Psalms 3*, 31.

Yhwh has compassion on those who fear him

For he knows our shape   (14)

   Mindful[10] that we are dust

A human[11]—like grass are his days   (15)

   Like a blossom of the field so he blossoms

When the wind blows on it, then it is no more   (16)

   And one cannot recognize its place any longer

Strophe 3

But the loyal love of Yhwh is from forever to forever   (17)

on those who fear him[12]

   And his righteousness on the children of children

To those who keep his covenant   (18)

   And to those who remember his instructions

Yhwh—in heaven he has set up his throne   (19)

   And his kingship rules over everything

Bless Yhwh, his messengers   (20)

   Heros of strength who do his word[13]

   By listening[14] to the sound of his word[15]

Bless Yhwh, all his troops   (21)

   His ministers—those who do his will

---

[10] "A form like the pass. ptcp. *Pā'ŭl*, but not to be confused with it, it is sometimes found from *intransitive verbs*, to denote an inherent quality" *GKC*§50f.

[11] Nominative absolute construction here, so also v. 19 (see *IBHS*, 76).

[12] As one can recognize, the length of this line has caused many interpreters to eliminate some words as glosses. Kraus states, "This verse is filled beyond capacity. In particular, ן מֵעוֹלָם should probably be considered a filler; so one could in any event conclude from the parallel member. Also עַל־יְרֵאָיו would have to be removed from v. 17 and could serve as a complement in v. 18" (*Psalms 60–150*, 289). Hossfeld and Zenger argue that the tricolon was intended (*Psalms 3*, 31). Indeed, given the often surprising changes which occur in poetry, in the absence of outside evidence it is best to leave the text as it stands.

[13] 4QPs[b] has the plural form, דבריו both here and at the end of the verse, the LXX has the plural at the end of the verse. Either is possible.

[14] Gerundive, or explanatory ל + infinitive; see *IBHS*, 608.

[15] Kraus argues that the phrase לשׁמע בקול דברו should be understood as an explanatory gloss (*Psalms 60–150*, 289). However, this is an unnecessary emendation.

Bless Yhwh, all his works (22)
    In all the places of his rule
Bless Yhwh, my soul

4.3   DETERMINATION OF THE RHETORICAL UNIT

The boundaries of Ps 103 have not been particularly contested. The both internal and external evidence clearly support the psalm as a unity.[16] More contested has been its form-critical categorization. Claus Westermann classifies this as a descriptive praise psalm.[17] He further groups this as an "imperative psalm" along with Pss 100; 145; 148; 150; 95A; and Add Dan 1:29ff.[18] This is a type of descriptive praise psalm that developed late in Israel's history evidenced by the "one-sided praise of God's grace."[19] However, other commentators understand this as an individual thanksgiving psalm, which has merged into a hymn.[20]

Mowinckel further argues that Ps 103 has moved so far beyond its traditional form category that it could be classified separately as a "psalm of confidence" along with Pss 23 and 71.[21] Gerstenberger, Anderson, and Brueggemann classify the psalm as a *communal* hymn not individual.[22]

---

[16] One discordant voice in this consensus is Paul Humbert who has argued that vv. 19–22 are actually the beginning of Ps 104, not the end of Ps 103 ("La relation de Genèse 1 et du Psaume 104 avec la liturgie du Nouvel-An israélite," in *Opuscules d'un hébraïsant*, ed. P. Humbert [Neuchâtel: Secrétariat de l'Universit,' 1958], 78–80). Briggs and Briggs have argued that vv. 19–22 are a Maccabean era liturgical addition to the psalm (*The Book of Psalms: Vol. 2*, 327). However, the inclusio and the number of lines in the psalm, twenty-two (equal to the number of letters in the Hebrew alphabet), both point to its original unity.

[17] Westermann, *Praise and Lament*, 132.

[18] Ibid., 131–32.

[19] Ibid., 136.

[20] Mowinckel, *Psalms in Israel's Worship*, 2:38; Kraus, *Psalms 60–150*, 164.

[21] Mowinckel, *Psalms in Israel's Worship*, 2:132.

[22] Bernhard Anderson, *Out of the Depths: The Psalms Speak for Us Today* (Philadelphia: Westminster, 1983), 241; Erhard Gerstenberger, *Psalms: Part 2 and*

On the one hand, this form-critical debate highlights one advantage of a rhetorical approach, which takes each psalm as a unique articulation. On the other hand, this debate reveals deeper interpretive issues related to the setting (individual vs. corporate; liturgical vs. private; pre- vs. post-exilic) to be addressed below.

4.4   STRUCTURE

Many scholars have lamented the ambiguity surrounding the structure of this psalm.[23] John Stek lists twenty-seven different proposals for dividing and sub-dividing the psalm.[24] While Jan Fokkelman states, "I have checked fifty authors on their strophic divisions of the psalm and came to the sad conclusion that 48 of them have missed the point."[25] Indeed, Fokkelman has presented the most persuasive argument for the division of the psalm based on both linguistic markers and content.[26] While I will use different terminology than he did, this strophic division is indebted to his careful analysis.

Strophe 1: vv. 1–8:
Call to Praise God for his Benefits

vv. 1–2:	Self-deliberation: call to praise
vv. 3–5:	Accumulation: Reasons for praise
vv. 6–8:	Past deeds of Yhwh – graciousness formula

Lamentations, FOTL 15 (Grand Rapids: Eerdmans, 2001), 215. Walter Brueggemann, *The Message of the Psalms: A Theological Commentary* (Minneapolis: Ausburg, 1984), 160–61. Brueggemann categorizes it as a hymn of "new orientation."

[23] E.g., Dion, "Psalm 103: a Meditation on the "Ways" of the Lord," 13–14; Timothy Willis, "'So Great is His Steadfast Love': a Rhetorical Analysis of Psalm 103," *Biblica* 72 (1991): 525–26; D. F. O'Kennedy, "The Relationship between Justice and Forgiveness in Psalm 103," *Scriptura* 65 (1998): 110; J. P. Fokkelman, "Psalm 103: Design, Boundaries, and Mergers," in *Psalms and Prayers, OtSt* 55, ed. B. Becking and E. Peels (Leiden: Brill, 2007), 110; Pierre Auffret, "Un père envers des fils: Nouvelle étude structurelle du psaume 103," *Theoforum* 37 (2006): 25–26.

[24] John Stek, "Psalm 103: Its Thematic Architecture," in *Text and Community* (Sheffield: Sheffield Academic, 2007), 23–25.

[25] Fokkelman, "Psalm 103: Design, Boundaries, and Mergers," 109.

[26] Ibid., 109–18.

Strophe 2: vv. 9–16:
Interpretation of Steadfast Love and Compassion[27]
vv. 9–10:	Yhwh's Forgiveness
vv. 11–13:	Yhwh's Compassion
vv. 14–16:	Human Frailty

Strophe 3: vv. 17–22:
Summary and Call to Praise
vv. 17–19:	Summary of Yhwh's Compassion and Steadfast Love
vv. 20–22:	Universal call to praise

4.5 DESCRIPTION OF THE WORLD OF THE PSALM: ITS INTERNAL ARGUMENT

In the previous chapter, this section was comprised of three main parts: a description of the implied author and audience of the psalm; a description of the world of the psalm; and an analysis of its internal argument. This psalm will require a somewhat different approach. One important feature of this psalm is the way in which it utilizes the language and theology from Exod 32–34. One could aptly describe Ps 103 as a liturgical rumination on Exod 32–34. Michael Fishbane has argued that Ps 103 is an "Aggadic exegesis" of the Exodus text.[28] So, the primary way to describe the world of the poem for this psalm is to reflect on the rhetorical significance of the Exodus narrative in this psalm. Thus, the first part of this section analyzing the world of the psalm will describe the connections between Exod 32–34 and Ps 103. This will serve as an important foundation for our rhetorical analysis.

---

[27] This title was used in Hossfeld and Zenger, *Psalms 3*, 33.

[28] Michael Fishbane, *Biblical Interpretation in Ancient Israel* (Oxford: Oxford University Press, 1985), 409–39.

4.5.1   PSALM 103 AND EXODUS 32–34

In the previous chapter we described the "world" of the psalm primarily by closely engaging the images and logic of the poem itself. Poets tend to highlight certain parts of the "real" world to create the "small-world" of their poem to achieve particular effects.[29] There is another way in which a psalm can create a world though. By utilizing the language and imagery of a culturally foundational narrative, the poet can exploit that narrative as a part of the "world" of the poem. Michael Fishbane puts it this way, "the purveyors and creators of aggadic exegesis [read: the psalmists] appear to live with 'texts-in-the-mind'—that is, with texts which provide the imaginative matrix for evaluating the present, for conceiving of the future...for providing the shared symbols and language of communication."[30] The goal of this section is to demonstrate that there are close links between Ps 103 and Exod 32–34.[31] The way in which the psalmist utilizes the imagery from the Exodus narrative will be described in the rhetorical analysis below.

Figure 1 is a chart indicating both lexical and thematic connections between Ps 103 and the Exod 32–34 narrative. Some of these connections are more compelling than others, but taken together they clearly demonstrate the close links between the texts.

---

[29] Umberto Eco, *The Limits of Interpretation* (Bloomington: Indiana University Press 1990), 64–82.

[30] Fishbane, *Biblical Interpretation in Ancient Israel*, 436.

[31] Hossfeld states, "scriptural references to Exodus 33–34 are frequently encountered throughout Psalm 103.... From these observations it has become clear that Psalm 103 knows extensive parts of the Sinai narrative. It subjects especially Exodus 32–34 to a close interpretation." (*Psalms 3*, 32). So also Matthias Franz, *Der barmherzige und gnädige Gott: Die Gnadenrede vom Sinai (Exodus 34, 6–7) und ihre Parallelen im Alten Testament und seiner Umwelt,* vol. 20 (Stuttgart: Kohlhammer, 2003), 231–33.

Figure 1

Psalm 103		Exodus 32–34	
1	Psalmist commands to bless Yhwh's holy name (שֵׁם)	33:9, 34:5	Yhwh proclaims his name in both of these texts (שֵׁם)
3, 10, 21	Yhwh forgives sin (עָוֹן), and he does not act toward us according to our iniquity (חַטָּאָה), and he removes from us our transgressions (פֶּשַׁע)	34:7	Yhwh forgives iniquity, transgression and sin (עָוֹן, פֶּשַׁע, חַטָּאָה)
3	Yhwh heals diseases	32:35	Yhwh struck the people with a plague
4	Yhwh redeemed your life "from the pit" (מִשַּׁחַת)	32:7	The people had "corrupted" themselves (שִׁחֵת)
5	Yhwh satisfies with jewelry (עֲדִי) as a result of forgiveness.	33:4–6	Because of their sin, the people are commanded not to wear their "ornaments" (עֲדִי). Root is used 3x in 3 verses.
7	Yhwh made known his ways to Moses (יוֹדִיעַ דְּרָכָיו לְמֹשֶׁה)	33:13	Moses requests that Yhwh make known to him his ways (הוֹדִעֵנִי נָא אֶת־דְּרָכֶךָ)
8, 13	Root (רחם) used of Yhwh 3x in these verses.	33:19	Yhwh declares that he will be have compassion on those whom he will have compassion (רחם)
8	Graciousness formula (רַחוּם וְחַנּוּן יְהוָה אֶרֶךְ אַפַּיִם וְרַב־חָסֶד)	34:6	Graciousness formula[32] (רַחוּם וְחַנּוּן אֶרֶךְ אַפַּיִם וְרַב־חֶסֶד וֶאֱמֶת)

---

[32] Label used for this verse by Hossfeld and Zenger, *Psalms 3*, 33.

10	Yhwh does not act toward us according to our חֲטָאָה	32:21, 30, 32, 34	Use of חֲטָאָה to describe Israel's sin
12	Sins and transgressions removed far from us (רחק)	33:7	Tent of meeting pitched "far" (רחק) from the camp
13	Yhwh has compassion upon us like the compassion of a father on children (אָב עַל־בָּנִים)	34:7	Yhwh visits the iniquity of the fathers on the children and grandchildren (בָּנִים אָבוֹת עַל־בָּנִים וְעַל־בְּנֵי)
14	Yhwh is "mindful" (זָכוּר) that we are dust.	32:13	Remember (זכר) the promise You swore to the patriarchs.
18	Yhwh's loyal love is on those who guard his covenant (לְשֹׁמְרֵי בְרִיתוֹ)	34:10–11	Yhwh makes a covenant (בְּרִית) and commands the people to guard it (שמר)
20	All Yhwh's messengers (מַלְאָכָיו) commanded to bless him.	33:2	Yhwh promises to send his messenger (מַלְאָךְ) to drive out the Canaanites

While there are other texts lurking in the background of Ps 103,[33] the narrative of Exod 32–34 is its primary background.[34] Exod 32–34 provided Israel with a foundational understanding of its propensity to sin and of Yhwh's graciousness and forgiveness. An audience of near contemporaries would have picked up on these connections and understood the psalm as a liturgical reflection on the Exodus text, a device which helped the psalmist achieve his/her rhetorical goals.

---

[33] E.g., Gen 2:7 and Ps 103:14.

[34] See the close connection between rhetorical criticism and intertextuality explained by Patricia Tull, "Rhetorical Criticism and Intertextuality," in *To Each Its Own Meaning: An Introduction to Biblical Criticisms and Their Application*, ed. S. McKenzie and S. Haynes (Louisville: Westminster, 1999), 156–82.

4.5.2   THE IMPLIED AUTHOR AND AUDIENCE

The poem begins on an inward note. The psalmist commands his own soul.[35] It is almost as if the psalmist is trying to rouse himself up to worship Yhwh, as if he needed some extra motivation. The command to not forget Yhwh's benefits (v. 2) implies that he knows he might. The psalmist follows the imperatives to the self with a series of participial phrases rehearsing past acts of Yhwh to ground his motivation for blessing.

While the psalm begins on a personal and even inward note, the participle phrases make clear that the psalmist envisions himself as more than just an isolated individual. The psalmist does not bless Yhwh for benefits he has received personally.[36] Rather the language utilized in vv. 3–13 connects back to the Exod 32–34 narrative. The psalmist understands himself as part of the exodus community, and is perhaps best understood as a representative Israelite, one who shares in the blessings and failings of the people of Israel. Therefore, the transition to the first common plural in v. 10 is quite natural. A. F. Kirkpatrick describes the psalmist as one in whom, "national sorrows and sufferings have so deeply entered into... [his] heart that he speaks of them as his own, so here he so completely identifies himself with the destines of the nation that its joys are his own, and he gives thanks for national deliverance and national mercies as though they had been vouchsafed to him individually."[37] The psalmist has a clear understanding of Yhwh's history with his people, including: the people's propensity to sin, Yhwh's graciousness and forgiveness, and the dra-

---

[35] The psalmist addressing his own נֶפֶשׁ is not unusual in the psalter (e.g., Pss 104:1; 146:1; 57:9; 35:9). Other psalms envision the psalmist addressing his כָּבוֹד (Ps 30:13), or his "mouth," "tongue," or "heart" commanding it to engage Yhwh in worship (e.g., Ps 13:6; 35:28; 51:16–17; 63:6; 71:8, 15, 24; 119:172; 145:21). See the classic analysis of this device by Gunkel and Begrich, *Introduction to the Psalms*, 27. This genre of text where the poet addressing the self has been labeled, "the dialogue of a man with his soul." See Dahood, *Psalms III: 101–150*, 25.

[36] Contra, Kraus, *Psalms 60–150*, 290; Gene Rice, "An Exposition of Psalm 103," *JRT* 39 (1982): 55; Terrien, *The Psalms*, 705

[37] Kirkpatrick, *Book of Psalms*, 600.

matic difference between Yhwh's eternality and human transience. Most of these themes are drawn from the Exodus narrative. However, the psalmist does not simply draw on language and theology from Exod 32–34 and apply it to worship. Rather, he subtly transforms the message of the Exodus text by highlighting particular themes (e.g., Yhwh's compassion) and downplaying others (e.g., Yhwh's anger) in order to meet his rhetorical goals. In sum, the psalmist is one who is steeped in the tradition and history of Israel. From his reflection on foundational Israelite traditions, he is motivated to praise Yhwh from a particular understanding of the nature of humans and of Yhwh.

The implied audience of the poem is not a stable entity. In contrast to Ps 19, which begins at a cosmic level and ends on an inward note, this psalm moves in the opposite direction. The poem begins on an inward note with the psalmist addressing his own soul (vv. 1–2). Thus, in the beginning of the poem the author and audience are merged into one. Yet, as the psalmist begins to rehearse to himself the benefits (גְּמוּל) of Yhwh, the circle of addressees widens. In verse 10, the poet includes the nation of Israel along with him as the speaker. Thus, the psalm moves from the psalmist addressing himself to the nation collectively addressing itself. The circle widens in vv. 20–22 to include the messengers of Yhwh (מַלְאָךְ), the hosts of Yhwh (צָבָא),[38] and finally "all his works (כָל־מַעֲשָׂיו)."

It seems that in motivating himself to bless Yhwh, the psalmist had become convinced that every created being needed to bless Yhwh as well. In sum, the implied audience grows in this way: the psalmist's soul → the nation/those gathered to worship ("us") → the messengers and hosts of heaven → all the works of Yhwh → the psalmist's soul.

4.5.3   THE INTERNAL ARGUMENT OF PSALM 103

The rhetorical goal of the psalm on the surface is transparent. The psalmist is seeking to convince himself and everyone else to bless

---

[38] In the ancient world the "hosts" (צבא) were often identified with the stars. See H. Neihr, "Host of Heaven," in *Dictionary of Deities and Demons*, ed. K. Van der Toorn and B. Becking (Leiden: Brill, 1999), 429.

Yhwh.[39] Based on this, the internal argument of the psalm could be classified as deliberative rhetoric. That is, the psalmist is trying to convince an audience to act in a particular way in the present and future. However, there is more going on in this psalm. By utilizing the language and imagery from Exod 32–34, the psalmist is attempting to convince the audience of a particular view of who Yhwh is. By simply reading the narrative of Exod 32–34, it would be easy to come away with a very different view of Yhwh than is presented by this psalm. Yhwh desired to destroy the entire nation and was barely dissuaded by Moses (32:10). Yhwh struck Israel with a plague *after* Moses had 3,000 people killed as a form of punishment (32:35). Yhwh then declared that he would not go up with the people of Israel lest he destroy them (33:3, 5). However, there is also a pervasive theme of Yhwh's compassion and grace in this narrative. He does engage Moses in dialogue, does not destroy the people, and does end up going with them. The psalmist clearly emphasizes this aspect of the narrative, and thus attempts to persuade the audience of a particular view of Yhwh. This could be helpfully classified as judicial rhetoric. That is, an attempt to portray Yhwh's past actions in a certain light. The connection between the two ways of looking at the psalm is logical. Based on Yhwh's character as revealed specifically in Exod 32–34, the psalmist calls on himself and others to bless Yhwh.[40]

4.6 THE POSSIBLE HISTORICAL SETTINGS/SITUATIONS OF THE PSALM

There has been little agreement as to several aspects of the setting of the psalm. Some scholars have understood this psalm as an individual praising God for healing or some other need that was surprisingly

---

[39] The verb ברך is used six times in the imperative in this psalm.

[40] Because of the similarity in function between the internal and external argument of the psalm, the argument of the psalm will only be analyzed once under the heading "the external argument." Places where there is a difference in emphasis between the internal and external arguments will be noted.

met.[41] Robert Foster has nuanced this view. He also believes it is the praise of an individual. However, instead of the reason being personal benefits the psalmist has experienced, the psalmist "reflects personally on the benefits given to the community in the *new* Exodus of the return from exile."[42] Thus, the psalm is understood as an individual praise based on a corporate blessing. Other scholars argue that the psalm is primarily a communal praise psalm rooted in cultic worship. In this view, the "I" of the psalm is likely a cultic singer who is leading the worship, but this should not be understood as an individual praise psalm.[43] Most of these scholars do not cite a specific reason why the praise is uttered, other than that one of the primary functions of the cult is to praise Yhwh.[44] Still other scholars do not see any connection with the cult.[45] Based on language and content, this poem is likely exilic or post-exilic.[46]

The above discussion may make us despair the possibility of determining a social setting for the psalm when there is no consensus on such basic matters of individual vs. communal or cultic vs. non-cultic. However, there is another factor to consider. Michael Fishbane

---

[41] Terrien, *Psalms*, 705; Rice, "An Exposition of Psalm 103," 55; Kraus, *Psalms 60–150*, 290; Willem VanGemeren, "Psalms," in *Expositor's Bible Commentary*, ed. F. Gaebelein (Grand Rapids: Zondervan, 1991), 650.

[42] Foster, *"Topoi* of Praise in the Call to Praise Psalms," 80. This is similar to the view of Kirkpatrick who argues that it is the praise of an individual who has identified himself with the nation, see Kirkpatrick, *Book of Psalms*, 600.

[43] Goldingay, *Psalms: Psalms 90–150*, 165; Allen, *Psalms 101–150*, 19–20; Gerstenberger, *Psalms: Part 2 and Lamentations*, 216–17.

[44] Allen states that each worshipper would have different reasons for praising, "For some the crippling handicap of sin had earlier manifested itself in illness...Others were there at the that time who had known oppression and harassment—until Yahweh had marvelously vindicated them" (*Psalms 101–150,* 21–22). Gerstenberger comes closest to offering a specific reason for the cultic praise, "In reality, this little hymn is a comforting song to the afflicted members of the Yahweh community" (*Psalms: Part 2 and Lamentations,* 216).

[45] Hossfeld and Zenger, *Psalms 3*, 31.

[46] As most scholars acknowledge, with the notable exception of Dahood, *Psalms III: 101–150*, 24–25.

has analyzed how Ps 103 uses the Exod 32–34 text. He argues that the psalmist was engaged in aggadic exegesis.[47] He defines aggadic exegesis in this way:

> *Aggadah* was ... applied to moral and theological homilies, didactic expositions of historical and folk motifs, expositions and reinterpretations of ethical dicta and religious *theologoumena*.... Aggatic exegesis is primarily concerned with utilizing the full range of the inherited *traditum* for the sake of new theological insights, attitudes, and speculations ... in contrast to legal exegesis, *fullness* is a significant condition for its emergence. That is: it is precisely because certain features of the received *traditum* are comprehensible, and predominate in the imagination or memory of its tradents—or, at any rate, it is precisely because certain features of the *traditum* are actively present in the mind of those tradents entrusted with its preservation and reformulation—that they are reused in aggadic exegesis.[48]

This type of textual reflection, he demonstrates, has a particular social setting. He argues that there are three exigencies which call forth aggadic exegesis:

> [These categories] concern crisis with regard to the convenantal traditions; and with regard to the continuity or survival of the traditions from one historical epoch to another. Catalysing these categories, moreover, are such dynamic tensions as **covenantal allegiance versus rebellion** (or disinterest); **cognitive coherence versus dissonance**; and **cultural memory and hope versus the irrelevance of the past and despair**.... First, in connection with those crises which affected the continuity of the entire covenantal *traditum*, one can observe the important role of aggadic exegesis in **the attempt of teachers to restore covenan-**

---

[47] Fishbane, *Biblical Interpretation in Ancient Israel*, 414.

[48] Ibid., 281–83.

tal allegiance in its totality. That is, on occasions of religious rebellion or simply passive disaffection, when the demands of the covenant are disavowed in practice, the aggadic rhetoric of ancient Israel frequently reused specific pieces of the *traditum* in order to realign the community with its entire heritage.[49]

Thus, the social situation of this type of exegesis is one in which the community has a weakening of adherence to their covenantal heritage. This could be due to a number of factors: rebellion, cognitive dissonance, or the apparent irrelevance of the received tradition. This type of exegesis then is thoroughly rhetorical. It is aimed at strengthening adherence to Israel's religious heritage in a climate where that adherence has weakened. As such, this type of exegesis could be understood as a species of epideictic rhetoric. It attempts to reverse the thoughts and attitudes of its hearer. The way in which aggadic exegesis functions in Ps 103 is primarily through the "reinterpretation or transformation of a specific element of the *traditum*."[50] As we will see, Ps 103 functions in a similar way to the Chronicler who "reworked *traditum* in light of prevailing contemporary notions of religious praxis or divine activity."[51]

While it is not essential for us to tie this psalm to a specific historical situation, it is important to understand the social situation from which this psalm was written. Based on the language of the psalm and the way in which the poet utilizes the exodus tradition, the situation seems to be one of relative political stability, but with a weakening of the belief in the relevance of the covenantal tradition. An example of this type of setting would be the post-exilic situation. The nation had political stability under the Persian regime. However, there was a sense that God had not fully restored the nation after the exile. This could easily have led people to believe either that the covenantal traditions did not matter anymore, or that they had so broken the covenant

---

[49] Ibid., 409. Emphasis mine.

[50] Ibid., 410.

[51] Fishbane, *Biblical Interpretation in Ancient Israel*, 410.

that Yhwh had given up on them. The psalm is best understood as a response to this type of situation. It is a public document intended both to praise Yhwh and to persuade the community to a deeper adherence to their God through a liturgical interpretation of a central covenantal text.

4.7   ANALYSIS OF THE ARGUMENT OF THE PSALM: ITS EXTERNAL ARGUMENT

J. Clinton McCann has rightly argued that Psalm 103 intends to be comprehensive. This can be demonstrated through the nine-fold use of כל (vv. 1–3, 6, 19, 21–22). This psalm "affirms that God, who rules over all and does all good things for all persons in need, is to be praised in all places by all creatures and things with all of their be-ing."[52] This is an apt introduction to the rhetorical goal of the poem. It seeks to convince the self and others to "bless" Yhwh. This is obvious from the six-fold imperative use of ברך (vv. 1–2, 20–22). However, the goal is more than simply provoking praise of Yhwh. The psalmist spends the majority of the poem describing who Yhwh is, primarily in terms of Yhwh's relationship with his people. Humanity is described as transient, frail (vv. 14–16), and prone to sin (vv. 3, 10–12). In that context, Yhwh relationship to Israel is characterized by רחם and חסד.[53] Emphasized is the fact that Yhwh's anger does not last forever in con-trast to his חסד. He does not just punish sin, but thoroughly forgives (vv. 3, 9, 10, 12). As Patrick Miller has emphasized, a theological con-fession in praise is not a neutral act.[54] Rather, it intends to shape the beliefs and attitude of the audience. The primary means of persuasion is the interpretive use of language drawn from the deep well of Israel's religious heritage.

---

[52] J. Clinton McCann, *Psalms,* NIB 4 (Nashville: Abingdon, 1996), 1090. This insight is also supported by the fact that there are 22 lines in the poem, equaling the number of letters in the Hebrew alphabet.

[53] Both roots are used four times: רחם (vv. 4, 8, 13); חסד (vv. 4, 8, 11, 17).

[54] Patrick D. Miller, *They Cried to the Lord: The Form and Theology of Biblical Prayer* (Minneapolis: Fortress, 1994), 202–3.

4.7.1   STROPHE ONE: CALL TO PRAISE

This section is comprised of a call to praise along with an enumeration of reasons why Yhwh is worthy of praise. The three sub-sections of this unit fall into nearly identical units of length:

vv. 1–2: 17 words
vv. 3–5: 18 words
vv. 6–8: 19 words

From the first word, the psalmist speaks in the imperative. The seven imperatives are clustered with three in vv. 1–2 and four in vv. 20–22. This clustering at the opening and closing of the psalm colors the whole. The psalm functions as one rousing imperative to bless Yhwh. One would assume that the imperative would have strong suasive force. However, Perelman and Olbrechts-Tyteca reveal,

> Contrary to appearances, the imperative does not have persuasive force: all its power comes from the hold of the person commanding over the one carrying out the orders; the relation is one of relative forces, without any implication of adherence. When actual force is lacking or when one does not consider using it, the imperative assumes the tone of a prayer.... On account of the personal relation which it implies, the imperative form is very effective for increasing the feeling of presence.[55]

Thus, the rhetorical function of the imperative in a context like this is to increase presence and to engage the audience in the poem. Imagine a sports radio announcer commanding the players on the field. Even though the players cannot hear the announcer, by speaking in this way the announcer draws the listener in as a participant in the game.

Verses 1–2

The first two verses are a neatly balanced set of lines.[56] These two verses contain three imperatives.[57] In some ways these lines seem

---

[55] Perelman and Olbrechts-Tyteca, *New Rhetoric*, 158.

[56] The number of syllables is identical between the two lines of vv. 1 and 2.

[57] Or four if you include the ellipsed imperative of v. 1b.

straightforward – they are commands to bless Yhwh. However, the question arises as to what exactly it means to bless (ברך) Yhwh. *HAL-OT* defines the word, "to endue someone with special power."[58] But how is it possible to endue Yhwh with special power? *HALOT* answers this question by stating that when Yhwh is the object, the word denotes a declaration that God is the source of special power. Thus, it is equivalent to saying, "praise God."[59] However, Sheldon Blank has persuasively argued that "blessing" in prayer connotes more than simply praise. He states, "Blessing has a quality that praise does not share. A blessing is a giving, a gift, an offering. To 'bless' the Lord is to bring Him an offering. It is right to say we 'offer' a blessing…The words of a blessing are material and ponderable like incense and animals."[60] While it is difficult to argue that offering a blessing is equivalent to animal sacrifice, it is clear that it is more than simply praising Yhwh. It is a way to offer something tangible, a verbal offering.[61] Additionally, the command to "bless" is a self-involving action. In speech-act theory, blessing would be considered behabative speech.[62] This type of speech has to do with the attitude of the speaker toward the object.[63] When used with God as an object in the Old Testament, to bless God is a way to respond to God's provision or action on one's behalf.[64] It implies an attitude of thankfulness, but as stated earlier, to bless God is also to offer him something – an offering of words. J. L. Austin recognized that this type of speech was especially liable to infelicities, or

---

[58] *HALOT*, I.160.

[59] Ibid.

[60] Sheldon Blank, "Some Observations Concerning Biblical Prayer," *HUCA* 32 (1961): 87, 89.

[61] See Miller, *They Cried to the Lord*, 180–81.

[62] J. L. Austin, *How to Do Things with Words* (Oxford: Oxford University Press, 1962), 159.

[63] Donald Evans, *The Logic of Self-Involvement: A Philosophical Study of Everyday Language with Special Reference to the Christian Use of Language about God as Creator* (London: SCM Press, 1963), 34–35.

[64] E.g., Gen 24:48; Deut 8:10; Judg 5:2.

insincerities.[65] It is all too easy to bless with one's mouth, but not with one's actions.[66] Perhaps this is why the psalmist adds the line "and all my inward parts" (וְכָל־קְרָבַי). It is a way of recognizing that it is very easy to bless merely with words, but not intention.

Additionally, when one analyzes how the command to bless Yhwh functions rhetorically, several other factors need to be considered. As stated above, the command does not have persuasive force simply because it is a command. Rather, the imperative functions as an effective way to increase the presence of this activity. The presence of this command is reinforced through anaphora (v. 1a, 2a). Culturally, the command to bless Yhwh would be similar to the command frequently heard today to "support our troops" or "get out to vote." They are activities or mindsets that culturally we know we should do. The imperatives function to highlight these issues for us.

Further, the psalmist does not command the gathered community. Rather, he commands his own נֶפֶשׁ. This creates what Fokkelman calls, "the rhetorical act of splitting," which "creates an opening where the listeners can step in."[67] That is, in commanding his own soul, the hearer/participant in the psalm can use the language to address his/her own soul. This type of speech works indirectly and is more effective for it. As has been long recognized, *identification* is essential for any persuasion to take place. Kenneth Burke emphatically states, "You persuade a man only insofar as you can talk his language by speech, gesture, tonality, order, image, attitude, idea, identifying your ways with his."[68]

The psalmist here provides an exceptionally good means of identification with the audience by encouraging the audience to address their own soul, thus identifying themselves as the author of the

---

[65] Austin, *How to Do Things with Words*, 159.

[66] Cf. Isa 29:13.

[67] Fokkelman, "Psalm 103: Design, Boundaries, and Mergers," 117.

[68] Kenneth Burke, *Rhetoric of Motives* (Berkeley: University of California Press, 1969), 55; Kenneth Burke, "On Persuasion, Identification, and Dialectical Symmetry," *Philosophy & Rhetoric* 39 (2006): 333–39.

psalm. This rhetorical feature has been recognized since Longinus, who referred to "that kind of elation wherein the audience feels as though it were not merely receiving, but were itself creatively participating in the poet's or speaker's assertion. Could we not say that, in such cases, the audience is exalted by the assertion because it has the feel of collaborating in the assertion?"[69] Also, addressing one's own soul creates a context of self-deliberation. Perelman and Olbrechts-Tyteca describe this as one of the most effective means of persuasion because it seems to have a greater degree of authenticity.[70] Why would one be false with the self?

The final clause of v. 2 serves as a transition to the following section which enumerates many of Yhwh's deeds. The language shifts from a positive command to a negative prohibition. The psalmist cautions his soul not to forget Yhwh's benefits. Forgetting Yhwh is a religiously culpable act for ancient Israel often associated with idol worship.[71] In Israel's sacred history, they tended to forget Yhwh when things were going well economically and politically.[72] This could be a subtle clue to the social situation of the psalmist. It is when things are going well the congregation needs to be reminded what Yhwh has done for them in the past. This is the force of the negative command. They are to remember the benefits Yhwh has bestowed upon them.

The final word of v. 2 serves as a kind of double entendre. The word usually indicates a punishment meted out against the wicked.[73] Given the allusions to Exod 32–34 later in the psalm, one might think it has a nuance of judgment in this context. In other words, "bless Yhwh, or he will pay you back for it – don't forget he is a judge!" Yet, surprisingly, the psalmist goes on to enumerate the blessings Yhwh

---

[69] Burke, *Rhetoric of Motives*, 57–58.

[70] Perelman and Olbrechts-Tyteca, *New Rhetoric*, 41.

[71] E.g., Deut 8:19; Judg 3:7; 1 Sam 12:9–12; Isa 17:10; Jer 3:21–25; Ezek 22:12; Deut 32:18; Ps 106: 21.

[72] E.g., Deut 32:15–18; 1 Sam 12:9; Hos 13:6; see also the cycle of the Judges (Judg 3:7).

[73] גְּמוּל has this sense in 12 out of 17 occurrences in the Hebrew Bible.

has bestowed. Thus, the psalmist is already shaping the listener's perception of Yhwh. Yhwh's recompense, rather than being primarily
judgment, is "first of all forgiveness!"[74]

Verses 3–5

These verses consist of three beautifully structured lines of poetry. The first line constitutes two perfectly matched cola. Each has a
substantive participle with an object phrase marked by לְכָל followed by
a noun with an unusual form of the 2fs enclitic (כִי-). The next two
lines deviate from this pattern in some way, which gives a natural progression to the unit.[75] The first five cola exhibit grammatical anaphora
in that each colon begins with a substantive participle. The sixth colon
is introduced with a reflexive verb, used here as a passive.[76] In these
verses, the psalmist continues to address his soul and enumerate many
of Yhwh's benefits. Yhwh forgives, heals, redeems, crowns, satisfies,
and renews.[77] The piling up of beneficial divine actions is an example
of the rhetorical device of accumulation.[78] Through utilizing this device, the psalmist creates an overall impression of Yhwh as a life-
giving source of blessing. Each of these divine actions has a connection back to Israel's exodus tradition.

הָרֹפֵא לְכָל־תַּחֲלֻאָיְכִי   הַסֹּלֵחַ לְכָל־עֲוֺנֵכִי

הַמְעַטְּרֵכִי חֶסֶד וְרַחֲמִים   הַגּוֹאֵל מִשַּׁחַת חַיָּיְכִי

תִּתְחַדֵּשׁ כַּנֶּשֶׁר נְעוּרָיְכִי   הַמַּשְׂבִּיעַ בַּטּוֹב עֶדְיֵךְ

There is a logical connection between several of these cola.[79]

---

[74] McCann, *Psalms*, 1091.

[75] Verse 4a substitutes the לְ prefix with a bound מִן. Verse 4b attaches the
3fs object suffix to the participle and omits a preposition to mark the object phrase.
Verse 5a introduces the object phrase with a בְּ. Verse 5b utilizes a hithpael stem verb
followed by a complement phrase introduced by כְּ.

[76] *GKC* §54g

[77] This list assumes some rather negative things about the world. The
psalmist assumes a world of sin, sickness, death, slavery, lack, and disintegration.

[78] Perelman and Olbrechts-Tyteca, *New Rhetoric*, 144.

[79] Goldingay, *Psalms: Psalms 90–150*, 168–69.

In the first line, Yhwh forgives sin and heals diseases. The Old Testament authors frequently assume a connection between sin and sickness.[80] This particular pairing seems to be inspired by a combination of Exod 15:26 with 34:9. It is in the first text that the divine self-designation of Yhwh as a healer is given: אֲנִי יְהוָה רֹפְאֶךָ.

The full context of Exod 15:26 more fully supports the connection between sickness and forgiveness,

> And he said if you indeed listen to the voice of Yhwh your God and do what is right in his eyes (וְהַיָּשָׁר בְּעֵינָיו תַּעֲשֶׂה) and listen to his commandments and guard all his statutes; every sickness (מַחֲלָה) which I placed on the Egypt, I will not place on you, for I am Yhwh who heals you.

The emphasis here is to motivate Israel to obedience so that Yhwh will not strike them with plagues. It is on the basis of this theology that Yhwh declares he will wipe out the people after the Golden Calf debacle (Exod 32:7–10). It is also the basis for why Yhwh states he will not go up with the people into the land (Exod 33:4–5). Moses seeks to dissuade him from this the following way (Exod 34:9): "And he [Moses] said, 'if I have found favor in your eyes (בְּעֵינֶיךָ), O Lord, may the Lord go up in our midst for a stiff-necked people they are, and forgive (וְסָלַחְתָּ) our sins (לַעֲוֹנֵנוּ) and our trespasses and maintain possession of us." Moses here intercedes to Yhwh requesting that the people not be punished, not because of their obedience, but on the basis of Yhwh's forgiveness. That is, Moses pleads with and convinces Yhwh to be a forgiving God.

The psalmist gives no hint of the struggle Moses underwent to alleviate Israel's punishment through convincing Yhwh to act out of forgiveness. Rather, the psalmist simply pairs Yhwh as healer (Exod 15:26) with Yhwh as forgiver (Exod 34:9). The resonance with the exodus tradition gives the psalm a weightiness. Yet, the psalmist recasts and refocuses the theology of the very passage to which it alludes. Michael Fishbane describes this type of interpretive practice in this way,

---

[80] See Kraus, *Psalms 60–150*, 291.

"*Theologoumena* which were disclosed by the deity become the basis of prayers...and praise. What appeared, therefore, as an instruction or a ceremony to one generation is frequently decontextualized in aggadic *traditio* and presented to a later group in a very different form and for very different reasons."[81] Fishbane here indicates that later writers selectively took up themes from earlier texts and used them for different ends. The selection of data in a discourse and its interpretation are thoroughly rhetorical concerns.[82]

The second line serves as a kind of merism. Yhwh not only redeems his people from slavery, he also treats them like royalty. The first colon combines the verb גאל with the complement שָׁחַת.[83] Given the close connection to the exodus event in this psalm, גאל should be understood as an allusion to redemption from slavery in Egypt.[84] Thus, the noun שַׁחַת becomes a metaphor referring to slavery in Egypt.[85] The second colon describes how Yhwh "crowns" (עטר) his people. Yhwh lifts people up from slavery and treats them like royalty.[86] This pro-

---

[81] Fishbane, *Biblical Interpretation in Ancient Israel*, 425.

[82] Perelman and Olbrechts-Tyteca, *New Rhetoric*, 115–26.

[83] This pairing is unique in the Hebrew Bible. Some common complements to גאל include: redemption of people from slavery/debt servitude (e.g., Lev 25:48–54); redemption of property (e.g., Lev 25:25–33; 27:13–33); redemption of Israel from Egypt (e.g., Exod 6:6; 15:13; Ps 74:2; 77:12; Ps 106:10); redemption of Israel from exile (e.g., Isa 44:22–24; 48:20; 52:3–9; Ps 107:2); redemption of the blood of a slain family member (e.g., Num 35:19–27; Deut 19:6; Josh 20:3–9).

[84] See Exod 6:6; 15:13.

[85] The noun שַׁחַת means "pits," but gets metaphorically used to connote a "trap" or "the grave" or death (*HALOT*, 1472–3). See also Keel, *Symbolism of the Biblical World*, 70. This interpretation of the phrase is contra, Dahood, *Psalms III : 101–150*, 25–26; Kraus, *Psalms 60–150*, 291; and Hossfeld and Zenger, *Psalms 3*, 34. Two other commentators take שַׁחַת to refer metaphorically to the exile, see Kirkpatrick, *Book of Psalms*, 601; McCann, *Psalms*, 1092. It is certainly possible that an audience of near contemporaries would have also connected with word with their exilic experience, thus it could be a double reference to the exodus/exile.

[86] Keel additionally describes how several references in these verses indicate that Yhwh is treating the psalmist like royalty. He "crowns" and "satisfies with good" (v. 5), and he acts as a physician for the psalmist (v. 3). Keel reminds us that in several ANE texts, the physician is often pictured with royalty. (*Symbolism of the*

vides a powerful motivation to bless Yhwh—he takes the psalmist from rags to riches. To be crowned with חֶסֶד וְרַחֲמִים metaphorically connotes being surrounded by these attributes.[87] This phrase also brings to mind the context of Exod 34, which is referenced in the following line.

The first colon of the third line serves as a reversal of Exod 33:5–6. Because of their sin, they were commanded to go without their finery.[88] Now that Yhwh has forgiven, this punishment can be taken away. The participle הַמַּשְׂבִּיעַ is particularly colorful. Yhwh does not simply reverse a punishment, he provides an abundance. The second colon declares that Yhwh will renew the full vitality of the psalmist. The word נְעוּרָיְכִי could refer back to the return from exile.[89] The eagle is used metaphorically in the Hebrew bible for Yhwh's actions related to both the exodus and the return from exile.[90] The import of the metaphor here is that Yhwh will return the psalmist to full vitality of life. Used of the nation as a whole, to have one's youth renewed like an eagle would be a way of stating that the golden era of the past would return again.

Verses 6–8

A transition takes place in v. 6.[91] The focus is no longer the individual dialoguing with his/her soul, but more clearly on the wider

---

Biblical World, 197).

[87] Goldingay, *Psalms: Psalms 90–150*, 168–69. One commentator sees a connection between this "crowning" and the crowning of a king for his wedding day in Song of Songs 3:11, see Jean-Luc Vesco, *Le Psautier de David: traduit et commenté*, vol. 2 (Paris: Les Éditions du Cerf, 2006), 948.

[88] This was a fitting punishment in that it was with their finery that they made the golden calf.

[89] Some texts reference Israel as in her "youth" (נְעוּרִים) at the time of the exodus (Hos 2:17; Jer 2:2).

[90] E.g., Exod 19:4; Isa 40:31.

[91] Fokkelman, "Psalm 103: Design, Boundaries, and Mergers," 115–16; O'Kennedy, "The Relationship between Justice and Forgiveness in Psalm 103," 109; Gerstenberger, *Psalms: Part 2 and Lamentations*, 218.

community.[92] In this section the allusions to the exodus tradition become more explicit.

The first line is a general statement celebrating the fact that Yhwh upholds justice.[93] He does so especially for the "oppressed" (עֲשׁוּקִים). When celebrating the administration of justice, it is important to mention that the oppressed are treated fairly since this is the group that would be the most vulnerable to oppression and injustice. Yet, this line also causes the worshipper to identify with the oppressed. The psalmist has been dialoguing with his soul up to this point. It is a natural move for the singer to continue to identify him/herself as the object of Yhwh's concern in this verse. The following two lines can be understood as a specific way in which Yhwh has helped the oppressed in the past.

Verse 7 introduces a kind of *chreia* in which an important figure from the past is referenced along with a short saying, or maxim associated with him or her.[94] The reference in v. 7 is back to Exod. 33:13. Two things about this allusion are worth noting: 1) When describing Yhwh's acts of righteousness and justice in relation to the Exodus narrative, one would imagine that the ten plagues and the crossing of the Red Sea would be highlighted.[95] However, here the psalmist looks to the fact that Yhwh disclosed himself to Moses as an example of an act of righteousness; 2) in the Exodus passage, Moses requests

---

[92] The 2fs pronouns are no longer used. The object of Yhwh's help shifts from the singular to the plural (עֲשׁוּקִים). See also Goldingay, *Psalms: Psalms 90–150*, 169.

[93] Some scholars have argued that צְדָקוֹת here refers specifically to the "mighty deeds of Yhwh." E.g., Kraus, *Psalms 60–150*, 292. However, when paired with מִשְׁפָּט as in this context, the term has a more general reference to Yhwh's character as expressed in regular acts of justice (e.g., Jer 9:23; Gen 18:19; 2 Sam 8:15; 1 Kgs 10:9). The upholding of justice was a responsibility of the deity in the ANE, see Walton, *Ancient Near Eastern Thought and the Old Testament*, 106–08.

[94] Richard A Lanham, *A Handlist of Rhetorical Terms* (Berkeley, CA: University of California Press, 1991), 188.

[95] As it is in other contexts, e.g., Ps 105. See also Dion, "Psalm 103: A Meditation on the 'Ways' of the Lord," 15.

(or begs, see the full context) Yhwh to make his plan for Israel known. However, in this psalm, Moses is the passive recipient of Yhwh's revelation. The emphasis is not on the struggle of Moses with Yhwh, but on the results of the struggle. Additionally, the reference to Moses is not arbitrary. In Israel's tradition, there is no one who had a more thorough grasp of Yhwh's character than he (Exod 33:11).[96]

Verse 8 is the rhetorical center of the psalm.[97] The psalm has been building up to this point and following this confession come statements which flow from it. The verse is close to the exact wording from Exod 34:6.[98] This oft-repeated confession is at the heart of Israel's belief about the nature of Yhwh.[99] For Israel this statement functioned as a maxim. That is, it embodied traditional Israelite beliefs.

Maxims are powerful shaping forces in a culture. Perelman and Olbrechts-Tyteca explain,

> Maxims not only condense the wisdom of the nations—they are also one of the most effective means of promoting this wisdom and causing it to develop: the use of maxims makes us put our finger on the role played by the accepted values and on the procedures for transferring these values. It is true that a maxim can always be rejected ... but so great is its force, so great the presumption of agreement attaching to it, that one must have

---

[96] The appeal to authority is one of Aristotle's twenty-eight topics for developing *enthymemes*; see Aristotle, *On Rhetoric*, 2.23. Many have seen the appeal to authority as a species of logical fallacy (*argumentum ad verecundiam*), however, more recent rhetoricians have acknowledged the suasive force of authority, especially in the religious realm. See Perelman and Olbrechts-Tyteca, *New Rhetoric*, 305–10.

[97] Hossfeld and Zenger, *Psalms 3*, 35; Rice, "An Exposition of Psalm 103," 58.

[98] The poet made some slight modifications in the phrase so that it fits the binary poetic form.

[99] E.g., Ps. 86:15; Joel 2:13; Jon 4:2; Num. 14:18; Neh 9:17; Dan 9:9. See also Hermann Spieckermann, "Barmherzig und gnädig ist der Herr," *ZAW* 102 (1990): 1–18; Josef Scharbert, "Formgeschichte und Exegese von Ex 34:6f und seiner Parallelen," *Biblica* 38 (1957): 130–50; Thomas B. Dozeman, "Inner-Biblical Interpretation of Yahweh's Gracious and Compassionate Character," *JBL* 108 (1989): 207–23.

> weighty reasons for rejecting it … the maxim, as described by
> Aristotle, is what we today would call a value judgment….[100]

This maxim serves both to ground and support the participial statements
enumerating Yhwh's benefits (vv. 3–6) and the following statements
celebrating Yhwh's forgiveness and compassion (vv. 9–18).

Additionally, stating that Yhwh is compassionate (רַחוּם) and
merciful (חַנּוּן) serves an important rhetorical function. One of the main
reasons why we label people with particular traits is because the stability of a person is never fully assured. Thus, labeling a person with certain attributes is a "linguistic technique … to stress the impression of
permanency."[101] The psalmist by declaring that Yhwh is by nature a
God of compassion and mercy helps the worshipper to understand that
God is not completely free or spontaneous in his response to the world.
His actions are driven by his attributes toward humanity. His nature as
compassionate, merciful, and loyal (חֶסֶד) give "cohesion and significance" to all his past and future acts.[102] These adjectives become the
lenses through which the community can evaluate and understand
what Yhwh has done.

At the same time, the general attributive phrases in v. 8 provide
the poet the opportunity to define their meaning. In the Exodus context, stating that Yhwh is compassionate and merciful connotes that
Yhwh was willing to set aside his natural anger at Israel through the
intercession of Moses. The psalmist, while not denying this, develops
the attributes in a different direction.

---

[100] Perelman and Olbrechts-Tyteca, *New Rhetoric*, 165–66.

[101] Ibid., 294.

[102] Ibid., 295.

4.7.2 STROPHE TWO: INTERPRETATION OF STEADFAST LOVE AND COMPASSION

This strophe interprets and defines the maxim recited in v. 8.[103] This strophe is comprised of three smaller units. In a series of negative statements, vv. 9–10 describe what Yhwh will not do because of his compassion and mercy. Verses 11–13 utilize a series of comparisons to unpack Yhwh's acts toward Israel. Finally, vv. 14–16 ground Yhwh's compassion in his awareness of the transient nature of humanity. Nevertheless, all three of these units are also bound by linguistic features that transcend the shifts in content. Verses 10–16 are driven by assonance created through the repetition of the כ.[104] Additionally, beginning in v. 10 the object of Yhwh's compassion alternates between 1ˢᵗ person and 3ʳᵈ person:

1cp	v. 10: "our sins" (כַחֲטָאֵינוּ) and "our guilt" (כַעֲוֺנֺתֵינוּ)
3pl	v. 11: "those who fear him" (יְרֵאָיו)
1cp	v. 12: "…from us our transgression" (מִמֶּנּוּ אֶת־פְּשָׁעֵינוּ)
3pl	v. 13: "those who fear him" (יְרֵאָיו)
1cp	v. 14: "our frame" (יִצְרֵנוּ) and "we are dust" (עָפָר אֲנָחְנוּ)
3sg	v. 15: "Mankind, like grass are his days" (אֱנוֹשׁ כֶּחָצִיר יָמָיו)

This indicates that the poet had a flexibility regarding how the speaker is referenced in the psalm. The "I" of vv. 1–5 has become the "we" of the community.[105] However, the group the psalmist identifies with is not just the covenant community, but by v. 15 it is humanity as a

---

[103] This would be an example of what M. Fishbane calls lemmatic deduction, or inference. That is, a particular *traditum* is cited or summarized and then a conclusion is either deduced or inferred from the topos as a whole. See ibid., 419.

[104] In this strophe, the כְּ preposition is used 6x, the conjunction כִּי 4x, and כֵּן 1x. Most of these uses occur at the beginning of a colon. The כ series which is so prominent in these verses brings to mind the sequence in the Baal cycle (UT 49:II:28–31), *klb arḫ l'glh klb ṯat limrh km lb 'nt aṯr b'l* ("like the heart of a wild cow for her calf, like the heart of the wild ewe for her lamb, such was the heart of Anath toward Baal") (cited by Dahood, *Psalms III: 101–150*, 29).

[105] Fokkelman, "Psalm 103: Design, Boundaries, and Mergers," 117–18.

whole (אֱנוֹשׁ). For if Yhwh has compassion on people simply because of their transient nature, that is certainly a feature that not just Israel possessed.[106] Thus, this strophe exegetes the maxim to indicate not only how Yhwh interacts with Israel in light of their failure, but also how he interacts with all humankind.

Verses 9–10

These two lines are held together by anaphora.[107] Verse 9 explains the maxim (v. 8) utilizing language from prophetic oracles of salvation.[108] Thus the psalmist places the community in the context of God's unconditional promises of salvation.[109] There is also a connection between v. 9 and the opening line to strophe 3 (v. 17). Verse 9 utilizes two terms connoting perpetuity negatively (לְעוֹלָם, לָנֶצַח); whereas v. 17 utilizes two similar terms positively (מֵעוֹלָם וְעַד־עוֹלָם). The contrast here is between Yhwh's contention and anger (v. 9), which do not last forever and his חֶסֶד that does. Verse 9 does not deny the reality of Yhwh's anger, but its duration.[110] This is an argument based on quantity.[111] That is, Yhwh's חֶסֶד is a more central feature of his actions toward Israel because of its permanence; whereas, his wrath and anger are not as central because of their transience. We can see here how important the maxim is to bring stability to Yhwh's character. Simply reading the Exodus narrative, one could emphasize how Yhwh's actions of changing his mind (Exod 32:14) and not carrying out the punishments he pronounced demonstrates his arbitrary nature. This psalm

---

[106] Ibid., 118.

[107] That is, the four negative particles at the head of each colon (לֹא).

[108] E.g., Isa 54:7–8; 57:16; Jer 3:12. See Hossfeld and Zenger, *Psalms 3*, 35.

[109] Both the Isa 54 and 57 texts are classified by Westermann as Group I oracles. That is, unconditional salvation oracles. See C. Westermann, *Prophetic Oracles of Salvation in the Old Testament*, trans. K. Crim (Louisville: Westminster, 1991), 62–63; 188–89.

[110] Fokkelman, "Psalm 103: Design, Boundaries, and Mergers," 111.

[111] Aristotle, *Topics*, III.2; P. Slomkowski, *Aristotle's Topics*, Philosophia Antiqua: A Series of Studies on Ancient Philosophy 74, eds. J. Mansfeld and et. al. (Leiden: Brill, 1997), 146–50; Perelman and Olbrechts-Tyteca, *New Rhetoric*, 85–89.

however helps the worshipper to see that Yhwh's character is indeed consistent. His anger is only momentary and fleeting, while his compassion and חֶסֶד are enduring.

Yhwh's compassion and mercy are further explained by the fact that he has not repaid Israel according to a strict sense of justice (v. 10). Terrien explains, "the psalmist clearly objects to a theology of strict justice based on retribution, in punishment or reward."[112] Both terms used to describe failure connect back to the golden calf incident (Exod 32:21, 30–31; 34:9). In the Exodus narrative, the psalmist emphasizes the fact that Yhwh did not repay the community according to their actions, but had mercy on them. However, this is more than a rumination on the past. By using the 1cp pronouns, the psalmist and the community can identify their own failures as the referents of חֵטְא and עָוֹן.[113]

Verses 11–13

This unit provides the second explanation of the maxim (v. 8) through a series of three comparisons. The first two comparisons are spatial in nature, while the third is relational. The unit is bracketed by the phrase עַל־יְרֵאָיו at the end of the first and last lines. This unit also connects back to the maxim (v. 8) through repetition of two of the main roots from that verse (חסד and רחם). As discussed in chapter 3, analogies function to "facilitate the development and extension of thought."[114] They force the worshipper to tease out the exact connection between the two sets of terms. Thus, the worshipper becomes involved in the creative process. This, in turn, increases the intensity of adherence to the theme being illustrated.[115]

---

[112] Terrien, *Psalms*, 704.

[113] The self-involving element of this line is emphasized by the four-fold repetition of the 1cp enclitic.

[114] Perelman and Olbrechts-Tyteca, *New Rhetoric*, 384. For a full discussion, see §3.5.2.2.

[115] H. S. Lee and K. J. Holyoak, "Absence Makes the Thought Grow Stronger: Reducing Structural Overlap Can Increase Inductive Strength," in *Proceedings of the Thirtieth Annual Conference of the Cognitive Science Society*, ed. V. B. L. Sloutsky, and K. McRae (Austin: Cognitive Science Society, 2008), 297–302.

The כִּי in v. 11 functions adversatively to contrast with the previous colon.[116] The first analogy can be displayed:

A: as the heavens are high B: over the earth
A': his loyal love is strong B': over those who fear him.

In the ancient world, the heavens were thought of as a solid dome. This dome seemed to be "spatially...endless."[117] That is, it encompassed the entire earth. Keel states, "the infinite expanse of the sky and the sure stability with which it abides in its lofty height made a profound impression on the ancient Near East."[118] The thrust of the analogy is this: just as the heavens completely encompass the earth, so Yhwh's חֶסֶד surrounds those who fear him. It is significant that the poet chose the heavens encompassing of the earth as the image to explain Yhwh's חֶסֶד. The first set of terms in an analogy can increase or decrease the value of the object of the analogy. For example, the poet could have used a different image (e.g., "As a sheath surrounds a sword..." or "as shame surrounds the fool..."). However, by using heavens and earth, the poet increases the value and status of Yhwh's חֶסֶד.[119]

Verse 11 also shifts the object of Yhwh's חֶסֶד to the 3rd person. It is significant that when discussing sin and guilt, the poet uses the self-involving 1cp (v. 10), but when referencing "God-fearers" the poet switches to the 3rd person. This shift creates just a space of difference between the worshipper and the "God-fearer," which gives the community an ideal to strive toward. The poet is not only trying to shape the worshippers view of God, but also of the self.

Verse 12 stretches the limits of metaphorical language almost to the breaking point.[120] The actual analogy is as follows: A: As the

---

[116] כִּי frequently has this sense following a negative clause (*HALOT*, 470).

[117] Keel, *Symbolism of the Biblical World*, 31.

[118] Ibid., 31.

[119] Perelman and Olbrechts-Tyteca, *New Rhetoric*, 378.

[120] One of the main dangers of analogical language is taking it too far, which the poet is close to here, see I. A. Richards, *The Philosophy of Rhetoric* (Oxford: Oxford University Press, 1965), 133.

east is far from B: the west // So, Yhwh has removed A': our sins from B': us. The phrase from the "east to the west" is a merism meaning "as far as possible." Indeed, "east" is partially defined by the fact that it is not "west" and *vice versa*. East and west are relative spatial terms. It is not logically possible for the east to be in the west. The poet applies that polarizing certainty to the distance between our sin and us. This is not a distance that is natural by definition. It is a reality Yhwh had to create. He removed (הִרְחִיק) transgressions from the people.[121] These are failures that are so identified with the people, that the poet has used a 1cp enclitic on the terms for sin no less than three times in these verses (פְּשָׁעֵינוּ, כַּחֲטָאֵינוּ, and כַּעֲוֹנֹתֵינוּ). The reason the poet is able to accomplish this daring analogy is that he is exploiting a polyvalence in the root רחק.[122] Beginning in v. 9, the poet sets up a legal metaphor with the verb רִיב. This legal flavor continues into v. 12. Bradley Gregory has demonstrated the root רחק was used in ANE texts as a technical legal term to indicate, "a cessation of litigation by an unsuccessful claimant and his relinquishment of all future claims to the property and person of the defendant."[123] Thus, while the root רחק in the first colon of v. 12 refers to spatial distance, in the second colon it takes on the additional connotation of a legal background. Yhwh has removed the transgressions of the people by dropping the charges against them.

Verse 13 gives the final comparison used to explain the maxim (v. 8). The analogy shifts from spatial to relational. The analogy is explicitly tied back to v. 8 through a double use of the root רחם.[124] The

---

[121] Technically this is an additional metaphor. It is not the transgressions which were removed, but the punishment, or consequences of them.

[122] Bradley Gregory, "The Legal Background of the Metaphor for Forgiveness in Psalm CIII 12," *VT* 56 (2006): 549–51. See also the important nuancing of this background by William D. Pickut, "Additional Observations Relating to the Legal Significance of Psalm CIII 12," *VT* 58 (2008): 550–56.

[123] Gregory, "The Legal Background of the Metaphor for Forgiveness in Psalm CIII 12," 549. Gregory here is citing Y. Muffs, *Studies in the Aramaic Legal Papyri from Elephantine* (Leiden: Brill, 1969), 48.

[124] McCann argues that the root רחם is actually a motherly image. Thus, Yhwh in the role of father acts with the compassion of a mother (McCann, *Psalms*, 1092; see

comparison between Yhwh's compassion on those who fear him with a
father's for children is more than just an analogy. Perelman and Olbrechts-Tyteca label this type of statement a double-hierarchy.[125] They
explain, "a double hierarchy is very different from an analogy, since the
first is based on a real connection, while the second suggests the comparison of relations belonging to different spheres."[126] That is, the
psalmist is taking a relationship which exists in the human sphere (par-
ent/child) and utilizing that to describe a relationship between two different spheres (divine/human).[127] The use of an analogy to comprehend
one sphere in terms of another can be very powerful as a way of understanding the unknown by the known.[128] In another context, T. Swann
Harding famously stated, "The scientists who first described electricity
as a 'current' forever shaped the science in this field."[129] Similarly, the
person who first described God as a father has drastically shaped how
Judaism and Christianity understand the divine/human relationship.[130]

This analogy is particularly powerful in this psalm for a couple
of reasons. First, it grounds the maxim that Yhwh is compassionate
(רחום, v. 8) through providing a rationale for this stance toward Israel.
Yhwh is not just Israel's deity, judge or king; but acts toward them as
a father. Thus, his actions toward Israel do not have to be based on a
strict sense of justice. Second, the image of God as father is grounded

---

also G. Vanoni, *"Du bist doch unser Vater" (Jes 63, 16): Zur Gottesvorstellung des
Ersten Testaments* [Stuttgart: Verlag Katholisches Bibelwerk, 1995], 43).

[125] Perelman and Olbrechts-Tyteca, *New Rhetoric*, 377.

[126] Ibid.

[127] This is, of course, true for every relational analogy between God and
humans (king, judge, friend, etc ...).

[128] Perelman and Olbrechts-Tyteca, *New Rhetoric*, 384.

[129] T. Swann Harding, "Science at the Tower of Babel," *Philosophy of Science* 5 (1938): 347.

[130] See a similar prayer in Mesopotamian Literature in the context of a confession, "Like the heart of a mother, may your heart return to its place for me, Like a
natural mother and a natural father may you return to me" (cited in Miller, *They
Cried to the Lord*, 20).

in the exodus tradition (e.g., Exod 4:22).[131] Thus, the analogy points back to the creation of Israel as a nation. Additionally, speaking of Yhwh as a father serves to strengthen the adherence of the speaker to Yhwh. Israel is not just in a formal covenant relationship with Yhwh, but is more fundamentally grounded in a familial relationship with the deity.[132] A familial tie is even stronger than a political/covenantal tie and maintained on a different basis. While Israel affirms both analogies as central, to achieve its rhetorical goals, this psalm focuses on the familial.

Verses 14–16

This unit provides one additional reason for Yhwh's compassion. The poet here reaches behind the exodus tradition to discuss humanity from a creation perspective (Gen 2).[133] Michael Fishbane argues that the poet here engages in an aggadic exegesis of Gen 2:7.[134] He states,

> Verse 14 is an aggadic adaptation of Gen 2:7 'And YHWH Elohim formed the man from the dust of the earth.' Human mortality, indeed mankind's created nature, is thus invoked in Ps 103:14 as a factor which should limit God's vindictive designs...Taken together one may venture to propose that Ps 103:14 is an exegetical reuse of Gen 2:7 while simultaneously punning on 8:21, so as to deepen the exegetical thrust. The Psalmist thus appeals to YHWH to refrain from requiting sin with punishment, both because he knows man's mortal nature

---

[131] Svetlana Knobnya, "God the Father in the Old Testament," *EuroJTh* 20 (2011): 139–48. She explains that God is explicitly described as a father sixteen times in the OT, and she demonstrates that there are numerous other instances where the idea of God as father is used without the word being present (140). References to God as father fall into two categories: 1) the larger category which is based on exodus imagery; and 2) God as the father of the king and his offspring.

[132] On the primacy of kinship terms for Yhwh, see Frank Moore Cross, *From Epic to Canon: History and Literature in Ancient Israel* (Baltimore: Johns Hopkins University Press, 1998), 3–21.

[133] Goldingay, *Psalms: Psalms 90–150*, 172.

[134] Fishbane, *Biblical Interpretation in Ancient Israel*, 349.

and also because of mankind's all-too-human will.[135]

Verse 14 states the argument and vv. 15–16 amplify it through analogy. The basic argument is that Yhwh has compassion on humanity because he is mindful of their creatureliness. This includes a deep understanding of the mortality and humility of our nature as עָפָר. Indeed, Yhwh's compassion is grounded in a "rationally impressive penetration [of] the frailty and futility of [human] life."[136] In contrast to v. 13 where Yhwh's compassion was grounded in the similarity between his relationship with Israel and the human relationship of a father's to a child, this verse emphasizes the vast difference between humanity and Yhwh. Yhwh can afford to be compassionate to humanity because humans are so transient and frail as opposed to his eternality (v. 17). As stated earlier, the object of comparison in an analogy is important rhetorically. In v. 11, the psalmist compared Yhwh's loyal love with the greatness of the heavens over the earth. The heavens were revered in the ANE, which increased the status of Yhwh's loyal love. In vv. 15–16, the poet compares humanity with grass to the diminution of the former.[137] Othmar Keel explains the force of this imagery, "Man before God is like the spring grass, which the scorching east wind can wither in the space of a day...The image is typical of Palestine-Syria, where the ground, watered almost exclusively by the spring rains, dries up in a very short time. The situation is different in Egypt and Mesopotamia, which possess rivers."[138] This analogy brings out a paradox in the psalm. The eternal Yhwh has compassion, grace, loyal love, and fatherly care for creatures who are here today and gone tomorrow.[139]

---

[135] Ibid., 349.

[136] Kraus, *Psalms 60–150*, 293.

[137] Perelman and Olbrechts-Tyteca, *New Rhetoric*, 378. It is also possible that v. 16 was a proverbial statement in Israelite culture (e.g., Job 7:10).

[138] Keel, *Symbolism of the Biblical World*, 240.

[139] As Perelman reminds us, the figure of paradox forces us to reinterpret a statement which appears to be inconsistent when taken literally, see Chaim Perelman and William Kluback, *The New Rhetoric and the Humanities: Essays on Rhetoric and Its Applications* (London: D. Reidel 1979), 84.

4.7.3 STROPHE THREE: SUMMARY AND CALL TO PRAISE

The final strophe is divided into two units. The first unit summarizes the message of the psalm, while the second unit renews the call to praise. This exuberant psalm fittingly concludes with a four-fold command to bless Yhwh directed at all things in heaven and on earth.

Verses 17–19

These verses are not as carefully structured lines of poetry compared with the rest of the poem. Indeed, some commentators view them as redactional.[140] Verse 17 summarizes the main theme of the poem while v. 18 qualifies the universal nature of the statement in v. 17. Verse 19 begins the transition to the closing unit of the poem. There is a tension in these verses between God's loyal love, which is multi-generational and the qualification that this is only for those who guard the covenant. As McCann has pointed out, this is the same tension found in Exod 34:6–7.[141] Yet, as throughout the psalm, the emphasis is different.

In an unusually long line, v. 17 gives an apt summary of the theme of the poem. Goldingay winsomely acknowledges, "Yhwh's lasting-ness stands over against humanity's transience. The prosody embodies the point: the line seems to go on forever."[142] This verse picks up on language from the maxim (חֶסֶד, v. 8) and from the explanation of the maxim (עַל־יְרֵאָיו, vv. 9–16). In contrast to Yhwh's anger or contention, which the poet declared is specifically not עוֹלָם (v. 9), Yhwh's חֶסֶד is מֵעוֹלָם וְעַד־עוֹלָם. As stated earlier, this is an argument based on quantity.[143] Yhwh's חֶסֶד is of greater import because it is of longer duration. The line concludes by paralleling Yhwh's חֶסֶד with his צְדָקָה. The latter word here emphasizes Yhwh's "loyalty to the community."[144] This loyalty extends to the children of children (לִבְנֵי בָנִים).

---

[140] E.g., Spieckermann, "Barmherzig und gnädig ist der Herr," 11 n. 29.

[141] McCann, *Psalms*, 1092.

[142] Goldingay, *Psalms: Psalms 90–150*, 174.

[143] Slomkowski, *Aristotle's Topics*, 146–50.

[144] E.g, Ezek 14:14. Ezekiel there argues that Noah, Daniel, and Job could

This is a significant phrase. It is included not just to emphasize the duration of Yhwh's loyalty. That was already stated more effectively in
the first colon. Rather, the language echoes Exod 34:7. Yet in quoting
the source text, the poet has changed the meaning. In Exod 34:7,
Yhwh qualifies his strong statement of forgiveness by adding, "but
who will in no way clear the guilty, visiting the iniquity of the fathers
on children, even on children of children (וְעַל־בְּנֵי בָנִים). The poet here
uses the language describing the duration of Yhwh's judgment and applies it to the duration of Yhwh's loyalty. This is an example of what
Fishbane describes as "exegetical meaning established by correlation."[145] It is as if the poet is staying, "You have heard it was said that
Yhwh's judgment extends to the children of children, but I say to you it
is his faithful loyalty that extends to them."[146]

The generous statement of Yhwh's loyalty is qualified by the
deuteronomic language of v. 18.[147] Qualifiers are important rhetorically because they enlarge the area of agreement with the audience. They
also reduce the need to question the overall theme of the discourse.[148]
Up to this point in the psalm, the poet could be in danger of being ac-
cused of an overly generous view of God's grace. This qualification
creates a bit of tension in the psalm. As Zenger states, "In contrast to

---

only deliver their own lives by their צְדָקָה. That is, their loyalty to the community
based on their intercession could still not save the community. It is this same sense
of communal loyalty that is in view here. See O'Kennedy, "The Relationship between Justice and Forgiveness in Psalm 103," 115; *HALOT*, 1006.

[145] Fishbane, *Biblical Interpretation in Ancient Israel*, 421.

[146] This functions as an implied antithesis. For the rhetorical function of
this device in the Sermon on the Mount, see Johan Carl Thom, "Justice in the Sermon on the Mount: An Aristotelian Reading," *NovT* 51 (2009): 328–33.

[147] In particular, the poet connects to Deut. 5:10, where the author of Deuteronomy also engages in an exegetical reflection on the Exod 32–34 passage. Deuteronomy states, "You shall not make for yourself a sculptured image, any likeness
of what is in the heavens above, or on the earth below. For I the LORD your God am
an impassioned God, visiting the guilt of the parents upon the children, upon the
third and fourth generations of those who reject Me, but showing kindness to the
thousandth generation of those who love me and keep my commandments" (JPS).

[148] Perelman and Olbrechts-Tyteca, *New Rhetoric*, 126-9.

the Magna Carta of forgiveness of sins in the basic psalm, here a different direction is envisioned…Israel's behavior is once more in play.
Despite all God's generosity, his judgment on human obedience to the
law must have its effect."[149] Yet, this line is not just a statement of or-
thodox deuteronomic theology. The statement has a different resonance coming at the end of this long poem celebrating Yhwh's grace.
It is an example of changing the tone of deuteronomic theology
through placing it in a new context, or through supplementation.[150] The
maxim concerning Yhwh's faithful love and grace was amplified and
explained for an entire strophe. The qualifying statement concerning
obedience simply gets one short line. This is not to deny the importance
of the theme, but to demonstrate that the rhetorical force of the psalm is
to highlight the generosity and grace of Yhwh, not human obedience. At
the same time, the poet connects our response to Yhwh with his response toward us. The worshipping community is called to be mindful
(זכר, v. 18) of Yhwh just as Yhwh is mindful (זכר, v. 14) of them.

Verse 19 completes the unit through celebrating Yhwh's lofty
status. Yhwh not only rules temporally (v. 17), but geographically as
well (בַּכֹּל). This is a standard motif in Israel's canonical witness, but
takes on new significance here.[151] This psalm emphasizes that Yhwh's
rule is one characterized by compassion, grace, and a deep and sympa-
thetic knowledge of the people he governs.

Verses 20–22

The psalm comes to a rousing conclusion with a four-fold
command to bless Yhwh. This functions as a climax. The climactic
utterance is notoriously effective. Kenneth Burke cites a common
phrase from the "Berlin Crisis" of 1948, "Who controls Berlin, controls Germany; who controls Germany controls Europe; who controls
Europe controls the world."[152] He comments on this,

---

[149] Hossfeld and Zenger, *Psalms 3*, 36.

[150] Fishbane, *Biblical Interpretation in Ancient Israel*, 423.

[151] E.g., Ps 47:2; 82:8; 93:1–2; 95:3–5; 96:10–13; 97:1; 98:2–3; 99:1–5.

[152] Burke, *Rhetoric of Motives*, 58.

As a proposition it may or may not be true. And even if it is true, unless people are thoroughly imperialistic, they may not want to control the world. But regardless of these doubts about it as a proposition, by the time you arrive at the second of its three stages, you feel how it is destined to develop—and on the level of purely formal assent you would collaborate to round out its symmetry by spontaneously willing its completion and perfection as an utterance. Add, now, the psychosis of nationalism, and assent on the formal level invites assent to the proposition as doctrine.[153]

The psalm concludes in the inverse of how it began. The psalm opened with a command to the self then gradually widened to include the whole community. In this final unit, the command to bless Yhwh is first given to the messengers and heavenly hosts, then is broadened to include the inhabitants of earth, and finally is reduced to a command to the self.[154] All these groups called to bless Yhwh belong to him and are thus under his authority. This is made clear from the three-fold use of the 3mp enclitic in the first colon of each of these lines:

Verse 20: מַלְאָכָיו
Verse 21: כָּל־צְבָאָיו
Verse 22: כָּל־מַעֲשָׂיו

The rhetorical functions of the command to "bless" Yhwh have been discussed and should be assumed here (see vv. 1–2). However,

---

[153] Ibid., 58–59.

[154] This final unit is comprised of a tricolon/bicolon/tricolon. This arrangement is unusual for the psalm, which is consistently comprised of bicolons up to this point. This alteration, along with other devices, alerts the reader that the hymn is coming to a close; *contra* Fokkelman who analyzes the psalm as having an additional tricolon comprised of v. 17b–18. However, it is better to see v. 17b as part of one long bicolon. See J. P. Fokkelman, *The Psalms in Form: The Hebrew Psalter in its Poetic Shape* (Leiden: Brill, 2002), 109. For the analysis of v. 17 as one long bicolon, see Goldingay, *Psalms: Volume 3: Psalms 90–150*, 174; Willis, "'So Great is His Steadfast Love'," 57; Dion, "Psalm 103," 21.

there are some additional rhetorical features to these closing lines that should be addressed. In v. 20, the messengers of Yhwh are command-ed to "bless Yhwh." The term מַלְאָךְ is used eight times in the Psalter. In most of these occurrences the מַלְאָךְ functions as the special agent of Yhwh to either punish or protect.[155] The high status of the messenger is strengthened in the psalm through the use of an epithet—"mighty men of strength who do his word" (גִּבֹּרֵי כֹחַ עֹשֵׂי דְבָרוֹ).

The function of this description is to remind the worshipper that these messengers are stronger and have a higher status then they do.[156] This line then functions as an *a fortiori* argument.[157] If the mes-sengers, these divine heroes, are commanded to bless Yhwh and obey his word, how much more should the worshipper?[158]

Verse 21 follows a similar structure and amplifies the argument of v. 20: command to bless Yhwh, aimed at the "hosts" of Yhwh, who are labeled as "his ministers who do his pleasure." The emphasis on obedience in both vv. 20 and 21 picks up the theme introduced in v. 18 and functions indirectly as an argument by example.[159]

The final line of the psalm broadens the command to bless

---

[155] Ps 35:6, 7; 78:49; 91:11; 104:4. In one other occurrence the messengers are commanded to praise Yhwh (Ps 148:2).

[156] On the function of an epithet, see Aristotle, *On Rhetoric*, III, 2, 1405b and Perelman and Olbrechts-Tyteca, *New Rhetoric*, 126–28.

[157] Aristotle, *On Rhetoric*, II, 23, 1397b. On the importance of *a fortiori* ar-gumentation in society in general, particularly in legal contexts, see Thomas Kyrill Grabenhorst, *Das argumentum a fortiori* (Schweiz: Peter Lang, 1990).

[158] The third colon in this verse is a bit awkward. Indeed, one commentator states, "The redundant third colon in v. 20b is hard to justify. Is it meant to indicate the complete obedience of the heroes in the sense of carrying out commands and being immediately prepared to receive new ones?" (Hossfeld and Zenger, *Psalms 3*, 37).

[159] One rhetorician describes how certain American magazines describe the life and career of successful businessmen. While it does not explicitly call the reader to follow the person's example, it functions to nudge the reader toward similar be-havior. See Perelman and Olbrechts-Tyteca, *New Rhetoric*, 351. The combination of *a fortiori* argument with an argument by example as a rhetorical device is labelled a "progressive argument" in the classic handbook by Richard Whately, *Elements of Rhetoric* (London: Longmans, 1867), 51–55.

Yhwh in the first two cola, then narrows it back to the self in the final colon. The final colon is a verbatim repetition of the first colon. As Goldingay points out, this does not mean that the words have the same force in both locations. He explains, "The psalm closes with the same bidding form which it started, though this does not mean that the words have the same significance. After all that the psalm has said, the exhortation to the self has much more power."[160] Indeed, this inclusion would cause the worshipper to reflect back on all the reasons presented to bless Yhwh. Additionally, it is clear at this point in the psalm that the self is not blessing Yhwh as an isolated individual, but is joining with the congregation of Israel from the past, the hosts of heaven, and the rest of all creation.

4.8   CONCLUSION

This psalm demonstrates how powerfully praise functioned to shape Israel's understanding of Yhwh. The primary goal of the psalm was to present an interpretation of what it means for Yhwh to be a God of compassion and grace, which would serve as a motivation for praise. As Claus Westermann recognized,

> The poet has no intention of contesting God's activity in wrath. But he makes a distinction. God's activity in wrath is limited; God's goodness knows no boundaries … The same is true of sin and its forgiveness. If God compensated man commensurate with the way he sins, then one might despair. But here too, God is inconsistent; his forgiving goodness is immeasurable. One might even say that the entire Psalm deals with the incomprehensible excess of God's goodness.[161]

This emphasis on the "excess of God's goodness" may not have comported well with either some interpretations of Exod 32–34 or with the

---

[160] Goldingay, *Psalms: Psalms 90–150*, 176.

[161] Claus Westermann, *Elements of Old Testament Theology*, trans. D. Scott (Atlanta: John Knox 1982), 139.

post-exilic experience.[162] Thus, in some ways the poem functioned similar to judicial rhetoric. It attempted to demonstrate how Yhwh could be understood as a gracious, compassionate, and forgiving God in light of the Golden Calf debacle specifically, and the historical situation of Israel generally. Psalm 103 provides a beautiful illustration of how the community could understand and appropriate the exodus tradition in a new context.

---

[162] E.g., the prayers in Ezra 9; Nehemiah 1, 9; and Daniel 9 all approach Yhwh in a penitential mood. The community is very conscious of its guilt before Yhwh. For a detailed examination of the function of these prayers, see Michael Matlock, *Discovering the Traditions of Prose Prayers in Early Jewish Literature*, LSTS 81 (New York: T&T Clark, 2012), 23–61.

CHAPTER 5
Rhetorical Analysis of Psalm 46

5.1 INTRODUCTION

The most difficult form category for Westermann is the declarative praise of the people.[1] The primary reason for this is that there are so few examples in the Psalter. As complete psalms, he concludes that only Ps 124 and 129 qualify.[2] Nevertheless, there are many psalms which are closely related to this group and should be discussed under this rubric, including the "Psalms of Zion."[3] Psalm 46 serves as a good example of a declarative praise of the people for our rhetorical analysis for a number of reasons. It contains two central images or themes in the Psalter: Zion and Yhwh as refuge.[4] Also, through Martin Luther's hymn *Ein feste Burg ist unser Gott* it has had a profound influence on western Christianity.[5] Additionally, in the previous chapter we discovered how a foundational narrative could serve as the "world of the poem." This psalm presents yet a different way the poem can create a world. Psalm 46 draws from common ANE imagery to create a sense of the chaotic danger in which God creates a space for his city and functions as a refuge for his people.[6]

---

[1] Claus Westermann, *Praise and Lament*, 81.

[2] Ibid., 81.

[3] Ibid., 92–93.

[4] See Jerome Creach, *Yahweh as Refuge*; Sidney Kelly, "Psalm 46: A Study in Imagery," *JBL* 89 (1970): 305–12.

[5] See the discussion of the modern appropriation of Psalm 46 in Susan Gillingham, *Psalms through the Centuries*, Blackwell Bible Commentaries (Oxford: Blackwell, 2008), 140–43, 56, 86–87, 218, 227–29, 259, 281. More recently, President Barak Obama read the entire text of Ps 46 at a memorial service on the tenth anniversary of the 9/11 attack.

[6] A version of this study was published as Ryan Cook, "Prayers that Form Us: Rhetoric and Psalms Interpretation," *JSOT* 39 (2015): 451–67.

5.2   *TRANSLATION*

To the leader, of the sons of Korah,
according to the *Alamoth*, a song.   (1)
Strophe 1
God is our refuge and protection   (2)
  help in difficulties,[7] readily found
Therefore, we will not fear when the earth[8] shakes[9]   (3)
  when the mountains sway in the heart of the seas.
Its waters[10] roar, they foam   (4)
  the mountains quake at its arrogance *Selah*
Strophe 2
A river, its streams make glad the city of God   (5)
  Elyon sanctifies his dwelling[11]
God is in its midst, it will not be shaken   (6)
  God will help it; as morning comes.
Nations have roared; Kingdoms have swayed,   (7)
  He gave his voice; earth wavers.
Yhwh of Hosts is with us   (8)
  Our refuge is the God of Jacob. *Selah*

---

[7] The plural form of צרה draws attention to both the amount of difficulties the psalmist faces as well as their general nature (see Job 5:19).

[8] Origen's transliteration of the Hebrew text along with the LXX includes the definite article. However, based on the parallel of "seas" at the end of the line, which also lacks the article, we should also understand it as lacking here. This is typical of the terse style of Hebrew poetry.

[9] בְּהָמִיר is an unusual form, not attested elsewhere in the Hebrew Bible. It is possible either to read this with the LXX and point it as a nifal infinitive, or to read it as a nifal infinitive from מוג. This assumes that the final ג was misread as ר by a scribe (the two letters are orthographically close in paleo-hebrew script).

[10] The 3ms enclitic here refers back to "seas." On a plural noun taking a singular enclitic, see GKC §132h.

[11] While having an adjective precede the noun is possible (see GKC §132c), what makes the MT reading difficult is that מֹשׁכֵּן is not a masculine noun. Thus, the LXX reading is plausible, which repoints כֹדשׁ as a piel perfect 3ms verb and understands a 3ms enclitic on מֹשׁכֵּן. As shown below, this reading also makes good sense in the overall flow of the poem.

Strophe 3

Come! Behold! The deeds of Yhwh[12]	(9)
That he has set desolations upon the earth.	
Making wars cease unto the end of the earth	(10)
Bow, he breaks and spear, he cuts up	
Shields,[13] he burns with fire.	
Slacken! And acknowledge! that I am God	(11)
I will be exulted among the nations	
I will be exulted among the earth	
Yhwh of Hosts is with us	(12)
Our refuge is the God of Jacob *Selah*	

5.3   DETERMINATION OF THE RHETORICAL UNIT

Fortunately, it is not difficult to determine the rhetorical unit. Psalm 46 is clearly a unified poem. The refrains celebrating God as refuge hold the psalm together and provide a sense of wholeness to the composition. Some scholars have added the refrain (vv. 8, 12) to the end of v. 3.[14] The primary argument for the insertion is for the symmetry of the strophes.[15] However, this insertion is not necessary. Hebrew poetry is not consistent enough in strophic divisions to emend the text on that basis alone with any confidence.[16]

The inclusion סלה at the end of the psalm is a bit odd. However, סלה is also the concluding word of two other psalms (Pss 3; 24), both of which stand as complete works.[17] The inclusion of the word

---

[12] Many mss, the LXX[AL], and the Syriac have אלהים here. This is likely due to the editorial influence of the Elohistic Psalter, of which this is a part.

[13] Reading the text as from the root עגילה following the LXX. The MT as it stands reads עֲגָלוֹת lit. "carts/wagons." The difficulty with this reading is that עֲגָלוֹת does not refer to war equipment in any of its other usages. See Mitchell Dahood, *Psalms I: 1–50*, 281.

[14] Hermann Gunkel, "Psalm 46: An Interpretation," *The Biblical World* 21 (1903): 28; Hans-Joachim Kraus, *Psalms 1–59*, 459.

[15] Gunkel, "Psalm 46: An Interpretation," 28.

[16] Cf. Pieter Van der Lugt, *Cantos and Strophes in Biblical Hebrew Poetry II: Psalms 42–89*, OtSt 57, ed. B. Becking (Leiden: Brill, 2010), 49.

[17] It is also the final word of Ps 9, which should be understood as continuing

here could be because v. 12 is a repetition of v. 8, which ends in סלה.

5.4   STRUCTURE

The structure of Ps 46 has not been particularly contested. Indeed, most scholars agree on a strophic division.[18] The consensus has been to view the psalm in three strophes: vv. 2–4; 5–7; 9–12. Some scholars have not included the refrains in the strophes (vv. 8, 12).[19] Samuel Terrien has dissented against this majority view, arguing that the poem is comprised of two strophes: vv. 2–8; 8–12.[20] Peter van der Lugt's analysis serves as a kind of rapprochement between the two perspectives. He argues that based on content the poem is divided into two cantos. The first canto is comprised of two strophes (vv. 2–4; 5–7) and the second is comprised of the final strophe.[21] My analysis will be based on the traditional three-strophe division. This division has the strength of being based both on linguistic markers (סלה) and shifts in content.

Strophe 1: vv. 2–4:   God is Our Refuge
    v. 2:   Theme: God as refuge
    vv. 3–4:   *A fortiori* argument: Lack of fear in chaos

Strophe 2: vv. 5–7:   God's City
    vv. 5–6:   Illustration 1: (v. 5–6)
    v. 7:   Illustration 2: (v. 7)
    v. 8:   Theme: refrain

---

into Ps 10 based on the acrostic form.

[18] Van der Lugt, *Cantos and Strophes in Biblical Hebrew Poetry II: Psalms 42–89*, 49.

[19] E.g., Jan P Fokkelman, *Major Poems of the Hebrew Bible: At the Interface of Hermeneutics and Structural AnalysisI*, SSN 41 (Assen: Uitgeverij Van Gorcum, 2000), 158–60.

[20] Samuel Terrien, *Psalms*, 370–71. See also Jean Noël Aletti and Jacques Trublet, *Approche poétique et théologique des psaumes: Analyses et méthodes* (Paris: Éd. du Cerf, 1983), 37.

[21] Van der Lugt, *Cantos and Strophes in Biblical Hebrew Poetry II: Psalms 42–89*, 45–51.

Strophe 3: vv. 9–12: Call to the nations

v. 9:   Apostrophe to fictive audience

v. 10:   Amplification-aggregation: the deeds of Yhwh

v. 11:   Apostrophe to fictive audience: Speaker is Yhwh

v. 12:   Theme: refrain

5.5   DESCRIPTION OF THE WORLD OF THE PSALM: ITS INTERNAL ARGUMENT

5.5.1   THE WORLD OF THE PSALM

This psalm is a study in the contrast between chaos and order. The psalm moves from chaos (vv. 3–4) to order (vv. 5–6); then again from chaos (v. 7a) to order (v. 7b); with a final exhortation (vv. 9–11). These movements are held together by the three nominal refrains (vv. 1, 8, 12), which give the psalm its overall theme of God as refuge. The chaos is depicted through two overlapping images: the waters and the nations.

In vv. 3–4, the poem presents a dizzying and apocalyptic scene of mountains tumbling into the sea and of the waters arrogantly rising up to envelope all things. This metaphorical use of the waters is a powerful image culturally. Authors use metaphors not simply to enhance understanding, but for their connotational value as well.[22] In an ANE mindset, the waters represented the forces of chaos, which if not controlled could make life impossible.[23] Thus, the scene here is the most perilous one could imagine.[24] J. Clinton McCann rightly compares this imagery with the more contemporary fears of a nuclear winter, or the results of excessive global warming.[25] The second chaotic image is of the nations (v. 7a). Othmar Keel has demonstrated that images of chaos were often associated with foreign nations, especially if

---

[22] Paul Ricœur, *The Rule of Metaphor: Multi-disciplinary Studies of the Creation of Meaning in Language* (Toronto: University of Toronto Press, 1977), 172.

[23] E.g., the role of Tiamat in the *Enūma Eliš*, or of Yam in *The Baal Cycle*. See also William P. Brown, *Seeing the Psalms*, 107.

[24] See Othmar Keel, *Symbolism of the Biblical World*, 24–25.

[25] J. Clinton McCann, *Psalms*, 865.

they were threatening Israel.[26] One can easily see the connection. Just as the waters were threatening and deadly to human life, an enemy nation brought destruction with it. Keel describes it this way,

> In national laments, the ravaging of the countryside is seen as an event of cosmic proportions. The earth begins to quake (Ps 60:2). The clamor of foes resounds like the surging of the floods of Chaos (cf. Ps 74:23 with Pss 65:7; 89:9 cj.). Pss 74 and 89 contrast the raging of the national enemies with the power of Yahweh, by which in primal times he conquered the Chaos dragon...The dragon embodies a cosmic power, as the symbolic animal of Babylon's destructive world domination. In Jer 51:34, the king of Babylon is compared to a dragon which devours Jerusalem as a monster swallows a man.[27]

Thus, this connection between the deadly waters surging with the nations is a natural one. In Ps. 46, through the repetition of the verbal roots מוט and המה (vv. 3–4, 7), the poet is able, in just four words, to make this connection by depicting the nations as a chaotic force of similar power and destructive effect as the waters.[28]

In the context of the world coming apart at the seams, vv. 5–6 portray God as carving out his city as a place of refuge.[29] Water, far from being a destructive force, becomes a source of joy and flourishing.[30] In v. 7b, Yhwh's voice is pictured as a protection against politi-

---

[26] Keel, *Symbolism of the Biblical World*, 100–9.

[27] Ibid., 107.

[28] William Brown correctly argues that the cosmic image of the waters and hills trembling is "mapped" onto the political realm. That is, the image of the chaotic waters becomes a metaphor for the chaos of the nations (*Seeing the Psalms*, 116).

[29] This fits well with the textual reading of v. 5b. Elyon "sanctifies" (קדש) his dwelling, in the sense of the basic meaning of the word, "to set apart." See *HALOT*, 1072.

[30] נהל in the Psalms is frequently used to denote the "sea" in parallel with ים or מים (with "sea": Ps 24:2; 66:6; 80:12; 89:26 with "waters": 72:8; 105:41; 107:33). In some of these contexts, the word clearly refers to "river" in contrast to sea, but in others it seems to denote 'sea' (ex., 24.2; 80.12; 93.3). If that is the case, the נהל here

cal and natural forces of chaos.[31] Thus, in the world of the psalm, the two dominate realities are the forces of chaos and the stabilizing presence and activity of Yhwh. The reality, which keeps the chaos at bay, is that "God is in its midst" (v. 6). However, God does not just bring peace. He defeats the forces of chaos through creating some chaos of his own. He turns the destruction back on the destroyers. Verse 8 declares that God's voice makes the earth waver. In verses 9–10, God wreaks desolations (שַׁמּוֹת) and breaks, snaps, and burns the implements of war. In sum, God is portrayed as a source of power greater than the forces of chaos and thus able to tame them. This is the thrust of the command to the nations to "slacken and acknowledge that I am God" (v. 11).

5.5.2 THE IMPLIED AUTHOR AND AUDIENCE

The implied audience is not obvious in the first two strophes of the psalm. The use of the first person plural pronouns could imply a reflexive tone to the psalm. That is, the speaker and audience are one. However, beginning in v. 8, the speakers call to another group and command them to "come and see" what Yhwh has done. This audience is made explicit as the "nations" in v. 11, where they are commanded to "cease and desist."[32] One can then read this audience back into the earlier strophes of the psalm. The poem becomes a confession of trust in Yhwh declared to foreign nations.

There are two implied speakers in the psalm: the congregation of Israel (vv. 2–10, 12), which is made clear by the plural pronouns, and Yahweh (v. 11). The brief speech of Yhwh serves as a climax to the psalm. However, the two speakers work together to communicate their message to the nations. Yahweh appears and speaks to the nations on behalf of the congregation. Thus, there are essentially two groups

---

"could have been represented in cultic symbolism by the 'bronze sea'. The waters divided from the sea would then have found concrete form in the lavers, which were of very imposing size," (*Symbolism of the Biblical World*, 140).

[31] Verse 7b is directed specifically against the "earth" (אֶרֶץ), but the parallel with v. 7a would indicate that the voice of Yhwh tames the nations as well.

[32] For a colloquial translation of הַרְפּוּ וּדְעוּ, see Gerald Wilson, *Psalms, Volume 1*, NIVAC (Grand Rapids: Zondervan, 2002), 718.

envisioned in the psalm: Israel with Yahweh and the nations. This makes for a polemical tone to the poem.

5.5.3   THE INTERNAL ARGUMENT OF PSALM 46

Within the world of the poem, the persuasive center of gravity is found in the four imperatives (vv. 9, 11). The nations are challenged to consider the awesome deeds of Yahweh, cease their rebellion, and acknowledge him as God. Based on the goal of persuading the nations to take a particular course of action, Ps 46 could profitably be understood as a kind of *deliberative* rhetoric.[33] The main presumption of the poem would be that God is a refuge for Israel (vv. 2, 8, 12).[34] This presumption is bolstered by appeal to an emotional state (vv. 3–4).[35] If God were not a refuge, how could one explain the community's lack of fear in the face of terrifying circumstances? The poet then presents two illustrations of how God is a refuge (vv. 5–6, 7).[36] Both of these illustrations show how God tames the forces of chaos. In vv. 9–10, the congregation appeals to the nation's own sense of sight for support of their presumption. They can see for themselves how Yhwh has defeated enemies.[37] Now that the presumption of the poem has been support-

---

[33] See the classic definition in Aristotle, *Rhetoric*, I.iii.10–30.

[34] On the differences between "fact," "truth," "presumption," and "value," see Perelman and Olbrechts-Tyteca, *New Rhetoric*, 68–79. A "presumption" would be a statement the speaker views as true, but would need to be reinforced and supported in an argument to be effective (70–71).

[35] George Kennedy has demonstrated that emotion is a primary means of persuasion in most cultures. See George Kennedy, *Comparative Rhetoric: An Historical and Cross-Cultural Introduction* (Oxford: Oxford University Press, 1998), 224.

[36] On the role of illustration, see Perelman and Olbrechts-Tyteca, *New Rhetoric*, 357–60. The argument of these two illustrations functions this way: In the first, God is pictured as present in his city. This presence transforms water from a source of chaotic terror to a source of blessing and joy. It also gives certainty that the city will not be shaken (cf. v. 3). In fact, his help is as assured as the sunrise (v. 6). In the second picture (v. 7), the nations are portrayed as rebellious forces, which God silences by the power of his word.

[37] Keel demonstrates how the description of Yhwh breaking bows, spears, and burning shields is a way of saying that Yhwh will be militarily victorious over his enemies. This is the image a conquering king would use to celebrate his defeat of

ed, the poet presents his main rhetorical point: the nations are to cease fighting and acknowledge God supremacy (v. 11).

5.6 THE POSSIBLE HISTORICAL SETTINGS/SITUATIONS OF THE PSALM

Issues related to the setting of Ps 46 have been robustly debated. This debate has raged over both its historical setting and over the social situation which elicited the poem. The two areas are not unconnected, but can be treated separately.

In regard to historical setting, older scholarship understood this psalm as a response to some specific historical event.[38] More recent scholarship under the influence of Gunkel has attempted to find a more general historical setting for all of the songs of Zion (Pss 46; 48; 76; 87).[39] Some argued that the Zion tradition was rooted in the cultic worship of pre-Israelite Jerusalem.[40] Thus, Ps. 46 would be the result of Canaanite themes and values, which were incorporated into Israelite religion. This would date the psalm to rather early in Israel's history. J. J. M. Roberts has nuanced this view by stating that the Israelites did not exactly borrow the Zion tradition from the Jebusite inhabitants of Jerusalem.[41] Rather, during the Davidic-Solomonic expansion, Israel had a need to theologically legitimize their regime to justify their imperial expansion.[42] One way of accomplishing this was to elevate Yhwh above El and Baal. So, Israel developed poems and traditions, which utilized Baal and El imagery to celebrate Yhwh. This functioned

---

an enemy (*Symbolism of the Biblical World*, 239–40).

[38] Many looked to the Assyrian invasion of 701 BCE (e.g., A. F. Kirkpatrick, *Book of Psalms*, 253); others point to the Scythian invasions in western Asia in the early reign of Josiah (e.g., Briggs and Briggs, *Book of Psalms*, 394). Still others look to some crisis in the Maccabean period.

[39] Gunkel and Begrich, *Introduction to the Psalms*, 264.

[40] The basic work on the Zion tradition remains Edzard Rohland, *Die Bedeutung der Erwählungstraditionen Israels für die Eschatologie der alttestamentlichen ProphetenI*, Th.D. diss. (Ruprecht-Karls-Universität Heidelberg, 1956).

[41] J. J. M. Roberts, "The Davidic Origin of the Zion Tradition," *JBL* 92 (1973): 329–44.

[42] Ibid., 340–41.

to demonstrate that Yhwh was the "undisputed head of the panthe-on."[43] Roberts argues that the uniquely Israelite elements in these texts are a result of Israel's "somewhat garbled understanding of Canaanite mythology."[44] The motif of nations threatening Jerusalem in these texts was likely due to the three revolts during the time of Solomon.

There have been several attempts to further nuance the histori-cal setting of this psalm, three of which are worthy of mention. First, Hans-Joachim Kraus agrees that Ps 46 needs to be understood within the context of the "Songs of Zion" group (46, 48, 76, 87).[45] After much consideration, Kraus argues that the setting of this psalm is to be found, not in the general context of the Davidic-Solomonic rule, but more specifically in an annual Zion festival in which the ark was con-veyed up to Zion in a procession and Yahweh was celebrated as the great King.[46] In his paragraph on the purpose of the psalm, he indicates that it highlights that the presence of Yahweh is what makes the city invincible.[47] This emphasis on the presence of Yahweh providing certi-tude contrasts with the prevailing theology of the day that viewed the temple of Yahweh as providing security (Jer 7:4).

An alternative setting has been proposed by Michael Goulder, who argued that the "sons of Korah" psalms were originally written for the Festival of Yahweh at Dan.[48] The order of the Korah psalms reflects the ritual order of this Festival. Thus, Ps 46 would have been sung as an evening song in the early days of this feast.[49] This psalm was a celebration of God's victory over the waters and over Israel's enemies.[50] The waters mentioned in the psalm are to be equated with the large spring that issues from Dan. Goulder further argues that the

---

[43] Ibid., 341.

[44] Ibid., 342.

[45] Kraus, *Psalms 1–59*, 459.

[46] Ibid., 461.

[47] Ibid., 464.

[48] Michael Goulder, *The Psalms of the Sons of Korah*, JSOTSup 20 (Sheffield: Sheffield Academic, 1982), 20.

[49] Ibid., 121–2.

[50] Ibid., 139.

history of Yahweh's deeds, especially those associated with Jacob, were recounted at the *Selah* points of the psalm.[51] The imperatives in v. 11 were voiced by Israel and addressed to the nations. These imperatives are "intended concretely and not figuratively" because "some of their [the nations] representatives are actually present in the rites... (47:9)."[52] Similarly, the mention of Yahweh burning chariots and weapons of war (v. 10) was ceremonially carried out in this festival. The weapons of enemies defeated in battle would have been burned as a part of this festival.[53] These northern psalms were then brought to the South after the Assyrian invasion and subsequently associated with the Jerusalem cult.

Finally, Erhard Gerstenberger recognizes several early themes in the psalm, including the mythical understanding of "waters" and the "Zion theology," which he argues could go back to pre-Israelite times. However, in its final form, the psalm derives from the post-exilic situation. He argues this based on the consistent use of the first person plural form, which he avers was a late development in psalm writing. Thus, the psalm is a communal affirmation of deep trust in Yahweh and an affirmation of a future hope of peace Yahweh would establish.[54]

The above discussion demonstrates that the attempt to tie the psalm to a specific historical context remains elusive. Another way forward would be to posit a social setting or arrangement that would have elicited this psalm. This would be attempted through a close look at the language of the psalm itself.

Based on the content of the psalm, Walter Brueggemann argued that it was written from the perspective of a strong, stable government concerned to maintain the status quo.[55] He states, "They [Israel's elite] were able to celebrate the present social arrangement under king as the ultimate rule of God...the psalm celebrating king and Zion

---

[51] Ibid., 141, 147.

[52] Ibid., 145.

[53] Ibid., 145.

[54] Gerstenberger, *Psalms: Part I,* 190–95.

[55] In this way Brrueggemann's social setting is similar to the one posited by Roberts above. See Roberts, "Davidic Origin of the Zion Tradition," 339–44.

had now silenced the hard tales of hurt, bondage and injustice...Such self-assured doxology...surely leads to social ideology."[56] Thus, the psalm was intended to push down voices from the margin to support the current regime.[57] However, when one examines other places in the Hebrew bible where similar language to Ps 46 is utilized, a different social situation emerges. The four passages most similar to Ps 46 are Ezek 38–39, Joel 3, Isa 17, and Nah 1.5–11.[58]

Figure 1

Ezekiel 38–39	Joel 3	Isaiah 17	Nahum 1:4–11
38:19 "on that day there will be a great earthquake (רעש) in the land of Israel. 38:20 "The fish of the sea, the birds of the sky, the wild beasts, all the things that creep on the ground, and all people who live on the face of the earth will shake (רעש) at my presence. The mountains will topple, the cliffs will fall, and every wall will fall to the ground.	3:16 Yhwh roars from Zion; from Jerusalem he gives his voice; the heavens and the earth shake (רעש). But Yhwh is a refuge (מחסה) for his people; he is a stronghold for the children of Israel	17:12 Ah, the thunder of many peoples; they thunder like the thundering of the sea! Ah, the roar of nations; they roar like the roaring of mighty waters! 17:13 The nations roar like the roaring of many waters but he will rebuke them, and they	1:4 He rebukes the sea and makes it dry; he dries up all the rivers... 1:5 The mountains quake before him; the hills melt; the earth heaves before him, the world and all who dwell in it. 1:7 Yhwh is good a stronghold in the day of trouble; he knows those

---

[56] Walter Brueggemann, *Israel's Praise: Doxology against Idolatry and Ideology* (Philadelphia: Fortress, 1988), 110–11.

[57] This social setting would fit well with the historical setting proposed by J. J. M. Roberts, see above.

[58] Understanding Ps 46 in light of these texts was first proposed by Amos Ḥakham in *Da'at Mikra,* see the discussion in Arie Folger, "Understanding Psalm 46," *JBQ* 41 (2013): 41.

39:3 I will knock your bow out of your left hand and make your arrows fall from your right hand 39:9 Then those who live in the cities of Israel will go out and use the weapons for kindling—the shields, bows, arrows, war clubs and spears—they will burn them for seven years.		will flee far away, chased like chaff on the mountains before the wind and the whirling dust before the storm.	who take refuge in him.

The social setting of these texts is from the perspective of a minor, threatened community.[59] The similarity of the language and imagery would point toward a similar social setting for Ps. 46. This makes sense with the content of the psalm since the time one would most need the reminder that God is a refuge is when that very fact is in doubt.[60]

Both sides in this debate agree that the psalm was written for corporate worship based on the use of the first person plural pronouns. The fundamental question is this: is the setting one in which a strong, stable regime is attempting to shore up its power through celebrating the invincibility of its capital (i.e., Zion) and thus silence opposition? Or, does the setting reflect a minor, threatened community confessing

---

[59] Ezekiel was likely written by a Jewish deportee in Babylon during the sixth century. See L. S. Tiemeyer, "Ezekiel, Book of," *DOTP*, 214. Joel is notoriously difficult to date, but Duane Garrett points out that whatever the date, the situation is the aftermath of a locust plague where, "the survival of the people, their livestock and even of local wildlife seemed in doubt" ('Joel, Book of', in *DOTP*, 449). Nahum and Isaiah 17 were written under the shadow of the Assyrian empire. See Victor Matthews, *The Hebrew Propets and Their Social World: An Introduction* (Grand Rapids: Baker Academic, 2012), 106–7, 126–29.

[60] In an interesting example from the psalm's later use, Greg Earwood reminds us that Martin Luther wrote the hymn based on Ps 46 during one of his chronic bouts with depression. See Greg C. Earwood, "Psalm 46," *RevExp* 86 (1989): 79.

trust in Yhwh as a refuge despite circumstances? This is a difficult question to decide. The metaphor of the deity as a refuge is not used in other ANE cultures, so it is difficult to find texts to compare it with.[61] Of course, it is possible for a speaker to use the same psalm to function either ideologically to silence opposition, or as a confession of trust. However, this study will primarily examine the psalm from the latter context for two reasons: 1) the similarity of the language in Ezekiel, Joel, Nahum, and Isaiah tip the scales toward this context; and 2) Israel only had an empire-like state for a very short time-period. Thus, even if the psalm originates from this era, much of its subsequent use in ancient Israel would have been in the context of minor, threatened community.

Thus, in its actual setting, the primary speaker of the psalm would be the worship leader, while the congregation would be both voicing the psalm and its main audience. The goal of the poem would be to instill in the community a disposition of belief and confidence in Yahweh in the midst of threatening forces. This would make the poem an example of epideictic rhetoric. Perelman and Olbrechts-Tyteca have argued at length for the importance of this genre of rhetoric. They state that the goal of this rhetoric is, "to increase the intensity of adherence to certain values, which might not be contested when considered on their own, but may nevertheless not prevail against other values that might come into conflict with them."[62] This captures effectively the dynamic between the speaker and audience of Ps 46. With this different rhetorical goal in mind, we will once again analyze the rhetorical features of the poem to consider how it would function.

---

[61] Creach, *Yahweh as Refuge*, 55. The closest ANE parallel to the theme of Yhwh as refuge is the prayer of Ashurbanipal in his petition to the goddess Ishtar for protections. He quotes Jacobson, "Ashurbanipal's attitude of childlike helplessness as he weeps before Ishtar was apparently—by virtue of the complete trust it expressed and its utter lack of self-assertiveness and reliance on own powers—most highly regarded as truly meritorious and pious. It stands for an attitude which may be termed quietistic, in that it holds that only by refraining from all action of one's own and thereby showing complete unflinching trust in divine help does one prove deserving of it." See Thorkild Jacobsen, *The Treasures of Darkness: A History of Mesopotamian Religion* (New Haven: Yale University Press, 1976), 237.

[62] Perelman and Olbrechts-Tyteca, *New Rhetoric*, 51.

5.7 ANALYSIS OF THE ARGUMENT OF THE PSALM: ITS EXTERNAL ARGUMENT

Based on its function as a type of epideictic rhetoric, the rhetorical center of gravity of the poem is the confession that God is present for Israel as a refuge and help. This is made clear through the three nominal refrains (vv. 2, 8, 12). This value is confessed in the midst of geographical and political chaos. Yhwh's presence as refuge is seen most clearly though the protection of his city (v. 6) and through his defeat of enemy nations (vv. 9–11).

5.7.1 STROPHE ONE

Verse 2

The opening refrain functions as a "value."[63] A value is essentially an attitude or belief that the addressed community would affirm, but would not necessarily be affirmed by outsiders. As such, the value needs to be supported and defended, which the poem does admirably. The forceful assonance spanning the end of the first colon through the second gives the refrain an aura of confident assertion, almost a slogan.[64] Additionally, the fact that the verse is a noun phrase is also important. Rhetorically, noun phrases are often used "to make a statement timeless and, in consequence beyond the limits of subjectivity and bias."[65] The declaration that God is a refuge, strength, and help, puts the statement beyond evaluation and into the realm of timeless

---

[63] For this use of the term, see Perelman and Olbrechts-Tyteca, *New Rhetoric*, 74–75. Jerome Creach calls this a "confession of faith." He goes on to list several types of confessions of faith, of which Ps 46:2 is a "simple confession" which most often occurs in a non-verbal sentence with a first-person suffix added to the predicate (e.g., Ps 59:10). Community confessions are not as common (e.g., Pss 62:9; 46:8; 33:20; 59:12; 115:9, 10, 11; 33:20). See Creach, *Yahweh as Refuge*, 44.

[64] אלהים לנו מחסה ועז עזרה בצרות נמצא מאד.

[65] Perelman and Olbrechts-Tyteca, *New Rhetoric*, 182. See also James L Kinneavy, et al., *A Rhetoric of Doing: Essays on Written Discourse in Honor of James L. Kinneavy* (Carbondale: Southern Illinois University Press, 1992), 333–35. He examines the function of noun phrases in scientific articles. One of the primary functions of noun phrases in that context is to create the sense of objectivity.

truth.[66] The use of the first common plural is also rhetorically significant.[67] By leading the congregation in a hymn in which they declare that God is a refuge "for us," the worshipper is led to make a self-involving statement. The worshipper has the value of "God as refuge" affirmed for them both through making this declaration themselves as well as by hearing others (community leaders and the congregation) state the value. The final two words of the line, that God is "readily found" (נִמְצָא מְאֹד) are an articulation of hope in the face of "troubles." The lack of specificity regarding the "troubles" (צָרוֹת) faced allows the psalm to be re-used in many different situations.

Verses 3–4

These verses not only draw a conclusion from the value stated in v. 2, they also present an argument designed to foster trust in God in any circumstance.[68] These verses present essentially an argument *a fortiori*. The congregation declares that even in a situation where the fabric of the cosmos was being undone and the land was reverting to a watery chaos, they would not be afraid. Thus, any lesser trouble the community faces, and any other difficulty would necessarily be lesser, they would likewise not fear. Once again, the use of the first-person plural is significant (לֹא נִירָא). Through the recitation of the psalm, the community voices their lack of fear in the face of chaos. This voicing itself helps to foster a disposition of trust. The argument here also puts any trouble now facing the congregation in perspective. Any difficulty

---

[66] William Brown has articulated how "refuge" in the psalter is the antithesis to another common theme, the pit. He states, "As 'refuge' marks the object of the psalmist's longing, so 'pit' constitutes the domain most feared by the psalmist. Whereas God's 'refuge,' the 'rock' of Zion, is the feature most elevated on the Psalter's theological landscape (61:2b–3), the 'pit' marks, as it were, the sinkhole in the psalmist's terrain, into which one descends to death. The 'pit' is the grave's metaphor (49:9) as much as 'refuge' is Zion's image, the locus of life. Not infrequently, the 'pit' is associated with the overwhelming waters, from which the psalmist pleads for deliverance [Ps 69:15]" (*Seeing the Psalms*, 26).

[67] Erhard Gerstenberger reminds us that the use of the 1 common plural has hardly any parallels among ANE hymns (*Psalms: Part 1*, 192).

[68] "Trust" being the positive way to state a lack of fear.

would seem smaller than the ultimate catastrophe described by vv. 3–4, thus it would seem more manageable. This is effectively leading toward v. 7, where the poem declares that God is over the nations.

5.7.2 STROPHE TWO

Verses 5–7

This strophe presents two illustrations describing how God is a refuge for his people.[69] Verses 5–6 portray God as carving out a geographical refuge for his people, the "city of God" (v. 5). The extra-positioning of "river" (נָהָר) highlights this city as a place where water has been transformed from a source of chaos to a source of joy (יְשַׂמְּחוּ)[70] The central image in this illustration is God's presence in his city. The city is a refuge because God has chosen to dwell there (v. 5).[71] God's presence in the city creates two realities for it. First, the repetition of the root מוט from v. 3 makes clear that the city will not be shaken the way the world is described in vv. 3–4. The second reality of God's presence is that God will surely help it. The very constancy of the sun rising in the morning is appealed to as an analogy. God's help is a sure as the sunrise.

The second illustration (v. 7) is a shrewd piece of rhetoric. A new, political subject is introduced: גוים and ממלכות. Yet, these entities are the subjects of the same verbs used of the "waters" in v. 4. Thus, the nations, which are real and visible threat, are described similarly to the "waters," a mythical threat, which the community already declared it did not fear. God is a refuge in this illustration because he is able to silence the nations by the power of his voice.

---

[69] On the role of illustration in discourse, see Perelman and Olbrechts-Tyteca, *New Rhetoric*, 357–60.

[70] As Waltke and O'Conner argue, the nominative absolute here serves "in context to contrast this element to a comparable item in another clause" (*An Introduction to Biblical Hebrew Syntax* [Winona Lake, IN: Eisenbrauns, 1990], 760). That is, it contrasts with the "waters" mentioned in v. 4. On the function of the river here, William Brown states, "The river is a sign and seal of God's refuge, a salvific order that pulses through the city as flowing streams, tvery streams longed for in Ps 42 and rechanneled in Ps 1 through the sustaining power of *tôrâ*" (*Seeing the Psalms*, 24).

[71] Hans-Joachim Kraus, *Psalms 1–59*, 463.

The poem, has set up well its repetition of the main "value" it
promotes (v. 8) through illustration (v. 5–7). The repetition of God as
refuge is itself suasive (v. 8).[72] Additionally, The mention of "Yhwh of
Hosts" on the heels of a verse concerning the nations is also significant. The nations may have armies, but Yhwh is the God of צבאות.

5.7.3   STROPHE THREE

Verses 9–11

The four imperatives in these verses serve as a crescendo to the
poem. These imperatives function in a slightly different way in reality
than in the world of the psalm. In v. 9, the congregation calls to a fictive audience of the nations to "Come! Behold!" (לכו חזו) what Yhwh
has done. Yet in calling to the nations they are also impacting their
own perception of Yhwh. In reminding the nations of the "desolations"
and great victories of Yhwh, they would be reminded of them themselves.[73] This connection of Yhwh with his mighty acts serves to enhance his prestige or honor among the congregation and it helps to foster trust in him, the main point of the poem.[74]

In v. 11, the speaker changes from the congregation to Yhwh.[75]
As stated earlier, in the world of the poem, the imperatives in this
verse would be a call for the nations to stop fighting and acknowledge
Yhwh. The congregation would understand that a fictive audience of
the nations was being addressed. Yet, these imperatives function suasively for Israel as well. Especially by shifting the speaker to Yhwh,
the congregation could envision themselves as addressed along with
the nations. For Israel this would be a call to not trust in their military

---

[72] Repetition is one of the earliest rhetorical devices one learns and it is utilized in every culture, at times in very sophisticated ways, see Kennedy, *Comparative Rhetoric*, 4, 14, 104.

[73] The imagery of breaking the bow and spear and burning the war cart refers to a victory in battle as pointed out by Kraus, *Psalms 1–59*, 463.

[74] On the connection between a person and his acts leading to prestige, see
Perelman and Olbrechts-Tyteca, *New Rhetoric*, 303–5.

[75] It is possible that this would have been voiced by a worship leader in a
cultic festival context, verse 11 would then be a response to the 'oracle' of Yhwh.

might or military alliances, but instead to "be still and realize that God is God."[76] As Jon Levenson has recognized, for Israel this psalm has an anti-political and pro-Yhwh thrust.[77] The two interpretations of these imperatives (that they command the nations to "cease and desist" and Israel to give up their trust in political or military might) are not mutually exclusive; rather they function at different levels of the poem.[78] In the second colon of v. 11, Yhwh supports his commands by pointing to a future reality. He will be exulted in the national (גוים) and natural (ארץ) realms, therefore it is in one's best interest to acknowledge him now.

The poem closes with a repetition of v. 8, which summarizes the main point of the discourse. Yhwh is with the congregation and he is their refuge. This value should lead the congregation to a deeper trust in him.

5.8 CONCLUSION

The extensive use of this psalm even to modern times testifies to the power of its imagery and message.[79] This chapter described the internal argument of the psalm as a type of deliberative rhetoric designed to convince the nations to "be still" and submit to Yhwh. However, in its actual use, the psalm functions as a kind of epideictic rhetoric designed to reinforce the value that Yhwh is Israel's refuge and strength in spite of circumstances that may indicate the opposite. Yet, it is not as if the psalm has two different arguments running concurrently. Rather, the poet creates a world in which a fictive audience of the nations is addressed in order to persuade the actual audience. This is one of the features that make art so compelling. In a celebrated essay, Kenneth

---

[76] Jon Levenson, *Sinai and Zion: An Entry into the Jewish Bible* (New York: HarperCollins, 1985), 154.

[77] Ibid., 151–54.

[78] This double application is intuitively grasped by Goldingay, *Psalms: Psalms 42–89*, 72.

[79] See Gillingham, *Psalms through the Centuries*, 140–43, 56, 86–87, 218, 227–29, 259, 281.

Burke analyzed Antony's speech in Shakespeare's *Julius Caesar*.[80] He argues that Antony's has one rhetorical goal in view within the world of the play. That is Antony addressing a Roman mob. However, the speech has another rhetorical goal when viewed from the actual setting, an Elizabethan-era theatre audience. It is important to understand both dynamics. The same is true in this psalm. The psalmist has the congregation address a fictive audience of the nations, persuading them to cease their fighting and acknowledge Yhwh. At the climax of the poem, Yhwh himself commands the nations. This dynamic helps the author achieve the actual goal of the poem, to deepen and affirm the value of Yhwh as a refuge to the community. That is, the poet had an epideictic function in view. Additionally, the poet utilizes self-involving speech, repetition, *a fortiori* argument, illustration, and exhortation to achieve the desired effect.

---

[80] Kenneth Burke, "Antony in Behalf of the Play," in *Rhetorical Analyses of Literary Works*, ed. E. Corbett (London: Oxford University Press, 1969), 103–14.

CHAPTER 6

Rhetorical Analysis of Psalm 116

6.1 INTRODUCTION

Psalm 116 has been widely used in both Christian and Jewish worship, albeit in quite different ways. Christians have generally used it as one of the primary psalms for funerals, while Jewish worship has utilized as a part of the Paschal, Hanukkah, and New Moon liturgies.[1] This diversity can be attributed to different interpretations of v. 15, which will be discussed below. For my purpose, this psalm provides a good example of a declarative psalm of the individual.[2]

In this chapter I will offer a rhetorical approach to Psalm 116 in the following way: a translation of the psalm followed by a discussion of the rhetorical unit; an analysis of its internal argument; a description of a plausible historical setting; and an analysis of its external argument.

6.2 TRANSLATION

The text of this psalm has several thorny textual and lexical difficulties. I have footnoted textual complications and indicated places where it is difficult to determine the original text with certainty.

I love (Yhwh)[3] for Yhwh heard[4]   (1)

---

[1] On Christian use, see Gillingham, *Psalms through the Centuries*, 55, 256–57. For the Jewish use, see Holladay, *Psalms through Three Thousand Years*, 134–55.

[2] Claus Westermann, *Praise and Lament in the Psalms*, 102.

[3] Some have suggested that it is odd for אָהַב to be lacking an object. Erhard Gerstenberger emphatically states, "the verb 'hb, 'to love,' used without a direct object, i.e., in an absolute state, does not make sense" (*Psalms: Part 2 and Lamentations*, 292). It is true that the verb normally takes an object. Waltke and O'Connor classify this verbal root as a "quasi-fientive," which "exhibits both stative and fientive charac-

my voice,[5] my pleading

For he inclined his ear to me   (2)

And in my days, I was calling out[6]

---

teristics," thus normally taking an object, see *IBHS* §30.5.3. However, there are times in the Hebrew Bible where אהב occurs without an explicitly stated object (Jer 5:31; Amos 4:5). Although even in those cases there is a verbal complement. There are two possible ways of understanding this line without resorting to emendation. One could argue that the כִּי clause complements the verb and fills the slot normally taken by the object. The כִּי clause indicates that what the psalmist loves is the fact that Yhwh hears. This solves one difficulty (אהב without an object), but creates another one. Every other instance where אהב is used with כִּי, the כִּי functions as causal (Gen 25:28; 37:3; Lev 19:34; Deut 10:19; 15:16; Hos 14:5). A better solution is to understand יהוה as an implied object. This allows the כִּי to function in a causal sense, thus parallel to v. 10. I grant that having an implied object is unusual. One possible reason for the psalmist to not explicitly state the object could be a reticence to proclaim, "I love Yhwh." While the Hebrew Bible often commands people to love Yhwh (e.g., Deut 6:5; 10:12; 11:1, 13, 22; Josh 22:5; Ps 31:24); states that someone loved Yhwh (e.g., 1 Kgs 3:3); or proclaims that Yhwh loves people (Deut 23:6; 1 Sam 12:24; 1 Kgs 10:9); nowhere reports someone saying, "I love Yhwh." Goldingay affirms that "there is no point in the Bible when someone says that they dedicate themselves to or love God," (*Psalms: Psalms 90–150*, 339) This translation is in agreement with several modern translations including NIV2011, NLT, NRSV, NASB95, and ESV.

[4] Most commentators emend this verb to a *qātal* as the BHS apparatus suggests, e.g., Leslie Allen, *Psalms 101–150*, 112; Hans-Joachim Kraus, *Psalms 60–150*, 385. However, Rainey has demonstrated that the *yiqtōl* in Hebrew has developed from the CS *yaqtulû* where the form was utilized as a preterite, see Anson Rainey, "The Ancient Hebrew Prefix Conjugation in the Light of Amarna Canaanite," *HS* 27 (1986): 4–19. This archaic preterite use of the *yiqtōl* can still be seen in some poetic texts in Hebrew, see Rainey, "The Ancient Hebrew Prefix Conjugation in the Light of Amarnah Canaanite," 15–16. In this case the use of the *yiqtōl* would be similar to its use in Ps 3:5a. In that text, the psalmist states, קוֹלִי אֶל־יְהוָה אֶקְרָא וַיַּעֲנֵנִי מֵהַר קָדְשׁוֹ סֶלָה. The verb "I called out" could be construed as a regular imperfect ("I cry out/will cry out"); however, the response to the cry is in the Past Narrative conjugation, indicating that this is a particular event. Similarly, here, the poet recounts an event that happened to him and utilizes the preterite form of the imperfect to do so.

[5] The LXX and Jerome's *Psalt. Hebr.* translate this phrase "the sound of my pleading" (LXX: τῆς φωνῆς τῆς δεήσεώς μου; Jerome: vocem deprecationis meae). This would indicate the absence of the final *yod* on קוֹל and taking it as part of a construct phrase. This is certainly possible since the *taw* and the *yod* look similar in a paleo-Hebrew alphabet.

The cords of death surrounded me (3)
And the snares[7] of Sheol found me
Need and grief I was finding
But on the name of Yhwh I was calling (4)
"Please Yhwh, deliver my life!"[8]
Gracious is Yhwh and righteous (5)
And our God is compassionate
Yhwh guards the naïve (6)
I was needy and he saved me[9]
Return to your rest, my soul (7)

---

[6] The *yiqtōl* form here represents the "calling out" to Yhwh as a past imperfective. That is, the emphasis is not on the completed act of calling out to Yhwh, but on the process of pleading to Yhwh. Similarly, vv. 3, 4. Taking the *yiqtōl* forms in vv. 1–6 as having a past time reference agrees with many modern translations including NIV2011, ESV, and NRSV. Some translations have vv. 1–2 as a present, but vv. 3–6 as a past time reference (NLT and NASB95).

[7] Here I am following the suggestion of several scholars and emending the text from מְצָרֵי to מְצֹדֵי (cf. *HALOT*, 622). "Snares" fits better into the context and ד and ר are easily confused letters in both Aramaic and Paleo-Hebrew scripts.

[8] Determining the bounds of a quotation in the psalms can be difficult. Rolf Jacobson has thoroughly studied direct discourse in the psalter grounding his analysis in quotation theory, see *'Many are Saying': The Function of Direct Discourse in the Hebrew Psalter*, JSOTSup 397 (New York: T&T Clark, 2004). Jacobson grounds his analysis in the work of S. A. Meier, *Speaking of Speaking: Marking Direct Discourse in the Hebrew Bible* (Leiden: Brill, 1992) and Cynthia Miller, *The Representation of Speech in Biblical Hebrew Narrative: A Linguistic Analysis* (Atlanta: Scholars Press, 1996). Recognizing that direct discourse is marked differently in poetry vs. narrative, Jacobson argues that direct discourse in the Psalms can be recognized by either a verb of speaking (קרא, שׂחק, דבר, חשׁב, נאם, שׁמע) and/or a shift in deixis (21). In Ps 116, the psalmist engages in self-quotation 3x (vv. 4, 10). The quotations in v. 10 are marked by verbs of speech (דבר and אמר). In v. 4, the direct discourse is marked by קרא and a shift in deixis. From speaking about Yhwh in the third person, the psalmist shifts to direct address. The analysis of the quotations in my translation of Ps 116 follow Jacobson's (65).

[9] The Hiphil Imperfect here is likely a later development of the form (יוֹשִׁיעַ). Bauer-Leader call this a "neubildung." See Hans Bauer, et al., *Historische Grammatik der hebräischen Sprache des Alten Testamentes*, vol. 1 (Tübingen: Georg Olms, 1922), 229. The translation takes this form as a preterite imperfect, see fn. 4.

For Yhwh has treated you well.[10]

For you rescued my life from death   (8)
   My eye from tear
   My foot from stumbling[11]

I will walk before Yhwh   (9)
   In the lands of the living.[12]

I believed because I said   (10)
   "I am very wretched"

I said in my panic   (11)
   "Every man is a liar"

What can I return to Yhwh   (12)
   For all his benefits for me?

A cup of salvation, I will lift   (13)
   To the name of Yhwh, I will call

My vows to Yhwh, I will fulfill   (14)
   In the presence of[13] all his people

Costly in the eyes of Ywhwh   (15)
   The death of his faithful ones

O, Yhwh, for I am your servant   (16)
   Your servant, the son of your handmaiden
   You released my bonds

To you, I offer a thanksgiving sacrifice   (17)
   At the name of Yhwh, I call

---

[10] This line incorporates two Aramazing 2fs object suffixes. This is due to stylistic reasons, but there could also be rhetorical significance, see below. Of the seven words in this line, five of them end in *yod*.

[11] Jerome and the LXX have plural body parts: "eyes" and "feet." It does not greatly affect the meaning.

[12] It is right after this word that the LXX and Jerome add the title "Hallelujah" and treat vv. 10–19 as a separate psalm.

[13] The MT here reads נֶגְדָה־נָּא. It is unusual to have the suffix ־נָא follow a preposition. Some scholars have argued that נגדה should be pointed as a verb from the Aramaic root meaning "to lead" (e.g., J. P. Fokkelman and Gary A. Rendsburg, "NGDH NH LKL 'MW (Psalm CXVI 14B, 18B)," *VT* 53 [2003]: 328–36). This is possible; however, Goldingay argues that it is just another example of an unusual sufformative in this psalm.

My vows to Yhwh, I will fulfill   (18)
   In the presence of all his people
In the courts of the house of Yhwh   (19)
   In your midst, Jerusalem
Hallelujah!

6.3   *DETERMINATION OF THE RHETORICAL UNIT*

The foundational step to a rhetorical analysis, or any reading of a text, is to determine the boundaries of the text in question. Psalm 116 is a bit ambiguous in this regard. Both Jerome and the LXX treat this unit of text as two psalms (vv. 1–9 and vv. 10–19). This has led some commentators to treat Ps 116 as two distinct psalms.[14] However, the division of the psalm into two parts is likely a liturgical expediency and does not reflect the history of composition.[15] This is evidenced by the parallel structure of vv. 1–9 and 10–19 and repeated key words and themes.[16] Additionally, while vv. 1–9 could work as a psalm in its own right, vv. 10–19 could not. The second half of the psalm depends on the first.[17] This could indicate that vv. 10–19 were a later addition to vv. 1–9. But even if that were the case, it would be appropriate to treat vv. 1–19 as a single unit since vv. 10–19 were intended to be read as an integrated part of the psalm.

So, if the analysis of Ps 116 should not be divided into two separate units, what about a larger unit of text? Many recent interpreters view this psalm as functioning as a part of a larger context, either as a part of Book V of the Psalter, or as a part of the *Hallel* collection (Pss 113–118).[18] However, in keeping with my methodology, I view it as

---

[14] E.g., Moses Buttenwieser, *The Psalms: Chronologically Treated with a New Translation* (Chicago: University of Chicago Press, 1938), xiv.

[15] Briggs and Briggs, *Book of Psalms: Vol. 2*, 238.

[16] The structure and thematic links will be further explored below. See Michael L. Barré, "Psalm 116: Its Structure and Its Enigmas," *JBL* 109 (1990): 61–78.

[17] Goldingay, *Psalms: Psalms 90–150*, 338.

[18] E.g., Jacques Trublet, "Approche canonique des Psaumes du Hallel," in *The Composition of the Book of Psalms*, ed. E. Zenger, BETL 238 (Leuven: Peeters, 2010), 339–76; Erich Zenger, "The Composition and Theology of the Fifth Book of

foundational to understand each psalm individually first before looking for potential links with other psalms in the collection(s). The placement of a psalm in the collection is a secondary context, which is an interesting and important area of study, but not the focus of this method.

6.4   DESCRIPTION OF THE WORLD OF THE PSALM: ITS INTERNAL ARGUMENT

As stated in earlier chapters, describing the world of the psalm potentially involves three parts. First, the implied speaker and implied audience need to be defined. That is, the speaker and audience that interact within the world of the poem itself. For example, if the heavens are commanded to praise Yhwh (eg., Ps 148:4), then they become a part of the implied audience of the poem.[19] Second, the world of the psalm needs to be described. Umberto Eco described how artists create "small-worlds," which highlight the specific parts of the "real" world they want to highlight to achieve their intended effect.[20] Thus, the geography and ethos of the world of the psalm will be elucidated. Third, the internal argument of the psalm may be described if necessary. That is, how is the implied speaker intending to persuade/shape the implied audience? Often the internal argument of a psalm will be somewhat different than the external argument (e.g., Ps 46). However, if there is significant overlap between the implied audience and the actual audience of a psalm, then the internal and external arguments of the psalm would be similar as well. In those instances, the argument of the psalm would need only to be analyzed once.

In most respects, this analysis of the internal rhetoric of the poem is similar to Kenneth Burke's rhetorical method as applied to the internal world of the psalm.[21] However, because of the dramatic nature

---

Psalms, Psalms 107–45," *JSOT* 80 (1998): 77–102; Yair Zakovitch, "The Interpretive Significance of the Sequence of Psalms 111–112.113–118.119," in *Composition of the Book of Psalms*, ed. E. Zenger (Leuven: Peeters, 2010): 215–27.

[19] For a theoretical discussion of the implied author, see Wayne Booth, *The Rhetoric of Fiction*, 70–77.

[20] Eco, *Limits of Interpretation*, 64–82.

[21] Kenneth Burke, *A Grammar of Motives* (Berkeley: University of Califor-

of the cultic scene this psalm envisages, Burke's method provides some additional insights that are helpful for the analysis. Burke's basic philosophy of rhetorical analysis he calls "dramatism."[22] In order to unpack the dramatic nature of a literary work, he employs the "Pentad" consisting of five elements: Act, Scene, Agent, Agency, and Purpose.[23] He describes the function of each of the elements in the following way:

> In a rounded statement about motives, you must have some word that names the *act* (names what took place in thought or deed), and another that names the *scene*, (the background of the act, the situation in which it occurred); also, you must indicate what person or kind of person (agent) performed the act, what means or instruments he used (agency), and the purpose…any complete statement about motives will offer *some kind* of answers to these five questions: what was done (act), when or where it was done (scene), who did it (agent), how he did it (agency), and why (purpose).[24]

Burke clarifies that there is some ambiguity at times between these categories. For example, the scene is the context, or setting in which the act occurs. However, there can be ambiguity between the scene and the act. Thus, Burke speaks in terms of ratios. Smith explains, "The formal relationships which exist among the terms of the Pentad are expressed in *ratios*. Thus, and act-scene ratio would identify or clarify the resources of ambiguity which exist between these two

---

nia Press, 1969). See also the helpful discussions in Arthur Y. Smith, "Kenneth Burke's Concept of Identification in the Perception and Evocation of Literature," *Communicator* 7 (1977): 69–76; Virginia Holland, "Rhetorical Criticism: A Burkeian Method," *Quarterly Journal of Speech* 39 (1953): 444–50; Dennis G. Day, "Persuasion and the Concept of Identification," *Quarterly Journal of Speech* 46 (1960): 270–73; Jessica Enoch and Dana Anderson, *Burke in the Archives: Using the Past to Transform the Future of Burkean Studies*, Studies in Rhetoric/Communication (Columbia: University of South Carolina Press, 2013).

[22] Burke, *A Grammar of Motives*, xxii.

[23] Ibid., xv.

[24] Ibid., xv.

terms. The nature of each term is a given context in which…the nature of the other terms is determined. In other words, these ratios link the five parts to one another so that they cannot be considered separately."[25] With that qualification in mind, it is possible to link the three areas I discussed for the analysis of the internal world of the psalm with Burke's Pentad:

> Act = the action of the implied speaker in the psalm
> Scene = a description of the internal world of the psalm
> Agent = the implied speaker and other actors in the psalm
> Agency = how the speaker persuades the audience
> Purpose = the rhetorical function

Thus, our discussion of the internal argument of Ps. 116 will take the following shape: a description of the implied speaker and audience of the psalm (agent); a description of the world of the psalm (scene); the internal argument of the psalm (act, agency, purpose).

6.4.1   THE IMPLIED SPEAKER AND AUDIENCE OF PSALM 116 (AGENT)

The first basic question is, what kind of person does the psalm itself imply is the speaker? Based simply on the pronouns used, the speaker is an individual throughout the psalm except in v. 5 where the community joins in. Thus, there are two speakers in this psalm, an individual and the community. The primary speaker would be the individual who is briefly joined in worship (v. 5).

It is possible to be even more specific about the identity of the individual. In the psalm, the closest the speaker comes to describing himself is in vv. 6, 15, 16. In v. 6, the speaker declares that Yhwh guards the פְּתָאיִם, a group to which the speaker presumably belongs. The word occurs 19x in the Hebrew Bible, mostly in Proverbs.[26] Chou-Wee Pan gives a helpful description of this type of person, "the פֶּתִי is an ignorant and simpleminded person who does not hate knowledge

---

[25] Smith, "Kenneth Burke's Concept of Identification in the Perception and Evocation of Literature," 72.

[26] 15x in Proverbs, 3x in Psalms, and 1x in Ezekiel.

but is receptive and always prepared to learn or to be taught."[27] "Naïve" would be a good translation for the term.[28] While not a morally negative term, it connotes a humble status. The nuance of humility led post-biblical Judaism to use this term positively. Indeed, this term is used in the Qumran material to refer to pious members of the community.[29] Although most scholars believe the psalm to be post-, or even late post-exilic,[30] the term likely did not have a positive connotation yet (Ezek 45:20). It is best to see the psalmist here as one of the simpleminded, or naïve. In the second half of v. 6, the psalmist says דַּלּוֹתִי ("I was needy"). The verb only occurs 7x in the Hebrew Bible.[31] While the adjectival form of the root could imply a lower social status, it does not necessarily do so in the verbal form (e.g., Isa. 38:14). The term connotes a situation of unnatural distress from which one needs deliverance. The distress in question could be physical, political, economic, or social.[32] Thus, v. 6 portrays the psalmist in a perilous situation. The psalmist is in unfamiliar distress and, being naïve, does not have the skill or knowledge necessary to handle the situation.

Verse 15 utilizes an important term which indirectly applies to the psalmist: חָסִיד. The root word חֶסֶד has been studied extensively.[33] In

---

[27] *NIDOTTE*, 3.716. See also Trevor Donald, "The Semantic Field of 'Folly' in Proverbs, Job, Psalms, and Ecclesiastes," *VT* (1963): 285–92.

[28] Cf. *HALOT*, 989.

[29] 1QpHab 12:4.

[30] E.g., Goldingay, *Psalms*, 339; Leslie Allen, *Psalms 101–150*, 112; Hans-Joachim Kraus, *Psalms 60–150*, 386.

[31] In Ps 79:8 and Judg 6:6, the verb refers to the political, economic, spiritual, and social hardship of the nation when defeated and oppressed by a foreign power; Ps 142:6 describes generally the plight from which the psalmist asks for deliverance. Isa 38:14, Hezekiah uses the term to describe the sickness from which he was delivered; Isa 17:4 and 19:6 use the verb to describe the diminished stature of the nation under divine judgment. Cf. *NIDOTTE*, 1.951–54.

[32] See above fn.

[33] E.g., Gordon Clark, *The Word Ḥesed in the Hebrew Bible*, JSOTSup 157 (Sheffield: Sheffield, 1993); Katharine Doob Sakenfeld, *The Meaning of Hesed in the Hebrew Bible: A New Inquiry*, HSM 17 (Atlanta: Scholars Press, 1978); Charles Whitley, "The Semantic Range of Chesed," *Biblica* 62 (1981): 519–26.

an important monograph on the term, Clark explains that a חֶסֶד relationship is one of bilateral commitment. The חֶסֶד "acts" between participants
may be described, "as a beneficent action performed, in the context of a
deep and enduring commitment between two persons or parties, by one
who is able to render assistance to the needy party who in the circumstances is unable to help him-or herself."[34] Naturally, in the relationship
between divine and human, the term is most often used of God's posture
toward his covenant people. In the adjectival form, the term is used to
describe "one whose life is lived in accordance with the principles of
חֶסֶד. Synonyms are יָשָׁר and תָּמִים."[35] Thus, the psalmist is described here
as one whose life is characterized as being faithful to the covenant. One
who looks to God for help. In a word, the psalmist is "pious."

Verse 16 describes the psalmist as עַבְדֶּךָ ("your slave"). The
psalmist continues in the second half of the line: עַבְדְּךָ בֶּן־אֲמָתֶךָ ("your
slave, the son of your handmaiden"). This claim to be, not just a slave,
but a slave born in the household serves both to "show that he is the
lowliest servant and slave"[36] and at the same time to indicate the close
relational connection between the psalmist and Yhwh. As one born in
the household, the psalmist could claim some of the benefits of being
considered part of the family (Exod 23:12).[37]

In sum, the implied author describes someone who was inexperienced, yet faithful/pious; poor and in deep distress, yet cared for and
delivered by Yhwh. This individual has come to voice his testimony to
Yhwh in the midst of the congregation, who join him in his thanksgiving (v. 5).

The audience of the poem is a bit ambiguous at first glance.
The addressees within the world of the poem are listed in the order
they appear in the poem as follows:

---

[34] Clark, *The Word Ḥesed in the Hebrew Bible*, 267.

[35] *NIDOTTE*, 2.213.

[36] Kraus, *Psalms 60–150*, 389.

[37] Bruce Wells discuss how the lowest rung of slavery, the chattel slave,
was made up of two groups: prisoners of war and children born to a chattel slave.
See Bruce Wells, "Law and Practice," in *A Companion to the Ancient Near East*, ed.
D. Snell (Oxford: Blackwell, 2005), 190–91.

Yhwh	4 ("Please Yhwh save my life!")
The Community	5 ("our God")[38]
The Psalmist	7 ("my soul")
Yhwh	8 ("You rescued my life")
The Psalmist	12–13 ("what will I return to Yhwh?")
Yhwh	16–17 ("Please Yhwh, for I am your servant...")
The Community	19 ("in your midst, Jerusalem")

Despite the different addressees, the audience of the poem is consistent throughout. The poem itself makes clear that the situation envisioned is one of corporate worship. Thus, it would not be unusual for the worshipper at times to address Yhwh then switch to address the community. Throughout the poem, the audience should be envisioned as being comprised of the gathered community in the presence of Yhwh for authorized worship.

In Burke's rhetorical analysis, it is not enough to simply list the speaker and audience of a speech, but to list all the other "agents" active in the discourse. In addition to the congregation, the psalmist, and Yhwh; there are two other agents the poem depicts as enemies of the psalmist: the "cords of death" / "pangs of Sheol" (v. 3); and "each person" (כָּל־הָאָדָם, v. 11) described as a "liar." Thus, the agents active in the psalm are as follows: the psalmist, the congregation, Yhwh, the cords of death, and each person (see fig. 1). These agents can be described in relation to time and in relation to their acts. Thus, the "cords of death" / "pangs of Sheol" and "each person" function primarily as negative agents acting upon the psalmist in the past. That is, they are a part of the story of deliverance the psalmist is narrating. Yhwh functions as a both an actor and recipient of action in the past and present. In the past, the psalmist called upon Yhwh, Yhwh heard and delivered. Thus, Yhwh's positive action counteracts the negative forces in the psalm.

Yhwh is also the present recipient of the offering of the psalmist. Thus, the only agents who stay completely in the past are the nega-

---

[38] Since they join the psalmist in worship here, one can assume they were present to hear the rest of the psalm as well.

tive forces. They stay in the past because they have been overcome by Yhwh. The congregation exists only in the present of the psalm. They are the main recipients of the testimony of the psalmist and even join him in worship. This chart also clarifies that all action in the psalm has the psalmist at the center. All other agents are understood through their relation to the psalmist.

Figure 1

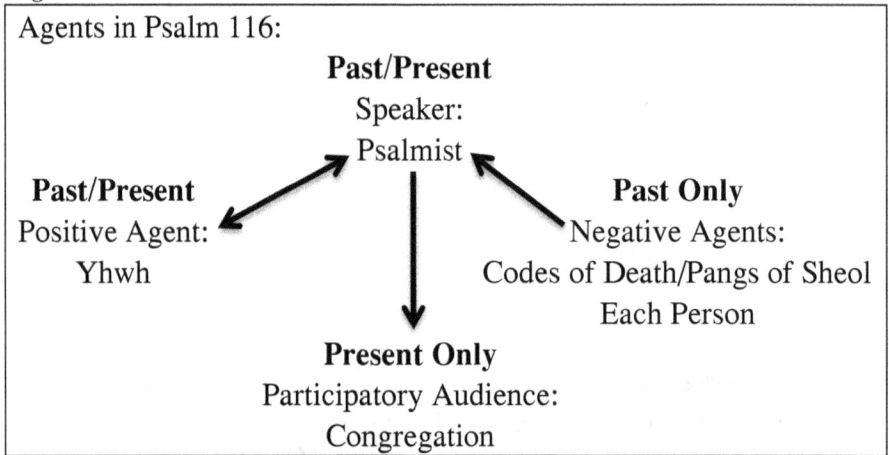

Agents in Psalm 116:

Past/Present
Speaker:
Psalmist

Past/Present
Positive Agent:
Yhwh

Past Only
Negative Agents:
Codes of Death/Pangs of Sheol
Each Person

Present Only
Participatory Audience:
Congregation

6.4.2   THE WORLD OF THE PSALM (SCENE)

There is an inherent ambiguity between agent and scene, or the audience of the poem and the world of the poem.[39] For example, part of the "world" of the poem is a world which is inhabited by a deity who is gracious, righteous, and compassionate (v. 5). Yet, Yhwh is also an agent in the poem. Indeed, the (slight) tension in the opening half of the poem revolves around whether or not Yhwh would act in response to the psalmist's plea (v. 4). Similarly, the "chords of death" are both part of the psalmist's world and actors within it. Additionally, the agents can act to change the scene. That is, Yhwh's action necessarily changes the nature of the world as experienced by the psalmist.

---

[39] See the discussion of the "Scene-Agent" ratio in Burke, *A Grammar of Motives*, 7–9 and idem, *Counter-Statement* (Berkeley: University of California Press, 1968), 150–52.

With this understanding of the relationship between the world of the poem and the agents within it, it is possible to describe the world created by the poet.

Bernd Janowski has mapped a "religious" topography of this psalm and described the topographical movements which take place in the psalm.[40] He identifies two movements in the psalm. The first is the movement of the psalmist from Sheol (v. 3) to the "lands of the living" (v. 9) and finally to the temple of Yhwh (v. 19).[41] This movement from Sheol to the temple geographically portrays the psalmist's movement from mortal distress to salvation. The second movement is found in vv. 6–7, which describes how Yhwh came down to help the "lowly."[42]

Janowski's discussion is helpful in providing us with an overview of the psalm's setting. The setting can, however, be described in more detail. The primary setting for the psalm is the temple (בְּחַצְרוֹת בֵּית יְהוָה, v. 19). In ANE culture, the temple was the center, or "focus of the universe."[43] It was the place from which everything else "takes its bearings."[44] As Jon Levenson aptly puts it, "The Temple and the world stand in an intimate and intrinsic connection. The two projects cannot ultimately be distinguished or disengaged. Each recounts how God brought about an environment in which he can find rest."[45] The temple was a kind of heaven on earth, the place where one could have the most intimate connection with the deity.[46] Additionally, the psalmist is

---

[40] Bernd Janowski, "Dankbarkeit: Ein anthropologischer Grundbegriff im Spiegel der toda-Psalmen," in *Ritual und Poesie: Formen und Orte religiöser Dichtung im Alten Orient, im Judentum und im Christentum*, ed. E. Zenger, Herders biblische Studien 36 (Freiburg: Herder, 2003), 98–111.

[41] Ibid., 106.

[42] Ibid., 107–8.

[43] Jon Levenson, "The Temple and the World," *JR* 64 (1984): 283. This connection between the cosmos and the temple derives from Mircea Eliade (*The Sacred and the Profane: The Nature of Religion* [New York: Harper & Row, 1961]) and has been developed more fully in connection with the Hebrew Bible by John Walton, *Genesis 1 as Ancient Cosmology* (Winona Lake, IN: Eisenbrauns, 2011).

[44] Levenson, "Temple and the World," 283.

[45] Ibid., 288.

[46] Gosta Ahlström, *The History of Ancient Palestine* (Minneapolis: Fortress,

surrounded by all the people of Yhwh (vv. 14, 18). Thus, the psalmist is in the place of integration and community both with Yhwh and the congregation. It is from this primary context that the psalmist tells the story of how he was delivered from the bonds of Sheol. Within the world of the poem, real-life is depicted not as the everyday world of work and family, but in worship at the temple with the congregation. The psalmist's primary identity is derived from his relationship with Yhwh (v. 16) and in his role in communal worship (vv. 14, 18).

In the narration of his plight (vv. 3, 8, 11), the psalmist describes a world that is both filled with adversaries and with the salvific presence of a God who listens. The author describes his trouble in these terms, "the cords of death surrounded me / the snares of Sheol found me / need and grief I find." "Death" and "Sheol" connoted for Israel the ideas of darkness, silence, absence of praise, decay, and forgetfulness.[47] "Death" and "Sheol" were thought of physically in terms of tombs and cisterns. Both of which had narrow entrances with either a vertical or horizontal entrance. They were dark, quiet places where one did not participate in life. In Ps 116, "death" and "Sheol" are envisioned as a prison. In the ancient world, empty cisterns were often used as prisons (Exod 12:29; Isa 24:22; Zech 9:11; Lam 3:53; Gen 40:15; Jer 38:6). Additionally, prisoners were often bound in fetters.[48] In conjunction with the statement that all people are deceptive (v. 11), this could indicate that the psalmist faced false accusations. Regardless, "Death" and "Sheol" are personified as the actors in the world of the psalm. They looked for and found the psalmist (מצא, v. 3). They bound him in ropes and snares. The image of being bound and plunged into the depths of "Sheol" is about as desperate as one can imagine.

However, the world of the psalm does not just contain negative forces. It also contains Yhwh, who is described in canonical terms as gracious, righteous, and compassionate (v. 5). Because Yhwh met the

---

1993), 256–57.

[47] See the excellent discussion in Othmar Keel, *Symbolism of the Biblical World*, 62–73.

[48] Ibid., 69.

psalmist in his need, thanksgiving and worship can occur, which the poem views as the ultimate goal of life.

6.4.3   THE INTERNAL ARGUMENT OF PSALM 116

A full discussion of the rhetorical structure and argument of the psalm will be detailed below in the analysis of the external argument of the psalm. Nevertheless, now that we have recognized the implied author, audience, and world of the poem; it is important to discern the internal rhetorical goal of the poem and discuss how the poet sets about achieving those goals.[49]

The psalm is comprised of a testimony declaring what Yhwh has done and an announcement that the psalmist will fulfill the vow he made to Yhwh in distress. This vow will be fulfilled by declaring Yhwh's praise to the congregation. Indeed, the psalm itself is the public testimony of the psalmist in fulfillment of his vow. The entire poem is a kind of speech-act whereby in voicing this poem to the congregation, he is fulfilling the promise he makes (vv. 13, 14, 17). Thus, for the implied speaker, the audience is Yhwh and the congregation. The dynamic between the two audiences is this, the poet voices his testimony in the hearing of the congregation before Yhwh in order to demonstrate that he is keeping the vow he made when in distress. Thus, within the world of the poem, the psalmist is reciting his testimony to the congregation in order to confirm and strengthen his status with Yhwh.

In this view, the poem could be understood as a type of judicial rhetoric. The psalmist gives public testimony to what Yhwh has done, thus fulfilling his vow and vindicating Yhwh's decision to deliver him. Labelling this poem a type of judicial rhetoric comports well with the testimony format of the psalm. Aristotle calls testimony a kind of non-artistic proof in judicial rhetoric.[50] The "testimony" form has some par-

---

[49] As discussed in the "methodology" section above (1.5.2.2), a poem can function rhetorically at two different levels, internally and externally. See Kenneth Burke, "Antony in Behalf of the Play," in *Rhetorical Analyses of Literary Works*, ed. E. Corbett (London: Oxford University Press, 1969), 103–14.

[50] See Aristotle, *Rhetoric*, I.2.2.

ticular advantages, namely, it is personal, it is able to make abstract and generalized statements concrete,[51] and it is valued not because of how ornate the speech is, but on how truthful the audience believes it to be.[52] However, the psalm also has some differences with traditional judicial rhetoric. Aristotle plainly states that the goal of judicial rhetoric is to determine someone's guilt or innocence.[53] Whereas in this poem the psalmist's goal is to demonstrate to Yhwh his faithfulness in fulfilling his vow, thus strengthening his ties to Yhwh. Ken Dowden in a helpful article on religious rhetoric states that the situation of the prayer is thus,

> The worshipper, like a Roman client, has no compelling hold over the god. Thus we should not be crude about the *do-ut-des* view of ancient religion ('I give so that you may give'), as though the worshipper purchased services from the god. What the worshipper does is seek to win goodwill and credibility by reference to the exchange of service and benefaction in which he has been engaged, much as a rhetorical author might suggest leaning on 'ancestral friendship' at this point.... [A prayer] has only two possible starting points, the actions of the god ... or the actions of the worshipper. It is therefore an argument *a persona*, starting from a person, in which we look at what has been done and said previously, because the present is usually judged on the basis of the past. This then is why the worshipper refers to instances of his own pious deeds—or to the track record of the god in acknowledging that he is worth support. These arguments both have something of the flavour of an *a fortiori* argument....[54]

---

[51] E.g., the slogan found in v. 5 of the poem has more significance because it is placed right after the testimony of deliverance (vv. 1–4).

[52] Robert Burns, "Rhetoric and the Law," in *Companion to Rhetoric and Rhetorical Criticism*, ed. W. Jost and W. Olmsted (Oxford: Blackwell, 2004), 447–50.

[53] Aristotle, *Rhetoric*, I.3.5–6.

[54] Ken Dowden, "Rhetoric and Religion," in *A Companion to Greek Rhetoric*, ed. I. Worthington (Oxford: Blackwell, 2007), 327.

Dowden's point here is that prayer attempts to strengthen the ties between the deity and the worshipper. Since the one praying does not have an extrinsic hold on the deity, he or she often appeals either to how the deity has helped them in the past or to how they have served the deity in the past.

In sum, within the world of the poem, the goal of the poem is to strengthen the ties of the psalmist to Yhwh by demonstrating both that Yhwh has cared for him in the past and by fulfilling the vows he made to Yhwh when in distress. This is accomplished through presenting a testimony in the presence of the worshipping community.

6.5   THE POSSIBLE HISTORICAL SETTINGS/SITUATIONS OF THE PSALM

Because of the anonymous and general nature of the psalm, most scholars have been cautious about identifying any specific person, or type of person as the speaker. Of those that have, there have been three main views. Hossfeld and Zenger argue that the speaker was one of the poor of the land. They state that in this psalm we have an "important witness to the spirituality of the poor."[55] They point to the fact that the psalmist self-describes as one of the פְּתָאיִם, and that he is depicted as "low" or "lowly."[56] In contrast, other interpreters argue that the speaker is envisioned as the king, or a royal personage.[57] The main argument for this view is that the speaker declares that "all people" have assembled for his sacrifice, something "all people" would not do for a common person, certainly not for one of the "poor." Some scholars also point to the simi-

---

[55] Hossfeld and Zenger, *Psalms 3*, 221.

[56] Ibid., 217. The "psalmist" will be referred to generically as "he" throughout this chapter. This is partly for stylistic reasons and also because the psalmist self-describes as an עֶבֶד (v. 16). The feminine equivalent of עֶבֶד would be either אָמָה or שִׁפְחָה.

[57] Dahood, *Psalms III: 101–150*, 145; Eaton, *The Psalms*, 400; and cautiously as a viable option, Goldingay, *Psalms: Psalms 90–150*, 338; Franz Delitzsch, *Biblical Commentary on the Psalms*, vol. 3, trans. F. Bolton (Edinburgh: T&T Clark, 1885), 215; Kirkpatrick, *Book of Psalms*, 687.

larity between the language of this psalm and Hezekiah's thanksgiving after his recovery from sickness as evidence (Isa 38).[58] One final view is that the "I" of the psalm represents the nation as a whole. The "death" that the psalmist was rescued from is the exile.[59]

While certainty is difficult, of the three views, the first is most likely. In addition to the reasons listed above, v. 16 provides further support. This description provided there gives a clue to the psalmist's social status. The same term is used to describe the psalmist in Psalm 86, which is often considered a "poor person's" psalm (Ps 86:16).[60] Additionally, there are other connections between the two psalms. In both psalms, the grace formula is present (Pss 116:5; 86:15); the psalmist pleads to Yhwh (Pss 116:1; 86:6); and the psalmist also affirms his deliverance from death (Pss 116:8; 86:13).[61] This supports Hossfeld and Zenger's contention that "the self-concept of the petitioner in Psalm 116 … is characterized as follows: he is materially and spiritually poor."[62]

It must be admitted that it is unlikely that a materially poor person would have had the time, leisure, or expertise to pen this psalm. Indeed, Karel Van der Toorn has persuasively argued that the psalms were primarily authored by scribes associated with the temple.[63] He states, "the scribes assisted worshippers in their devotional duties, including the recitation of prayers and, if need be, the composition in writing of songs of thanksgiving."[64] While certainty is impossible, Van

---

[58] Eaton, *The Psalms*, 687.

[59] Buttenwieser, *Psalms*, 641.

[60] See the discussion in, Hossfeld and Zenger, *Psalms 3*, 219.

[61] Ibid., 219.

[62] Ibid., *Psalms 3*, 220.

[63] Karel Van der Toorn, *Scribal Culture and the Making of the Hebrew Bible* (Cambridge: Harvard University Press, 2007), 51–108.

[64] Van der Toorn, *Scribal Culture*, 102. He further states more comprehensively, "The prayers and hymns brought together in the Psalter are, for the major part, the work of liturgists with a scribal background…. They are the work of cult specialists trained to translate situations and sentiments into the proper words of prayer and thanksgiving" (118). Van der Toorn's view is similar to and influenced by the work of earlier Psalms scholar Mowinckel, *Psalms in Israel's Worship*, 2:85–103.

der Toorn has made a strong case for probable authorship by temple/Levitical scribes. So, how does our understanding of the speaker as "materially and spiritually poor" comport with the view that the psalm was penned by temple scribes? The answer is that the temple scribes did not think of themselves as authors in anything like a modern conception. The scribe viewed himself as a part of the community and his work served to "express the common values, ideological and artistic, of the scribal community."[65] The dynamic in this psalm, then, would be that authorized temple personnel penned the poem to be used by an individual as a psalm of thanksgiving.

Regarding the setting, commentators are agreed that the imagery behind this psalm places it in the context of corporate worship at the temple, and more specifically in the context of the *tōdāh* sacrifice.[66] Additionally, most commentators affirm that the cause of the thanksgiving is not clear, although that does not prevent some from guessing.[67]

Despite this broad agreement, there has been significant debate as to the actual setting of the psalm. Although commentators agree that the imagery of the psalm is drawn from temple worship, they are not agreed as to whether or not that was the actual setting of the psalm. This is a debate that goes back to Gunkel. The basic question is this: was the psalm written for and primarily used in temple worship?[68] Or,

---

[65] Van der Toorn, *Scribal Culture*, 46.

[66] Weiser's comment is typical, "The psalm…is a thanksgiving which the poet recites in public worship in the presence of the congregation (vv. 5, 14, 18) after his prayer has been granted (v. 6 f., 16) and before he pays his vow (v. 18) and offers the sacrifice of thanksgiving (v. 17). He owes God thanks for delivering him from a danger that threatened his life (vv. 3, 8, 16). It cannot be established for certain whether sickness or persecution (v. 11) was the cause of his affliction." See Artur Weiser, *Psalms*, 719.

[67] The most common suggestion is that the psalmist was sick and has now been healed, see Robert Bratcher and William Reyburn, *A Translator's Handbook on the Book of Psalms* (New York: United Bible Societies, 1991), 978; Barré, "Psalm 116: Its Structure and Its Enigmas," 67. For commentators affirming the ambiguity of the cause of the thanksgiving, see Weiser, *Psalms*, 719; McCann, *Psalms*, 1148; Allen, *Psalms 101–150*, 114; Goldingay, *Psalms: Volume 3*, 340.

[68] So Weiser, *Psalms*, 719; Kraus, *Psalms 60–150*, 386; Samuel Terrien,

did the psalmist utilize imagery from the thanksgiving sacrifice in the temple in order to compose a poem designed for non-cultic/reflective use?[69] If the answer is the latter, then the setting described above of the psalmist joined with the worshipping community in the presence of Yhwh would only be the internal setting of the psalm. The actual setting would be individual or familial use of the psalm apart from the temple. The question then becomes how to discern between these two views. Those who take the former view, tend to understand a temple context as self-evident. The psalm itself discusses fulfilling vows in the presence of the people (vv. 14, 18–19). However, Hossfeld has argued that, "The saturation of the psalm with confessional expressions of trust..., the decline of addresses to YHWH..., and the reflective style, for example, in the self-exhortation (v. 7) or self-questioning (v. 12), force us to speak more of a thanksgiving song drawing on the ritual of a thanksgiving sacrifice."[70] Similarly, Spieckermann states, "Here ritual progression has not guided the formation of the text, but rather the desire to make a particular theological statement."[71] In a summary statement, Hossfeld states, "Psalm 116 is the thanksgiving song of an individual, shaped by borrowing from a ritual thanksgiving sacrifice and reflective statements..."[72] Thus, the primary audience for this psalm is an individual in personal, or familial worship. This view comports with Carleen Mandolfo's understanding of the dynamic between family and state cult.[73] She argues, along with Van der Toorn,

---

The Psalms, 778; Janowski, "Dankbarkeit: Ein anthropologischer Grundbegriff im Spiegel der toda-Psalmen," 99; Allen, *Psalms 101–150*, 114; Mowinckel, *Psalms in Israel's Worship*, 2:32.

[69] So, Hermann Spieckermann, "Lieben und Glauben: Beobachtungen in Psalm 116," in *Meilenstein: Festgabe für Herbert Donner zum 16. Februar 1995*, ed. M. Weippert and S. Timm (Weisbaden: Harrassowitz, 1995), 271–72; Hossfeld and Zenger, *Psalms 3*, 215.

[70] Hossfeld and Zenger, *Psalms 3*, 215.

[71] Spieckermann, "Lieben und Glauben: Beobachtungen in Psalm 116," 272.

[72] Hossfeld and Zenger, *Psalms 3*, 220–21.

[73] Carleen Mandolfo, *God in the Dock: Dialogic Tension in the Psalms of Lament*, JSOTSup 357 (Sheffield: Sheffield Academic, 2002), 150–55.

that "even on the family level, religious activity was conductive to compliance with culturally accepted codes of behavior."[74] Thus, it would not be surprising that temple scribes would write a psalm for the use of individuals/families.[75]

An additional support to Hossfeld and Spieckermann's view is the lack of a traditional call to worship in this psalm. Most of the texts identified by Westermann as declarative praises of the individual have a "call to worship" element.[76] Of the five texts that do not include a call to worship, three of them were clearly not meant for temple worship.[77] This leaves two other psalms that also do not have a call to worship, Pss 138 and 52. The lack of a summons to worship can be under-

---

[74] Mandolofo, *God in the Dock*, 155; Karel Van der Toorn, *Family Religion in Babylonia, Syria and Israel: Continuity and Change in the Forms of Religious* Life, Studies in the History and Culture of the Ancient Near East 7 (Leiden: Brill, 1996), 94.

[75] This idea of a scribe writing a psalm intended for use by an individual can also be seen in Ps 102. There the heading makes clear that it is for individual use even though the psalm mentions Zion and praise in Jerusalem (vv. 13–23). Granted the compositional history of this psalm is complex and debated as is the relationship between the heading and the text of the psalm. However, it demonstrates that, at least early in its reception history, a psalm with a corporate dimension was intended for use by an individual. This usage is paralleled in several Babylonian collections which indicate when a particular lament or thanksgiving poem was to be used, some of them in non-cultic situations. See Gerstenberger, *Psalms: Part 2 and Lamentations*, 211. Gerstenberger states that the dynamic of this psalm, "heralds a special kind of society, perhaps in between family and clan structures and state organization" (211). The setting he proposes for Ps 102 is similar to what I am proposing for Ps 116. Of Ps 102, he states, "The fundamental goal of our prayer is perseverance of Yahweh and the Zion community under adverse conditions.... The individual complaint of familial tradition is considered a proven *tĕpillāh* that may be used in the entreaty before God. It will fortify each individual member of the congregation, and will help to undergird praise and prayer of the community itself" (215).

[76] See Ps 30:4; 40:16; 66:1-2 107:1–2, 8, 15, 21–22, 31–32; 118:1–4. One could technically argue with Ps 66:1–2 since Westermann only categorizes Ps 66:13–20 as the declarative praise of the individual. But the fact that it is included as a part of Ps 66, which has a clear call to worship at the beginning of the psalm makes the call to worship an integral part of that poem. See Westermann, *Praise and Lament*, 102.

[77] Jonah 2:2–9; Lam 3:51–58; Job 33:26–28. In fact, these texts can be understood as utilizing the declarative praise of the individual form for their own ends.

stood in both of these psalms based on their implied audience.[78] As will be discussed below, there is a type of call to praise in this psalm (vv. 7, 13–15), but its highly personal nature reinforces the individual/familial context of the psalm. Thus, the fact that the congregation is not summoned to join in the psalmist's thanksgiving is an additional support that the poem was intended for personal/familial use.

It must be admitted that there is some ambiguity in regard to the context of this psalm. Strong cases have been made for both a temple and a personal/familial context for this poem. In my view, the evidence of the poem itself as articulated by Hossfeld and Spieckermann convince me that the personal/familial use of the poem is likely correct and my rhetorical analysis will assume this context. However, one could also analyze this psalm from a public/corporate worship context and come up with a somewhat different rhetorical function. The goal of this study is to demonstrate the value of a rhetorical analysis for praise psalms. It does not eliminate all ambiguities with regard to setting. The same rhetorical tools could profitably be utilized to analyze the psalm from a corporate worship setting if one disagrees with my analysis of the actual setting.

6.6   ANALYSIS OF THE ARGUMENT OF THE PSALM: ITS EXTERNAL ARGUMENT

6.6.1   RHETORICAL STRUCTURE

Although there have been a few different proposals on the poetic structure of Ps 116,[79] the language of the psalm supports understanding it in two parts, each part is comprised of two strophes.[80] Michael Barré has

---

[78] In Ps 138, the poet only addresses Yhwh throughout. In Ps 52, the poet addresses his enemy throughout.

[79] E.g., some understand the poem as composed of two strophes (vv. 1–11 / vv. 12–10) (e.g., Hossfeld and Zenger, *Psalms 3*, 216); others view it as comprised of eight strophes in two "halves," (e.g., J. P. Fokkelman, *Major Poems of the Hebrew Bible: At the Interface of Prosody and Structural Analysis. Volume 3: The Remaining 65 Psalms*, SSN 47 [Assen: Van Gorcum, 2003, 227).

[80] E.g., Kirkpatrick, *Book of Psalms*, 687; Barré, "Psalm 116: Its Structure and Its Enigmas," 61–78; Terrien, *Psalms*, 775–77.

written the most cogent defense of this position, and his proposal is outlined as follows:[81]

Part I (vv. 1–9)
    Strophe 1 (vv. 1–4): Description of the plight and petition
    Strophe 2 (vv. 5–9): Description of salvation and resolve
Part II (vv. 10–19)
    Strophe 3 (vv. 10–14): Commitment to thanks God
    Strophe 4 (vv. 15–19): Thanks offered

Barré's proposal is supported by numerous linguistic and semantic features of the psalm and is accepted here. However, the rhetorical structure is a bit different than the poetic structure, which is outlined below:[82]

Figure 3

Reason for Thanksgiving	v. 1:	Testimony-God has heard plea
	v. 2:	Testimony-God has heard plea
	v. 3:	Testimony-Narrative of plight
	v. 4:	Testimony-Narration of petition
	v. 5:	Maxim-Character of Yhwh
	v. 6:	Testimony-Description of salvation
Call to Thanksgiving/	v. 7:	Call to worship
Reasons for Thanksgiving	v. 8:	Summary of deliverance
	v. 9:	Psalmist resolves to walk before Yhwh
Reason for Thanksgiving	v. 10:	Testimony-Faith in God vs. self
	v. 11:	Testimony-Faith in God vs. humans

---

[81] Barré, "Psalm 116: Its Structure and Its Enigmas," *JBL* (1990): 78.

[82] In figure 3 I have listed each verse on a separate line. The reason for this is so that you can visually see the amount of text devoted to different aspects of the psalm, thus discerning emphasis.

Call to Thanksgiving	v. 12:	Question to self
Reasons for Thanksgiving	v. 13:	Answer
	v. 14:	Answer
	v. 15:	Maxim-Character of Yhwh
	v. 16:	Testimony-Description of Salvation
	v. 17:	Resolve to sacrifice
	v. 18:	Resolve to fulfill vows
	v. 19:	Resolve to fulfill vows

Both structures agree on a major break between vv. 9 and 10. However, there are differences in the structures at a smaller level. This should not be surprising. The poetic structure is concerned with features other than the argumentative structure. Thus, it is possible poetically to have a break in strophes between vv. 4 and 5, yet pragmatically v. 5 continues to give an additional reason, or grounding for giving thanks. In my analysis of the poem, I will outline it according to the poetic structure, but the discussion of the argument of the poem will be informed by the rhetorical structure given in figure 3. Understanding the psalm through both poetic and rhetorical lenses is vital for grasping how it functioned persuasively for an audience of near-contemporaries.

If the analysis of the historical setting of the psalm is correct, this psalm was composed for the use of individuals or families in their worship. The primary goal of this poem would be to encourage the individual to participate in cultic life. That is, the poet models for the auditor the proper response to answered prayer. In doing this, the poet instills the value of corporate worship for the auditor. The poet instills this value through narrating an answered prayer/deliverance and a proper response to that deliverance. Thus, this poem in its actual setting should be seen as a type of epideictic rhetoric. Aristotle stated that epideictic rhetoric was concerned with praise or blame.[83] Perelman and Olbrechts-Tyteca have argued that in addition to assigning praise or blame, epideictic rhetoric serves an essential role in affirming and

---

[83] Aristotle, *Rhetoric*, I.9.

deepening adherence to cultural values.[84] The values concerning who God is are deepened primarily in the "reason for thanksgiving" sections, while the "call to thanksgiving" sections primarily model how to respond to God. Yet, in this psalm the two sections are not so easily divided since the "call to thanksgiving" sections include additional reasons for thanksgiving. This is different than some praise psalms, which only include a call to praise (e.g., Ps 134; 150), or psalms where the call to praise and the reason for praise is more evenly divided (e.g., Ps 146). In fact, the ratio between the call to praise and the reason for praise could give a clue as to the *kairos* of the psalm, or the "speaker's immediate stance toward God and to the community as well as his or her goals for the way the relationship should be."[85] This possibility will be discussed at length in the next chapter.

6.6.2 RHETORICAL ANALYSIS: THE EXTERNAL ARGUMENT

The goal of the psalmist is to instill in the worshipper an understanding of who God is and of what the proper response to God should be when prayer has been answered. The primary way in which the author of the psalm achieves this goal is through encouraging the hearer/user to enter into the implied world of the psalm. That is, the hearer/user of the psalm would envision themselves as the "I" of the psalm. This would enable the hearer/user to see themselves inside the fictive scenario of the poem as reciting this testimony as their testimony before the worshipping community.[86] Even if one is far from the temple, this psalm

---

[84] Perelman and Olbrechts-Tyteca, *New Rhetoric*, 122–23.

[85] Davida Charney, "Maintaining Innocence Before a Divine Hearer: Deliberative Rhetoric in Psalm 22, Psalm 17, and Psalm 7," *BibInt* 21 (2013): 40.

[86] Harold Fisch discusses the dynamic between the 'I' of the psalmist and the 'I' of the worshipper in this way, "We have the cry of an 'I' that calls out to, and is answered by, the 'I' of the reader. 'Bless the Lord, O my soul' – a phrase read and re-read by thousands every day—becomes their words, the expression of their individuality on each and every occasion of reading or singing. It is in a sense written anew for every new context and occasion, remaining at all times sociolect and idiolect, and individual cry and collective affirmation..." (Harold Fisch, *Poetry with a Purpose: Biblical Poetics and Interpretation* [Bloomington: Indiana University Press, 1988], 118). What Fisch does not specifically discuss is how this interplay between the "I" of the psalmist

encourages the user to envision themselves as participating in a cultic ritual, thereby reinforcing the value of communal worship. This is a powerful way to deepen the values and behaviors the author wants to instill. Nevertheless, the author still uses a number of rhetorical devices to help make the poem more engaging and suasive to the user/hearer.

The rhetorical center of gravity for this psalm comes in vv. 13–14, 17–18. The goal of the poet is to instill the value of cultic worship including fulfilling vows. Undoubtedly, an audience of near-contemporaries would have agreed that fulfilling vows one made to Yhwh is a vital task. Thus, the psalmist is not trying to instill values or practices an audience of near contemporaries would resist. Rather, the psalmist is deepening adherence to the cultural value of corporate worship.[87] The fact that this is the rhetorical goal of the poem can be demonstrated a couple of different ways. One is through repetition. Verse 18 is a verbatim repetition of verse 14 and v. 17b is a repetition of v. 13b.

Additionally, while v. 13a and v. 17a are not verbally parallel, they are conceptually parallel. Lifting the cup of salvation (v. 13a) is a cultic act similar to offering a thanksgiving sacrifice (v. 17a), indeed they may be part of the same ritual. The repetition between these two elements in vv. 13–14/17–18 give a heightened sense of presence to the concept of fulfilling vows through public cultic act.[88] Moreover, repetition is one of the earliest devices and is utilized in every culture as one of the primary indicators of rhetorical emphasis.[89] Also demonstrating emphasis on vv. 13–14/17–18 is the fact that these verses are set up through a question and answer format (v. 12).

By asking the question, "What will I return to Yhwh for all of his benefits to me?" the psalmist is drawing attention to the answer (vv. 13–14), which gets repeated (vv. 17–18). Thus, there is a double emphasis on the content of these verses. One final argument for the

---

and the "I" of the worshipper functions as a suasive device.

[87] Perelman and Olbrechts-Tyteca, *New Rhetoric*, 48–49.

[88] Ibid., 175.

[89] Kennedy, *Comparative Rhetoric*, 4, 14, 104.

focus on these verses is from the narrative implied in the poem. Kenneth Burke stated that the rhetorical function of a poem could be determined by "dramatically showing how that motive *ended*: the maturity or fulfillment of a motive, its 'perfection' or 'finishedness'...The depicting of a thing's *end* may be a dramatic way of identifying its *essence*."[90] This poem tells a fairly simple story: the psalmist was in deep, life-threatening trouble, he cried out to Yhwh and made vows to him, Yhwh delivered him, now the psalmist has a responsibility to publicly fulfill those vows. More space is given to describe the final movement in the psalm. With the psalmist fulfilling his vows, the narrative will have come to its "perfection," or final point. It is this final movement that is described in vv. 13–14, 17–18.

6.6.3   PART ONE: VV. 1–9

Strophe 1: vv. 1–4

The first two verses introduce the psalm by narrating the story of the poem in condensed form. The opening verb gives the result, the psalmist now loves Yhwh. The two כִּי clauses give the reason for this outcome in ABAB form.

> The Psalmist loves Yhwh:
> | A | For (כִּי) Yhwh has heard |
> | B | his voice/pleading |
> | A' | For (כִּי) Yhwh inclined his ear |
> | B' | when he called out |

The opening *qātal* verb has been the cause of some discussion.[91] De-

---

[90] Burke, *Rhetoric of Motives*, 14–15.

[91] Most commentators have noted this verb form as unusual in Ps 116 and tried to make sense of it. For example, Terrien states, "the cry 'I love' without a direct object reveals the absolute degree of the psalmist's passion for His God" (*Psalms*, 777). Gerstenberger calls this introductory verb "odd," says that it "does not make sense," and is "rare" and states that its function must be "to call attention to Yhwh's audience" (*Psalms: Part 2 and Lamentations*, 292); see the extended discussion in §6.2 fn. 3

clarative praise psalms of the individual are said to generally begin with a non-indicative statement like, "I will extol you" or "I give you thanks," linguistically marked by a *yiqtōl* verb.[92] However, after examining the first word of each declarative praise of the individual, one is struck by the diversity of expression:

Figure 4

Psalm 18	definite article + demonstrative pronoun
Psalm 30	*yiqtōl*
Psalm 34	*yiqtōl*
Psalm 40	infinitive absolute/adverbial infinitive
Psalm 52	interrogative pronoun
Psalm 66:13	*yiqtōl*
Psalm 107	imperative
Psalm 116	*qātal*
Psalm 118	imperative
Psalm 138	*yiqtōl*
Jonah 2	*qātal*

Thus, while the *yiqtōl* is the most common introduction, it is by no means standard. Additionally, the fact that אהב is a quasi-stative would make it more akin to *yiqtōl* than other *qātal* verbs.[93] More to the point would be to state that this type of psalm does something at the beginning to capture and focus the reader/user's attention. Perelman and Olbrechts-Tyteca discuss how grammatical substitution of tense, or unusual grammatical constructions in general, can create a sense of presence and bring focus to a discourse.[94] If one studies psalms which open with a *qātal* verb, it becomes clear that the verb functions to em-

---

[92] This point is made both by Westermann, *Praise and Lament*, 102 and Gunkel and Begrich, *Introduction to the Psalms*, 201. Although, Gunkel also includes imperatives and jussives because his category of "individual thanksgiving song" is more expanded than Westermann's category "declarative praise of the individual."

[93] On the term "quasi-stative," see §6.2 fn. 3.

[94] They call this "grammatical enallage" (Perelman and Olbrechts-Tyteca, *New Rhetoric*, 177).

phasize the following clause, or the implied object of the verb.[95] For example, Ps 14:1, the verb אָמַר focuses attention on the speech of the fool, which is quoted in the second half of the line. Or, in Ps 122:1, the verb שָׂמַחְתִּי focuses attention on the cause of the rejoicing given in the second half of the line. Similarly in this psalm, the verb אָהַבְתִּי focuses attention on the cause of the love the psalmist feels. This is a rather striking introduction and perhaps necessary because of how common the confession that "Yhwh hears" is in the Psalter (E.g., Pss 4:4; 6:9, 10; 34:7, 18; 69:34; 78:21).[96] Something needs to be done to highlight this particular act of hearing. Both the *qātal* verb introducing the statement and the double object (קוֹלִי תַּחֲנוּנָי) serve to keep the sentiment from lapsing into a cliché.[97]

After the opening (vv. 1–2), the psalmist narrates his plight (v. 3) and call for help (v. 4). These verses vividly narrate the plight of the psalmist in the format of a testimony. In this context, the testimony of the psalmist functions like an illustration. Rhetoricians since Aristotle have carefully distinguished between an illustration and an example. An example is particular case, or situation, from which one can support an argument for a general rule. However, an illustration is used to "strengthen adherence to a known and accepted rule, by providing particular instances which clarify the general statement, show applications, and increase its presence to the consciousness."[98] The "known and accepted rule" in this case would be that Yhwh is gracious and compassionate (v. 5), a God who hears the cries of his

---

[95] Six other psalms begin with a *qātal* verb: Ps 14/53, 39, 45, 75, 85, 122.

[96] Indeed, the deity "hearing" the petitioner is a stock ANE image. Keel describes an Egyptian memorial stone which a worshipper erected after the god (Amon-Re) answered a prayer. The stele has the name of the deity and then right below the name are two large ears representing the fact that Amon-Re had heard the petition (*Symbolism of the Biblical World*, 192).

[97] Shorthand, or stock language can build adherence and communion between the speaker and audience, but if the hearer/reader recognizes it as a rhetorical device it becomes a cliché and loses its power, see Perelman and Olbrechts-Tyteca, *New Rhetoric*, 165.

[98] Ibid., 357.

people. Since the psalmist is not trying to prove this point, but rather to strengthen adherence to it, it functions illustratively.

Perelman and Olbrechts-Tyteca state that for an illustration to "create presence" it will "have to be developed with a wealth of concrete and vivid detail."[99] Additionally, illustrations should be chosen for their "affective impact."[100] While this psalm does not have a long narrative of the distress and salvation of the poet, it does detail psalmist's plight in a long tricolon. This tricolon consists of powerful images designed to appeal to the emotion and imagination of the hearers. In v. 3 the psalmist pictures himself like prey caught unaware by Death. It is "as if death were a hunter throwing ropes over his prey."[101] The actual plight of the psalmist is not described, but the vivid imagery leaves no doubt that the psalmist was in mortal danger. The psalmist creates the feeling of terror, helplessness, and surprise through personifying Death as a hunter stalking and binding him. The tricolon ends with an unexpected twist. The root מצא is used twice in this line with different agents. In the second colon, the *snares of Sheol* have found (מצא) the psalmist. In the third colon, the *psalmist* has found (מצא) "need and grief." At first glance this seems ambiguous, who found whom? This ambiguity creates the possibility of double causation. Viewed from one angle, the distress found the psalmist. From another angle, it is also possible to say that the psalmist had a role in creating his own plight. This nuance would keep the hearer/reader from possibly raising objections based on a strict sense of the retribution principle.[102] In this sense, the third colon serves as a type of prolepsis.[103] It also brings an authenticity to the plight. The vagueness of the causation makes the

---

[99] Ibid., 358.

[100] Ibid., 360.

[101] Goldingay, *Psalms: Psalms 90–150*, 341. See also the discussion concerning the plight of the psalmist above at §6.4.2.

[102] On the "retribution principle," see John Walton, "Retribution," in *Dictionary of the Old Testament: Wisdom, Poetry and Writings*, ed. T. Longman and P. Enns (Downers Grove: IVP Academic, 2008), 647–55.

[103] Lanham, *Handlist of Rhetorical Terms*, 120–21.

plight seem true to life.[104] While the difficulty seemed to come as a surprise making the psalmist feel like a victim, he realizes that he could have had some role in creating the situation.

In this desperate situation, the psalmist calls out to Yhwh (v. 4). Like most thanksgiving psalms and laments, the psalmist does not describe any steps he took to resolve the plight himself. Indeed, the way the plight was described makes a human solution impossible. Rather, the psalmist simply calls upon Yhwh in the imperative mood. It is this calling upon Yhwh that makes the thanksgiving possible. The correlation between the psalmist's request and the deliverance makes thanks to Yhwh necessary.

Strophe 2: vv. 5–9

The second strophe completes the testimony by narrating the psalmist's deliverance, it concludes with a call to the psalmist to act based on what Yhwh has done (vv. 7–9). There is an abrupt shift in the poem in v. 4. This is strikingly different than other declarative psalms of the individual, most of which have either a response from God, or a more extended narration of deliverance, or both.[105] Here, after narrating the plight as one of mortal danger, the psalmist shifts to discuss the nature of Yhwh through a maxim. As discussed in the chapter on Ps 103, maxims are powerful shaping forces in a culture.[106]

Additionally, stating that Yhwh is gracious and compassionate serves an important rhetorical function. One of the main reasons why we label people with particular traits is because the stability of a person is never fully assured. Thus, labeling a person with certain traits is a "linguistic technique…to stress the impression of permanency."[107] By declaring that Yhwh is righteous, gracious, and compassionate, the worshipper understands that Yhwh is not completely free or spontane-

---

[104] Perelman and Olbrechts-Tyteca, *New Rhetoric*, 134–35.

[105] See Ps 18:7–19; 30:11; 34:7, 15–22; 40:7; 52:5; 107:7, 10, 14, 16, 20, 29, 33–41; 118:7–18; 138:3, 7–8; Jon 2:6–7. The one other psalm that similarly has no narration of the deliverance or of God's response is Ps 66:19.

[106] See the discussion of maxims in 4.5.2

[107] Perelman and Olbrechts-Tyteca, *New Rhetoric*, 294.

ous in his response to the world. His actions are driven by his attributes. They give "cohesion and significance" to his past and future acts.[108] Thus, Yhwh's deliverance of the psalmist give further evidence of his character, but his character also serves as grounds for his deliverance.[109]

Verse 6 continues the narration of the deliverance, but the emphasis is not on the act of deliverance, but on the character of Yhwh revealed through the deliverance. Describing Yhwh's deliverance (v. 6) as a result of his "compassion" (v. 5) further reinforces the psalmist's belief that Yhwh is a compassionate God. The interplay between a person's act and essence is a powerful way to create an image, or a perspective on a person that can color the way one views all their acts.[110] Thus, by stating that Yhwh's deliverance was not just one of the acts of Yhwh, but that it flows out of his very essence shapes the hearer/reader's understanding of who Yhwh is. Additionally, the psalmist confesses that Yhwh saves the naïve (פְּתָאיִם) and the lowly (דלל). This further proves Yhwh's compassionate nature, but it also serves as a kind of *a fortiori* argument. If Yhwh's saves even the naïve and lowly, how much more is he likely to act for the hearer/reader of the psalm?

Verses 7–9 shift from the testimony to the response of the psalmist. These verses contain two resolutions of the psalmist (vv. 7a, 9), each grounded in additional reasons (vv. 7b, 8) arranged in a chiastic structure:

> Response of Psalmist (v. 7a)
> כִּי – Reason (v. 7b)
> כִּי – Reason (v. 8)
> Response of Psalmist (v. 9)

---

[108] Ibid., 295.

[109] Most commentators see only half of this relationship; e.g., Goldingay argues, "More literally, the worshipper has called out *in* Yhwh's name. The psalm will use that expression twice more for proclaiming Yhwh's name (vv. 13, 17). Here, too, it suggests proclaiming who Yhwh is, and therefore urging Yhwh to act in light of the revelation expressed by the name" (*Psalms: Psalms 90–150*, 341).

[110] Perelman and Olbrechts-Tyteca, *New Rhetoric*, 327–31.

In v. 7, the psalmist commands his נֶפֶשׁ to "return to your rest."[111] The imperative mood foregrounds the presence of this activity.[112] This command is further emphasized through alliteration.[113]

There is a debate concerning the referent of "rest." That is, what was the psalmist calling himself to do? Hossfeld and Zenger argue that "rest" here should be construed as the temple,

> *Rest* is not only to be understood as a spiritual or mental condition. What is meant is certainly a *place* of rest, which is the opposite of *Sheol* (v. 3), perhaps in close relation to the *lands of the living* (v. 9b). In view of the close parallels in Pss 23:2, 6 and 95:11 an association with an ultimate place of rest, the Temple, is possible."[114]

While the "temple" as the ultimate rest in view is plausible, it is significant that the temple is not mentioned directly at this point in the psalm.[115] The very fact that it is described indirectly could enhance the overall argument of the psalm. Perelman and Olbrechts-Tyteca muse, "there are also less direct methods of insisting on a point: one wonders whether one of the benefits resulting from the obscurity of certain texts is not that it quickens the attention; 'presence of mind' confers presence on what the writer desires to communicate."[116] That is, the cryptic reference to the temple actually brings it to the fore more powerfully for those who understand it. Thus, the allusion to the temple sets up the rhetorical goal of the poem admirably (vv. 13–14; 17–18). The command to return to rest would be another way of saying, "partici-

---

[111] For the rhetorical function of commanding one's נֶפֶשׁ, see above §4.5.2.

[112] Perelman and Olbrechts-Tyteca, *New Rhetoric*, 158.

[113] שׁוּבִי נַפְשִׁי לִמְנוּחָיְכִי כִּי יְהוָה גָּמַל עָלָיְכִי

[114] Hossfeld and Zenger, *Psalms 3*, 218. So also Goldingay, *Psalms: Volume 3*, 34. Contra, Kraus, *Psalms 60–150*, 387. For the temple as a place of rest, see Jon Levenson, *Creation and the Persistence of Evil: The Jewish Drama of Divine Omnipotence* (San Francisco: Harper & Row, 1988), 78–79.

[115] Janowski, "Dankbarkeit," 110.

[116] Perelman and Olbrechts-Tyteca, *New Rhetoric*, 145.

pate in cultic life." However, by focusing on the temple as a place of rest, the benefit of worship, not the obligation is foregrounded.

The command (v. 7a) and the resolution to "walk before Yhwh (v. 9) are given two further motivating clauses (v. 7b, 8). Both כִּי clauses cover the same content, Yhwh's deliverance of the psalmist. The first is abbreviated in which the psalmist reminds his soul that Yhwh has treated him well (גמל). This comports well with the reference to the temple. Since Yhwh has treated the psalmist well, the psalmist likewise should treat Yhwh well by fulfilling cultic duties. But it is not a direct command, or statement yet. This verse hints at the main rhetorical goal of the poem, which is yet to come.

Verse 8 gives the most detailed description of the psalmist deliverance in the poem. There is a shift from talking about Yhwh in the third person to addressing Yhwh directly in the second person. Through a repetition of מָוֶת (v. 3a, 8), the psalmist describes how Yhwh has rescued him from the "chords of death," which had entrapped him. He is now free to return to his "rest." The second colon utilizes accumulation, which is a type of repetition. This is a vital rhetorical device because emotion is appealed to through specific details. As Richard Whately illustrates, Shakespeare in *Julius Caesar* does not just refer to the conspirators as those who "killed Caesar," but as those "whose daggers have stabbed Caesar."[117] Similarly, the psalmist here does not simply say that Yhwh delivered him, but that Yhwh delivered "my נֶפֶשׁ from death, my eye from tear(s), my foot from stumbling" (v. 8). Just as the psalmist vividly described his plight in three phrases to arouse the emotion of fear and dread (v. 3), here he vividly describes his salvation in three phrases emphasizing the relief and joy of his salvation (v. 8).

The description of how Yhwh has saved the soul, eye, and foot of the psalmist well establishes the resolution to "walk before Yhwh in the land of the living" (v. 9). The phrase to "walk before Yhwh" is an allusion back to the piety of the patriarchs.[118] An allusion is a rhetori-

---

[117] Whately, *Elements of Rhetoric*, 195.

[118] Gen 17:1; 24:40; 48:15. The phrase in each of these texts is a hitpael

cal device which creates communion between the hearer and the referent.[119] The worshipper is encouraged to understand their worship in
continuity with the founders of the nation. Additionally, the phrase
בְּאַרְצוֹת הַחַיִּים could be a reference to the temple.[120] If that is the case,
then vv. 7 and 9 are semantically parallel. Both verses are indirect references to faithfully fulfill cultic obligations at the temple.

In sum, the first half of the poem is comprised mostly of reasons for thanksgiving in the form of testimony. Added to this are two
indirect references to the psalmist resolving to participate in the cultic
life of Israel.

6.6.4 PART TWO: VV. 10–19

Strophe 3: vv. 10–14

In this strophe, the psalmist begins by giving testimony of a
different kind followed up by a transition to the rhetorical focus of the
psalm, a question and beginning of an answer, which will continue into the following strophe.

The testimony narrated in vv. 10–11 begins in a structurally
parallel way to vv. 1–2. Both have a first-person singular *qātal* + כִּי +
yiqtōl. However, instead of narrating the plea and Yhwh's response,
the psalmist narrates the reasons why he trusted in Yhwh.[121] The

---

form of הלך followed by the prepositional phrase "before Yhwh."

[119] Perelman and Olbrechts-Tyteca, *New Rhetoric*, 177.

[120] Michael L. Barré, "'*rṣ (h)hyym* – 'The Land of the Living'," *JSOT* 41
(1988): 40–59. The same phrase is used in Ps 27:13 as a clear reference to the temple, so also Ps 52:7. Barré points out that in this passage, the "land of the living" is in
parallel to "before Yhwh" (46).

[121] There has been some confusion as to the best way to understand these
verses. Some translations take the כִּי (v. 10) as concessive (ESV, NRSV) others take
it as temporal (NASB). While these are grammatically possible, taken either of these
ways it is difficult to understand the logic of the poem. It is better to take the כִּי here
the same way it is taken in v. 1 as causal (KJV, NIV2011). This view is forcibly argued by Barré, "Psalm 116: Its Structure and Its Enigmas," 74–75. The reason the
psalmist trusted in Yhwh is because he was "very wretched," thus he could not help
himself; and everyone else was untrustworthy, Yhwh was the only option left.

psalmist declares that he believed in Yhwh because he had no other
choice. He was helpless in himself and no other human was reliable
either. In other words, Yhwh was the only source of hope left. Thus,
the psalmist had to either trust in Yhwh or despair. The psalmist makes
this point through self-quotation. He had said, "I am very wretched"[122]
and "all people are liars." These lines function as an argument by *expeditio*. That is, "the device of setting out numbered options and then
eliminating all but the one preferred."[123] This is also another way of
narrating how desperate the plight was.

The psalmist does not need to narrate the deliverance in this
part of the poem. It can be assumed from the first strophe. Rather, at
this point the poem shifts to its rhetorical focus. This is set up through
a question and answer format (vv. 12, 13–14). Asking a question and
then answering it is an ancient rhetorical device.[124] The function of the
device here is to highlight the answer (vv. 13–14).

Additionally, the question connects back to v. 7. Both v. 7 and
12 use contain the root words שׁוב, גמל, יהוה, and the preposition עַל.
Thus, of the seven words of v. 7 and the six words of v. 12, four of
them are shared. This strengthens the view espoused earlier that "rest"
is a reference to cultic participation. The command in v. 7 gets further
clarified by the question and answer in vv. 12–14.

The answer given in vv. 13–14 is striking for its detail. Scholars have long noted the lack of references to cultic acts in the Psalter.[125] Thus, it is unusual for the psalmist to describe a ritual at all,
which brings additional emphasis to this part of the poem. The psalmist does not just say that he will make a sacrifice, but states, "A cup of
salvation, I will lift." The detail makes the act more prominent. As Perelman and Olbrechts-Tyteca state, "To create emotion, it is essential

---

[122] ענה appears in the qal only 5x in the Hebrew Bible and has the nuance of
being helpless, or "wretched, emaciated…suffering" (*HALOT*, 852).

[123] Jeanne Fahnestock, *Rhetorical Style: The Uses of Language in Persuasion* (Oxford: Oxford University Press, 2011), 386.

[124] Ibid., 299; Lanham, *Handlist of Rhetorical Terms*, 87.

[125] E.g., Gunkel and Begrich, *Introduction to the Psalms*, 13; Keel, *Symbolism of the Biblical World*, 324.

to be specific."[126] Culturally, it is clear that the cup is not lifted to drink, but to be poured out as an offering to God (e.g., Gen 35:14; Num 28:7).[127] Additionally, v. 13 connects back to v. 4. The phrase וּבְשֵׁם יְהוָה אֶקְרָא is repeated in both lines. In the former, the psalmist's call was a plea for help. In the latter use, the call is a declaration of salvation. The identical language draws the two acts together. The first half of the psalm focuses on the testimony of the psalmist (vv. 1–9), the second half focuses on the act of the thanksgiving ritual (vv. 10–19). By connecting the two halves linguistically and semantically, the poet has created an association between the two events, the deliverance and the thanksgiving sacrifice. This is a quasi-logical argument whose function is to persuade the hearer/user that when a deliverance occurs, it should be understood as from Yhwh and therefore a thanksgiving sacrifice is necessary.[128] This first statement of the psalmist's resolve to offer a thanksgiving sacrifice concludes with a note that it will be a public act (v. 14b).

Strophe 4: vv. 15–19

The final strophe of the poem is signaled by an abrupt shift to a nominal sentence (v. 15) parallel to the shift earlier in the poem (v. 5). It also functions as a maxim designed to give a further rationale to thank Yhwh and as a justification for the salvation he provided. This maxim is followed up by one final narration of deliverance (v. 16), which serves as the grounds for the final resolution to offer thanksgiving.

There has been some debate concerning the meaning of v. 15. However, this debate is mostly due to an inaccurate translation in English. Most English translations follow the KJV and read something like the following: "Precious in the sight of the LORD is the death of his saints."[129] The implication with these translations is that the death of a

---

[126] Perelman and Olbrechts-Tyteca, *New Rhetoric*, 147.

[127] See Goldingay, *Psalms: Psalms 90–150*, 345.

[128] On association as a quasi-logical argument, see Perelman and Olbrechts-Tyteca, *New Rhetoric*, 191.

[129] So also NIV84/2011, ESV, NRSV, NASB, NJB, NCV, and HCSB. This tradition of translation goes back to the LXX, which translates יָקָר as τίμιος. Jerome's

saint is somehow viewed positively by Yhwh. The problem with this is
that it seems to go against the grain of the entire psalm. This psalm is
thanking God for deliverance from death. In light of this difficulty,
Barré has proposed an emendation for the word הַמָּוְתָה. He argues, "this
word has suffered a simple, minor corruption—namely the loss of one
letter. It should be read hm<n>wth, that is, hēmānûtāh, the well-
attested Aramaic word for "trust, faith(fullness)."[130] Thus, the line
would read, "Precious in the sight of Yhwh is the faithfulness of his
devoted ones." However, we need not resort to emendation, revocalization, and importation of a word from another language to solve this
difficulty. It is better to understand the word יָקָר as denoting "costly."
That is, the death of a saint is grievous to Yhwh, thus serving as a motivation for his help.[131]

The shift to a null-copula clause has a rhetorical impact.
Phrases of this kind are, "an effort to make a statement timeless and, in
consequence, beyond the limits of subjectivity and bias."[132] It states
something about the nature of Yhwh. Yhwh views the death of his
faithful ones as having a high price, thus serving as a motivation for
the deliverance of the psalmist. At the same time, the use of the root
יָקָר is also significant. Since the term does normally denote something
good,[133] one has to disassociate that connotation of the word when
used here. This makes it a type of irony, or as Fokkelman puts it, an
oxymoron.[134] In this context, the phrase could have multiple functions.
At the most basic level, an ironic statement, "requires a certain collu-

---

Psalt. Hebr. similarly reads gloriosa whereas the V more accurately reads pretiosa.

[130] Barré, "Psalm 116: Its Structure and Its Enigmas," 72. His view is en-
dorsed by Gerstenberger, Psalms: Part 2 and Lamentations, 294–95.

[131] See Goldingay, Psalms: Volume 3, 346; McCann, Psalms, 1149; Terri-
en, Psalms, 778; Kraus, Psalms 60–150, 388–89; Hossfeld and Zenger, Psalms 3,
219; John A. Emerton, "How does the Lord Regard the Death of His Saints in Psalm
116:15," JTS 34 (1983): 146–56.

[132] Perelman and Olbrechts-Tyteca, New Rhetoric, 182.

[133] E.g., the "word of Yhwh" (1 Sam 3:1), precious stones (Job 28:16; 2
Sam 12:30; 2 Chron 20:2), or the חֶסֶד of Yhwh (Ps 36:8)

[134] Fokkelman, Major Poems of the Hebrew Bible, 320.

sion between the rhetor and at least one audience member" and "can create social cohesion."[135] It could also have a deeper significance. Perelman and Olbrechts-Tyteca point out that irony can be a way of refuting a view that has currency.[136] Thus, it is possible that the poem was written in a situation where some did believe that the death of a saint was a noble thing. If so, by making this statement in the context of this psalm, which clearly proves the opposite, the belief that death could be viewed positively appears ridiculous.[137] Nevertheless, this is only a possibility and the psalm would have to be dated quite late for this to occur. Either way, the noun-phrase does ground the salvation of the psalmist in the very nature of Yhwh, as in v. 5.

Verse 16 again narrates the deliverance of the psalmist. The final *qātal* verb phrase simply states, "you released my bonds." This connects the deliverance back to v. 3, where the psalmist was in bondage. However, the emphasis on this verse comes in the first nine words. The phrase עַבְדֶּךָ אֲנִי is twice repeated with the addition בֶּן־אֲמָתֶךָ appended after the second phrase. Thus, in a line that narrates the salvation of the psalmist, the emphasis is clearly on the status of the psalmist as a servant of Yhwh. As stated earlier this would both highlight the speaker's lowly position and his close connection to Yhwh.[138] Additionally, it would remind the speaker/user of the obligation a servant has to a lord, thus supporting the rhetorical goal of the poem, which comes in the following verses (vv. 17–18). The emphasis on the status of the speaker supports the view that the poem was written for personal/reflective use and its goal was to model for the hearer/user the appropriate response to answered prayer.

Verses 17–18 again rehearse the psalmists resolve to participate in cultic life through offering a thanksgiving sacrifice thus fulfilling his vows. This resolve has been supported through the testimony of God's acts (vv. 1–4; 6; 8; 10–11; 16) grounded in God's very

---

[135] Fahnestock, *Rhetorical Style*, 116.

[136] Perelman and Olbrechts-Tyteca, *New Rhetoric*, 411–15.

[137] Ibid., 206.

[138] §6.4.1

nature (vv. 5; 15) and through describing the psalmist's position before Yhwh (vv. 6; 16). The repetition of the phrase וּבְשֵׁם יְהוָה אֶקְרָא functions, as it did in v. 13, to draw the two halves of the psalm together. Also repeated is the phrase נֶגְדָה־נָּא לְכָל־עַמּוֹ (cf. v. 14, "in the presence of all his people"). The public nature of this thanksgiving sacrifice gets amplified in v. 19. The combination of amplification and repetition gives presence to the rhetorical goal of the poem, to encourage the hearer/user to participate in cultic life.[139] Also adding to the emphatic nature of these final verses is the use of apostrophe. The psalmist earlier speaks to his own נֶפֶשׁ (v. 7) while speaking about Yhwh in the third person.[140] In this verse, he shifts to addressing Yhwh directly. In v. 19, the psalmist addresses the city of Jerusalem directly. In both of these uses of apostrophe, the psalmist declares to the new audience that he will fulfill his vows/sacrifice. This device has two functions. First, it is an "interactional device" arousing emotion and creating a sense of community between the audience and the addressee.[141] It also serves here to create a type of accountability. By the speaker declaring that he will fulfill his vows directly to Yhwh and the worshipping community, he creates an additional motivation to follow through on his promise.

6.7   CONCLUSION

Most previous scholarship on Ps 116 has focused either on its prehistory, ANE background, structure, or canonical placement. This psalm has been particularly used in the reconstruction of various Israelite rituals and festivals. The rhetorical approach offered here builds on insights from all of those areas, but focuses its interpretive energy on the poem as a whole. It is concerned with analyzing the poem both as a work of art (its internal argument) and as socially embedded suasive

---

[139] Both "amplification" and "repetition" are figures of speech that contribute to presence, see Perelman and Olbrechts-Tyteca, *New Rhetoric*, 174–75.

[140] Yhwh is spoken about in the third person consistently except in vv. 8 and 17. The direct address to Yhwh in v. 4 is a narration of a past event.

[141] Fahnestock, *Rhetorical Style*, 292.

discourse (its external argument). Distinguishing between these two levels is an important feature of this analysis.

My analysis of the internal argument of the psalm concluded the following: the psalmist, who envisions himself as a poor and inexperienced devotee of Yhwh, seeks to "win goodwill and credibility"[142] from Yhwh by demonstrating both that Yhwh has cared for him in the past and by demonstrating that he faithfully fulfills his cultic obligations. The psalmist achieves this through a lengthy public testimony declaring what Yhwh has done and a pronouncement that he is now fulfilling his end of the bargain. The scene is clearly the temple and part of the rhetorical force of the psalmist's argument to Yhwh is the public nature of his address. Both the goal and the form of the poem enable it to be helpfully viewed as a type of judicial rhetoric.

In the actual setting of the psalm, the primary goal of the poet was to instill in the worshipper a particular understanding of who Yhwh is and of how best to respond when prayer has been answered. This would make the poem a type of epideictic rhetoric. The primary way these values are instilled is through enabling the user/hearer to enter into the implied world of the poem. The user/hearer could envision themselves as the one offering the public testimony before the gathered community. This device would function to deepen the adherence to the values and practices highlighted in the psalm. More specifically, the poem uses several rhetorical devices to make the message of the poem more present, vivid, and suasive to the worshipper, including: repetition, grammatical substitution, illustration, personification, *prolepsis*, maxim, the interplay of act and essence, indirect speech, allusion, apostrophe, accumulation, question and answer, *expeditio*, quasi-logical arguments, irony, and amplification. All of this was designed to influence the user/worshipper to deepen their commitment to Yhwh as described in the psalm, to viewing answered prayer as coming from his hand, and to the importance of cultic life and public expressions of thanksgiving.

---

[142] Dowden, "Rhetoric and Religion," 327.

CHAPTER 7
Summary

7.1   INTRODUCTION

At the outset of this study, I quoted a 2008 review of scholarship on Hebrew Poetry by Jamie Grant in which he stated, "in terms of the study of the poem as a unit there has not been the same sort of dynamic movement or radical change in recent years. The key ideas have remained largely the same in recent ideas."[1] This study is an attempt to bring a different perspective to the interpretation of the praise psalms as complete poetic units. The goal of this study was to argue that a rhetorical analysis of praise psalms will foster a clearer understanding of how praise functioned to shape the beliefs and piety of ancient Israel so that the reader will better appreciate the social, psychological, and theological contribution of the praise psalms. It is to be hoped that by this point the reader will have seen the value of a rhetorical approach to the praise psalms.

This chapter is one final attempt to clarify how rhetorical criticism contributes to our understanding of these important texts. In addition to rehearsing some of the more salient findings of this study, I will also discussion a number of issues the study has raised. This chapter will be outlined as follows: I will discuss the praise psalms as epideictic rhetoric; analyze the relationship between the internal and external rhetorical functions; demonstrate how rhetorical analysis gives a different perspective on interpretive issues in these psalms; examine the call/cause ratio of the different praise psalms and how that could lend insight to the *kairos* of the psalm; and finally discuss the limits and potential of rhetorical analysis.

---

[1] Grant, "Poetics," 222.

7.2   PRAISE PSALMS AS EPIDEICTIC RHETORIC

One of the sustained arguments of this study is that praise psalms in their external context functioned in a way similar to epideictic rhetoric. While it was not my intention to make this argument at the outset of the study, a close examination of the psalms has convinced me that not just these four psalms, but praise psalms in general can be helpfully viewed as a species of epideictic rhetoric. This raises two related questions: what is epideictic rhetoric? And, how does drawing an analogy between epideictic rhetoric and praise psalms help in the study of praise psalms? These questions have been briefly addressed in different places above, but is worthy of a more expanded discussion.[2]

Epideictic (or "demonstrative") rhetoric is one of the three main genres of rhetoric outlined by Aristotle.[3] Each of these genres of rhetoric, Aristotle relates to "time." That is, judicial rhetoric deals with the past, deliberative rhetoric with the future, while epideictic deals with the present. However, in relating to the present, epideictic can also use events from the past or projections about the course of the future.[4] Each genre also has its own end in view. For judicial rhetoric, the end is the assignation of guilt or innocence. For deliberative it is the consideration of the advantageous or harmful. For epideictic it is the assignation of praise or blame.[5]

Of the three genres, Aristotle spends the least amount of time developing his views on epideictic. In his introduction to *Rhetoric*, George Kennedy affirms, "Epideictic discourse, in particular, needs to be looked at in a variety of ways not recognized by Aristotle. He thought of it as the rhetoric of praise or blame, as in a funeral oration or a denunciation of someone, and failed to formulate its role in the instilling, preservation, or enhancement of cultural values, even though this was clearly a major function."[6] However, partially under the influ-

---

[2] See §3.5.2.1; §4.5; §5.1.1; §6.6.1

[3] Aristotle, *Rhetoric*, I.3

[4] Ibid., I.3.4

[5] Ibid., I.3.5

[6] In the introduction to, Aristotle, *On Rhetoric: A Theory of Civic Discourse,*

ence of Aristotle and partially under the influence of the Sophists, epideictic rhetoric became understood by many scholars, ancient and modern, as primarily concerned with pleasing the audience and enhancing the reputation of the orator.[7] While the genre was originally represented by funeral orations, or praise of leaders, in the hands of the Sophists the speech became a way for the orator to demonstrate their verbal prowess.[8] The focus shifted from the content of the speech to the style in which it was delivered. Indeed, Yun Lee Too states,

> The characterization of epideixis as a useless genre aimed at pleasure may be in large part due to the Sophists themselves, the professional teachers, who by and large come from outside of the city-state to prey on young men for the sake of their own economic advancement and who are regarded as contributing nothing to the community they enter.[9]

It is this type of speech that allowed "rhetoric" to become a pejorative term. However, despite its ill repute, epideictic rhetoric has a function that is much deeper and more important than simply entertaining an audience or glorifying the speaker.

As early as Plato, epideictic speech has also been acknowledged for its educational function.[10] This broader understanding of the genre has been articulated and strongly advocated by Perelman and Olbrechts-Tyteca.[11] They argue that epideictic speech concerns values. They explain, "it is in this perspective that epideictic oratory has significance and importance for argumentation, because it strengthens the

---

2nd ed., trans. George Kennedy (Oxford: Oxford University Press, 2007), 21–22.

[7] Cf. Yun Lee Too, "Epideictic Genre," in *Encyclopedia of Rhetoric*, ed. Thomas Sloane (Oxford: Oxford University Press, 2001), 253–54.

[8] Cicero states that this genre "belongs to the Sophists" (cf. *Brutus* 12.47), cited by Too, "Epideictic Genre," 253.

[9] Too, "Epideictic Genre," 254.

[10] Cf. Too, "Epideictic Genre," 255.

[11] Perelman and Olbrechts-Tyteca, *New Rhetoric*, 47–51; see also Jeffrey Walker, "Aristotle's Lyric: Re-Imagining the Rhetoric of Epideictic Song," *College English* 51 (1989): 5–28.

disposition toward action by increasing adherence to the values it lauds."[12] They continue,

> The argumentation in epideictic discourse sets out to increase the intensity of adherence to certain values, which might not be contested when considered on their own but may nevertheless not prevail against other values that might come into conflict with them. The speaker tries to establish a sense of communion centered around particular values recognized by the audience, and to this end he uses the whole range of means available to the rhetorician for purposes of amplification and enhancement.... In epideictic oratory, the speaker turns educator.[13]

Perelman and Tyteca's discussion of epideictic is not intended to be prescriptive, but descriptive demonstrating how this type of speech has functioned through history. If speeches are mainly classified based on their goals, then the primary goal of epideictic rhetoric is not best described as assigning praise and blame, but as instilling and increasing adherence to communal values. This is one of the primary ways a society maintains an identity and shared cultural norms. Thus, epideictic rhetoric could be considered educational, but not in the classic sense. Epideictic speeches did not often directly appeal to the audience to accept and adhere to particular values.[14] They worked more indirectly.

With this goal in mind, praise psalms in general serve to instill and increase adherence to communal values in the same kind of indirect way that many of the Greek and Roman epideictic speeches did. This understanding of praise psalms is in accordance with the analysis in Menander's *Rhetor*.[15] In his division of speeches, Menander classifies "hymn to the gods" as a type of epideictic rhetoric.[16]

---

[12] Perelman and Olbrechts-Tyteca, *New Rhetoric*, 50.

[13] Ibid., 51.

[14] See, e.g., the paradigm example of epideictic, Pericles' *Funeral Oration*.

[15] D. Donald Andrew Russell and N. Nigel Guy Wilson, *Menander Rhetor* (Oxford: Clarendon, 1981).

[16] Ibid., 7.

Understanding praise psalms on analogy with epideictic is helpful because it emphasizes the formational function of praise. Normally, we are accustomed to think of praise as directed mainly toward the deity. It is interesting, however, how little speech is spoken directly toward Yhwh in the psalms I analyzed.[17] This indicates that the function of praise psalms was not just to glorify Yhwh, but to instill values and shape the perspectives of the user/audience. Labelling praise psalms as a type of epideictic rhetoric helps the interpreter focus on the formative nature of praise and allows the interpreter to understand the psalms from a different perspective. The praise psalms were intended to have this function.

7.3   THE INTERNAL AND EXTERNAL RHETORIC OF PRAISE PSALMS

Another sustained argument of this study is that praise psalms need to be analyzed from two different perspectives. As described in the chapter on methodology, there is an internal world of the praise psalms.[18] The internal world is made up of the implied speaker, audience, and projected world of the poem. There is also an external world of the praise psalms. That is, the praise psalms were written for actual situations with a real-life speaker, audience, and world in view. These two settings often do not line up with each other, nor were they intended to. For example, in Ps 46 the implied audience was comprised of the nations.[19] Now, the nations were never intended to be the actual audience. Since the two worlds of praise psalms often imply two different

---

[17] In the four psalms this study analyzed, Yhwh was addressed directly in 4 of 15 verses of Ps 19, in 0 of 22 verses in Ps 103, in 0 of 12 verse in Ps 46, and in 3 of 19 verses in Ps 116 (note, I did not include the call to Yhwh in v. 4 of this psalm since the psalmist is narrating a past event). In sum, these 4 psalms directly addressed Yhwh 10% of the time. For a more detailed look at the speaker and addressees implied in the psalms, see Mark J. Boda, "'Varied and Resplendid Riches': Exploring the Breadth and Depth of Worship in the Psalter," in *Rediscovering Worship: Past, Present, Future*, MNTS, ed. Stanley E. Porter (Eugene, OR: Wipf & Stock, forthcoming).

[18] See §2.5.2.2

[19] See §5.4.2.

settings, the rhetorical function can often be analyzed in two different ways for the same psalm. The question then becomes, what is the relationship between the internal and external worlds of the praise psalms? The answer is this: often the primary way the psalmists achieve their external rhetorical goals is by having the users enter into the internal world of the psalm.

To unpack this idea, I will examine the relationship between the internal and external author and audience of the four psalms analyzed in this study.

Figure 1

PSALM	INTERNAL SPEAKER	INTERNAL AUDIENCE	EXTERNAL SPEAKER	EXTERNAL AUDIENCE
19	Servant of Yhwh (v. 12), concerned with moral and ceremonial purity (vv. 13–15), personal connection to Yhwh (v. 15) (See §3.1.1).	The psalmist (self-speech) and Yhwh (§3.1.1).	Worship leader (See §3.4)	Worshipping community (See §3.4)
103	Representative Israelite (See §4.4.2).	The psalmist (self-speech), the worshipping community, the hosts of heaven, all the words of Yhwh (See §4.4.2)	Worship leader	Worshipping community – time of a weakening of belief in the relevance of the convenantal tradition (See §4.5).
46	The worshipping community and Yhwh (See §5.4.2)	The nations (See §5.4.2).	Worship leader (See §5.5.1)	Minor, threatened community at worship (See §5.5.1)
116	Poor, inexperienced, faithful devotee of Yhwh (See §6.4.1)	Yhwh, the community, and the psalmist – in sum the community at worship (See §6.4.1)	Individual or family (See §6.5)	Individual or family (See §6.5)

In Ps 19, the situation envisioned is that of a pious Israelite voicing this prayer to himself and Yhwh. The poem itself highlights features of the speaker as follows: the psalmist sees all of creation as revealing Yhwh, loves and delights in the Torah, and seeks to live a blameless life. However, the actual context was likely that of a worship leader overseeing authorized communal worship. Thus, the psalm was designed to allow its users to enter into the "fictional" world of the poem. In so doing, the users could envision themselves as the psalmist. Based on emphases within the poem, it is clear that the implied author serves as a model which the users of the psalm could emulate.[20] In this way, the goal of the poem – that an audience of near contemporaries would understand and deepen their adherence to the relationship the poem describes between themselves, the world, God, and the Torah – is achieved. That is, one of most powerful ways in which the psalmist achieves his rhetorical goals is by enabling the user to enter into the world of the poem.

Psalm 103 similarly allows the worshipping community to envision themselves as the psalmist. However, in this psalm, the psalmist is not so much held up as an "exemplar of spirituality," but as an authoritative interpreter of Yhwh's character. The goal of the poet was to reverse the trend of weakening adherence to Israel's religious heritage. In order to achieve this goal, the audience was encouraged to view the Exodus 32–34 narrative in a different way. The psalm highlights Yhwh's gracious and loyal nature. This understanding of Yhwh's nature would be ingrained in an audience by allowing each member of the community to voice these words as their own. Again, the play between the internal and external worlds of the psalm is one of the ways the psalmist achieves his goal.

In Ps 46, it is not the speaker that is different between the internal and external worlds of the poem, but the audience. The audience, by envisioning themselves (and Yhwh) voicing this poem to the nations, would have their belief that Yhwh was Israel's refuge and

---

[20] This is the insight picked up on by Allen, "David as Exemplar of Spirituality: the Redactional Function of Psalm 19," 544–46.

strength, in spite of circumstances, strengthened.

Psalm 116 is almost the inverse of Ps 19. In Ps 116, the individual, or family unit was the likely actual audience of the poem. However, by entering into the world of the poem, the audience would be able to envision themselves as joining with and participating in cultic worship. This would help achieve the goal of the poem – to instill in the worshipper a particular understanding of who Yhwh is and of how best to respond when prayer has been answered.

At this point, an objection could be raised. In my analysis, it looks like when the world of the poem portrays an individual at worship, it was actually designed for a communal setting (e.g., Ps 19); whereas when a psalm makes explicit its temple context, it was actually designed for individual/family use (e.g., Ps 116). However, this is only an apparent discrepancy. As stated in the chapter on methodology, the text of each poem needs to be closely examined to determine as closely as possible the textual intent.[21] In the case of Ps 116, Hossfeld, Zenger and Spieckermann make a strong case for the psalm as intended for individual or family use based on the text of the poem.[22] For Ps 19, the didactic and dramatic elements of the poem point to its intended use in corporate worship.[23]

Regardless of whether or not one agrees with my analysis of the setting of these psalms, the overall point that one of the primary ways that the psalmists achieve their rhetorical goal is by enabling the actual user of the poem to enter into the fictional, internal world of the psalm, is a valid and important one.[24]

---

[21] See §2.5.2.4

[22] Hossfeld and Zenger, *Psalms 3*, 215; Spieckermann, "Lieben und Glauben: Beobachtungen in Psalm 116," 266–75.

[23] See §3.4.

[24] This is not a new insight, but it is one that is not consistently employed. For an earlier discussion of the internal and external rhetorical functions of a psalm, see Howard, "Psalm 88 and the Rhetoric of Lament," 132–46.

7.4   INTERPRETATION HELPED AND ENRICHED BY A RHETORICAL APPROACH

While the foregoing analysis has demonstrated that a rhetorical approach certainly does not solve all of the interpretive issues regarding praise psalms, nevertheless, it does help give some additional options when confronted with difficulties and provides ways of enriching interpretation. In this section, I will address five different ways in which a rhetorical approach has helped or enriched the interpretation of praise psalms.

A rhetorical approach can help provide an explanation for an unusual lexical or grammatical choice. In Ps. 116:1, several commentators have noted how unusual the initial *qātal* verb is.[25] One option for understanding this without resorting to emendation would be to argue that the poet used an unexpected verb form to capture and focus the reader/user's attention.[26] In Ps 19, the shift in divine name from El to Yhwh can be understood as a part of the argument of the overall poem from general to specific.[27] Similarly, the abrupt shift in the cadence of Ps 19 in v. 8 can be explained as a part of the "argument" of the psalm. It could have encouraged the worshipper to understand that there is an orderliness and clarity in the Torah not present in the cosmic speech (vv. 1–7).[28] In Ps 103, the poet's use of the unusual form עֶדְיֵךְ (v. 5) can be understood as connecting the poem back to the Exodus 32–34 narrative, thus serving the goal of reinterpreting that narrative. In sum, a rhetorical approach gives one additional option for understanding the difficult language in some psalms.[29]

As discussed in the previous section, the realization that the language of praise psalms has both an internal and external rhetorical

---

[25] See §6.6.2.2

[26] A classic rhetorical trope, see Perelman and Olbrechts-Tyteca, *New Rhetoric*, 177.

[27] See §3.5.1.2

[28] See §3.5.2.3

[29] Obviously, many psalms do have textual issues that need to be emended as well (as this study has done in some cases).

function does help alleviate some scholarly debates. For example, some scholars understand the setting of Ps 19 as an individual at worship, while others understand it as designed for corporate worship. The reality is that there is truth to both settings, one is the internal and the other the external setting of the psalm.[30] For Ps 46, some have understood the line "Be still and know that I am God" (v. 11) as a call to the nations to cease their rebellion against Yhwh. Others have understood it as a command to Israel to give up their trust in political or military might and to trust in Yhwh alone.[31] Again, the first view is true with regard to the internal rhetorical function and the latter view is true with regard to the external rhetorical function.

The debate over the setting of Ps 116 can likewise be negotiated by appealing to the external and internal rhetorical functions of the poem.[32] This is not to say that all debates regarding setting or intention can be solved this way. I explicitly argued against some of the settings proposed for Ps 46 based on the language and logic of the poem.[33] Nevertheless, the rhetorical approach advocated in this study does help to resolve some of these tensions regarding setting.

A rhetorical approach also enriches interpretation by going beyond most traditional analysis in not simply noting stylistic features of a poem, but considering what the suasive impact of those features could be. For example, the shift in poems to nominal or stative sentences (Ps 19:8–11; 46:2; 116:5, 15) can be, not just stated, but explained based on how that shift would have affected an audience of near contemporaries. For this particular device, the shift to the nominal/stative function in a number of ways. They could serve to outline areas of agreement between the speaker and user, thus serving the rhetorical goal of the poet. If the phrases are describing a person (e.g., Yhwh), they function as a label, which is "a linguistic technique ... to

---

[30] See §3.4

[31] See §5.5.5

[32] See §6.5

[33] See §5.5.1

stress the impression of permanency."[34] The same kinds of suasive techniques can be described for the following stylistic features of the psalms:[35] extra-positioning (46:5); personification (19:2–3; 8–11); allusion (19:2–3; 103); illustration (19:5; 46:6–7); analogy (19:6, 11); the use of the imperative (103:1–2, 20–22; 46:9–11); self-deliberation (103:1–2, 116:7); maxims (103:8); shift in person (103:10–15; 116:4–19; 46:7–8); use of imagery (46:3–4; 116:3, 6–7, 13–14); repetition (103:1–2, 20–22; 116:13–14, 17–18). The point is not that these stylistic features of the psalms have gone undetected. Rather, the point is that interpreters rarely go beyond labeling the feature to ask what the suasive import of the feature could be. Rhetorical theory has provided helpful categories and terms to analyze suasive import. It can help explain not just the fact that a particular image was used, but perhaps the reason why. It is important to note that this analysis is not a science. One cannot state that a particular stylistic device has this particular rhetorical function in every case. Nevertheless, rhetorical theory outlines a number of ways in which these devices can function suasively, which greatly aids in their interpretation.[36]

However, it must be admitted that there are limits to what a rhetorical approach can bring to the text. There is a subjective element to rhetorical analysis. In their monumental work on rhetorical analysis, Perelman and Olbrechts-Tyteca candidly state:

> Now the meaning and scope of an isolated argument can rarely be understood without ambiguity: the analysis of one link of an argument out of its context and independently of the situation to which it belongs involves undeniable dangers. These are due not only to the equivocal character of language, but also to the fact that the springs supporting the argumentation are almost

---

[34] Perelman and Olbrechts-Tyteca, *New Rhetoric*, 294.

[35] For the suasive import of these stylistic features, see the discussion of that particular verse in the body of the dissertation.

[36] In addition to the seminal work of Aristotle, several modern works are particularly helpful in this regard, including Perelman and Olbrechts-Tyteca, *New Rhetoric* and Fahenstock, *Rhetorical Style*; Burke, *Rhetoric of Motives*.

never entirely explicitly described. In establishing the structure
of an argument, we must interpret the words of the speaker,
supply the missing links, which is always very risky. Indeed it
is nothing more than a plausible hypothesis to assert that the
real thought of the speaker and of his hearers coincides with
the structure which we have just isolated. In most cases, moreover, we are simultaneously aware of more than just one way
of conceiving the structure of an argument.[37]

Their analysis of the limits of rhetorical analysis certainly rings true
for my analysis of the praise psalms. There are other ways one could
conceive of the "argument" of each of the psalms analyzed. However,
it is not an entirely subjective enterprise. There are boundaries to interpretation set by the language, culture, and content of the poems
themselves as discussed in the chapter on methodology.[38] Within those
boundaries, a rhetorical approach cannot eliminate all ambiguity, but
this is true for any interpretive method. The benefit of a rhetorical approach is that we can utilize the wisdom of the rhetorical tradition to
propose ways in which the language of the praise psalms functioned to
shape the beliefs, attitudes, and piety of an audience of near contemporaries. This kind of analysis is especially helpful for those attempting
to utilize the psalms in worship in a modern context.

7.5   THE KAIROS OF THE PRAISE PSALMS

In the introductory chapter, I discussed the problem of setting for praise
psalms.[39] One advance that this study has explored is to discern both an
internal and external setting as discussed above.[40] However, it may be
possible to say more than what has been for the external setting of the
praise psalms. Many rhetorical theorists have utilized the concept of
kairos in their analysis of the setting of a discourse. *Kairos* is notoriously difficult to define. In English, it has been translated translated as, "the

---

[37] Perelman and Olbrechts-Tyteca, *New Rhetoric*, 187.

[38] §2.5.4.

[39] §1.7

[40] §7.3

right time," "due season," "occasion," "the propitious moment," "opportunity."[41] The term refers to not only the speaker, audience, and place of
a speech, but to the relation between the three. It is the situation which
called forth the speech. Lloyd Blitzer calls this the *exigence* of the
speech, which is another way of saying the problem addressed by the
text.[42] Rhetorician Davida Charney has recently applied rhetorical theory to the study of individual psalms of lament.[43] In her study she defined
kairos in this way, "the situational nexus in which a speaker attempts to
move specific listeners at a particular place and time to change their attitudes, beliefs, or actions."[44] Charney points out that rhetorical scholars
have often analyzed the topics an author chose to dwell on for clues to
the *kairos* of a speech. She states,

> In general, authors allocate space and time by anticipating what
> points the audience will consider most controversial and there-
> fore most in need of elaboration and supporting appeals. When
> an issue is complicated or unfamiliar, an author may choose to
> focus entirely on the issue or problem elements without offer-
> ing any time of solution. When a problem is well understood,
> an author may devote the bulk of the discourse to the solution.
> Thus the shape of a psalm, the amount of space devoted to spe-
> cific points relative to others, offers important clues to the
> speaker's assessment of the *kairos*, the speaker's immediate
> stance toward God and to the community as well as his or her
> goals for the way the relationship should be.[45]

In her analysis, she examined the ratio of text devoted to the following

---

[41] Jane Sutton, "Kairos," in *Encyclopedia of Rhetoric*, ed. Thomas Sloane
(Oxford: Oxford University Press, 2001), 412–15.

[42] Blitzer, "The Rhetorical Situation," 1–14; See also Michael Carter, "*Stasis* and *Kairos*: Principles of Social Construction in Classical Rhetoric," *Rhetoric
Review* 7 (1988): 97–112.

[43] Davida Charney, "Maintaining Innocence Before a Divine Hearer: Deliberative Rhetoric in Psalm 22, Psalm 17, and Psalm 7," *BibInt* 1 (2013): 33–63.

[44] Ibid., 39.

[45] Ibid., 40.

areas of lament psalms: the address, complaint, and proposal for recip-
rocal action (or "praise," "thanksgiving"). She averred that the different ratios devoted to each section of a lament betrayed the author's
perception of the *kairos*.

It is possible to apply this insight to the praise psalms. At the
most basic level, praise psalms are made up of two elements: the call
to praise and the cause of praise. The other typical "form" elements of
praise psalms can be subsumed under one of those two labels. The ratio between these two elements of a praise psalm could provide insight
into the *kairos* of the psalm, that is, the speaker's stance toward the
audience and rhetorical goals. Figure 2 is an analysis of the call/cause
ratio of the psalms studied:

Figure 2

PSALM 19	PSALM 103	PSALM 46	PSALM 116
v. 1 - Cause	**v. 1 - Call**	*v. 1 - Cause*	*v. 1 - Cause*
v. 2 - Cause	**v. 2 - Call**	*v. 2 - Cause*	*v. 2 - Cause*
v. 3 - Cause	*v. 3 - Cause*	*v. 3 - Cause*	*v. 3 - Cause*
v. 4 - Cause	*v. 4 - Cause*	*v. 4 - Cause*	*v. 4 - Cause*
v. 5 - Cause	*v. 5 - Cause*	*v. 5 - Cause*	*v. 5 - Cause*
v. 6 - Cause	*v. 6 - Cause*	*v. 6 - Cause*	*v. 6 - Cause*
v. 7 - Cause	*v. 7 - Cause*	*v. 7 - Cause*	**v. 7 - Call**
v. 8 - Cause	*v. 8 - Cause*	**v. 8 - Call**	**v. 8 - Call**
v. 9 - Cause	*v. 9 - Cause*	**v. 9 - Call**	**v. 9 - Call**
v. 10 - Cause	*v. 10 - Cause*	**v. 10 - Call**	*v. 10 - Cause*
v. 11 - Cause	*v. 11 - Cause*	*v. 11 - Cause*	*v. 11 - Cause*
v. 12 - Cause	*v. 12 - Cause*		**v. 12 - Call**
v. 13 - Cause	*v. 13 - Cause*		**v. 13 - Call**
v. 14 - Call	*v. 14 - Cause*		**v. 14 - Call**
	v. 15 - Cause		**v. 15 - Call**
	v. 16 - Cause		**v. 16 - Call**
	v. 17 - Cause		**v. 17 - Call**
	v. 18 - Cause		**v. 18 - Call**
	v. 19 - Cause		**v. 19 - Call**
	v. 20 - Call		
	v. 21 - Call		
	v. 22 - Call		

This is a general analysis designed to bring out the emphases in the psalms.[46] Psalms which give more space to the cause, or reasons for praise would be more didactic in function. That is, the author/speaker would envision themselves more as a teacher attempting to shape the auditor's views, attitudes, and perceptions toward God, whereas psalms which give more space to the call to worship, function to motivate the community or individual to engage in worship. This analysis supports the external rhetorical goals outlined for the four psalms. For Ps 116, I argued that the rhetorical goal was to encourage the individual to participate in cultic life, which is supported by the greater emphasis on the call section.[47] In Ps 19, I argued that the goal was to shape the auditor's view of the heavens and Torah and was thus didactic in function.[48] Again, this conclusion is supported by the cause/call ratio. Psalm 103 was concerned with re-shaping the community's perspective on Yhwh, emphasizing his compassionate, gracious, and forgiving nature. Finally, Ps 46 was designed to instill in the community a disposition of belief and confidence in Yhwh amid threatening forces. Both of these more "didactic" functions are also supported by this analysis.[49]

7.6   FUTURE AREAS OF STUDY

The rhetorical approach outlined and applied in this study raises a number of areas of study for future research. The goal of this brief section is to outline some of them. Most obviously, this type of study could be expanded and applied to all the praise psalms. This would enable the interpreter to have a broader basis by which to make comparisons between psalms, thus honing the analysis. For example, the *Kairos* of the praise psalms could be more sharply described if one in-

---

[46] In this analysis, I looked at sections of text and discerned the overall intent of the section. Thus, there are some portions within Ps 116:12–19 that could be described as giving a reason for praise (vv. 15–16), but the overall thrust of the section was calling, or resolve to praise.

[47] See §6.6.1

[48] See §3.4.

[49] See §5.5.1 and §4.5.

cluded the data from all the praise psalms. Additionally, one could also rhetorically analyze how praise language functions in other types of psalms (e.g., lament). Another helpful avenue of study would be to apply this methodology to the praise psalms from other ANE cultures. This would provide a fruitful way to compare and contrast how Israel's praise is similar to and different from its neighbors.

As discussed in the chapter on methodology, Speech Act Theory approaches to the psalms are a growing area of study.[50] It would be helpful to bring rhetorical criticism into closer dialogue with Speech Act Theory. The two approaches share similar values. That is, they are both concerned with the pragmatics of praise language. For example, in this study, I called for analyzing the psalms both for their internal and external rhetorical function. In some ways, this is similar to what Speech Act Theorists would call the psalms locutionary and illocutionary functions.[51] A closer rapprochement between the two methods has the potential to help understand the praise psalms better.

7.7   CONCLUSION

The stated goal of this study was to apply rhetorical criticism to the interpretation of praise psalms to better understand the suasive and formative aspects of Israel's praise. This was a modest goal and one that has been but modestly achieved. The beauty and power of Israel's praise poetry profoundly shaped how its users understood God, themselves, the nation, and the world. This is not a byproduct of the praise psalms, but it is one of the reasons they were written. Rhetorical analysis provides us with one additional tool to unpack how they achieved this goal. However, both the depth of praise psalms and the profundity of the western rhetorical tradition indicate that there is more profitable work to be done in this area. This study should not be seen as an exhaustive application of rhetorical criticism to the praise psalms, but as an invitation to further study and conversation.

---

[50] §2.5.5.

[51] A point raised by David M. Howard, Jr. in personal communication.

הללו־יה

BIBLIOGRAPHY

Abrams, M. H. *The Mirror and the Lamp: Romantic Theory and the Critical Tradition*. London: Oxford University Press, 1953.

_____. *Doing Things with Texts: Essays in Criticism and Critical Theory*. Edited by Michael Fischer. New York: Norton, 1991.

_____. "Poetry, Theories of." Pages 942–54 in *The New Princeton Encyclopedia of Poetry and Poetics*. Edited by Alex Preminger and T. V. F. Brogan. Princeton: Princeton University Press, 1993.

Achinstein, P. "Models, Analogies, and Theories." *Philosophy of Science* 31 (1964): 328–49.

Ahlström, Gosta. *The History of Ancient Palestine*. Minneapolis: Fortress, 1993.

Allen, Leslie C. *Psalms 101–150*. WBC 21. Waco, TX: Word, 1983.

_____. "David as Exemplar of Spirituality: The Redactional Function of Psalm 19." *Biblica* 67 (1986): 544–46.

_____. "The Value of Rhetorical Criticism in Psalm 69." *JBL* 105 (1986): 577–98.

Aletti, Jean Noël and Jacques Trublet. *Approche poétique et théologique des psaumes: Analyses et méthodes*. Paris: Cerf, 1983.

Alter, Robert. *The Art of Biblical Poetry*. Rev. and enl. ed. New York: Basic, 2011.

Anderson, Arnold Albert. *The Book of Psalms*. Grand Rapids: Eerdmans, 1981.

Anderson, Bernhard. *Out of the Depths: The Psalms Speak for Us Today*. Rev and Exp ed. Philadelphia: Westminster, 1983.

Aristotle. *Art of Rhetoric*. Translated by J. H. Freese. LCL 22. Cambridge: Harvard Universtiy Press, 1926.

Athanasius. *Letter to Marcellinus*. Translated by Robert Gregg. Mah-
    wah, NJ: Paulist, 1980.

Auffret, Pierre. "Un père envers des fils: Nouvelle étude structurelle
    du psaume 103." *Theoforum* 37 (2006): 25–43.

Augustine, *Expositions of the Psalms*. Translated by Maria Boulding. 6
    vols. Hyde Park, NY: New City, 2000–2004.

Austin, J. L. *How to Do Things with Words*. Oxford: Oxford
    University Press, 1962.

Baldwin, C. S. *Medieval Rhetoric and Poetic (to 1400)*. New York:
    Macmillan, 1928.

Balla, Emile. *Das Ich der Psalmen*. Forschungen zur Religion und Li-
    teratur des Alten und Neuen Testaments 16. Göttingen:
    Vandenhoeck & Ruprecht, 1912.

Barker, Kit. "Divine Illocutions in Psalm 137: A Critique of Nicholas
    Wolterstorff's 'Second Hermeneutic.'" *Tyndale Bulletin* 60
    (2009): 1–14.

Barré, Michael L. "'rṣ (h)hyym – 'The Land of the Living.'" *JSOT* 41
    (1988): 37–59.

_____. "Psalm 116: Its Structure and Its Enigmas." *JBL* (1990):
    61–78.

Bartha, P. *By Parallel Reasoning: The Construction and Evaluation of
    Analogical Arguments*. New York: Oxford University Press,
    2010.

Bartholomew, Craig and Ryan O'Dowd. "The Poetry of Wisdom and
    the Wisdom of Poetry." Pages 47–72 in *Old Testament Wisdom
    Literature: A Theological Introduction*. Downers Grove, IL:
    InterVarsity Press, 2011.

Barton, John. *Reading the Old Testament: Method in Biblical Study*.
    Rev. and exp. Louisville: Westminster, 1996.

_____, ed. *Cambridge Companion to Biblical Interpretation*.
    Cambridge: Cambridge University Press, 2000.

Bauer, Hans, Pontus Leander, and Paul Kahle. *Historische Grammatik
    der hebräischen Sprache des Alten Testamentes*. Volume 1.
    Tübingen: Georg Olms, 1922.

Bellinger, Jr., W. H. "Psalm 61: A Rhetorical Analysis." *Perspectives in Religious Studies* 26 (1999): 379–88.

Berger, Peter and Thomas Luckmann, *The Social Construction of Reality: A Treatise in the Sociology of Knowledge*. New York: Doubleday, 1966.

Bizzell, Patricia and Bruce Herzberg, eds. *The Rhetorical Tradition*. 2nd ed. New York: Bedford/St. Martin's, 2001.

Blank, Sheldon. "Some Observations Concerning Biblical Prayer." *Hebrew Union College Annual* 32 (1961): 75–90.

Bitzer, Lloyd. "The Rhetorical Situation." *Philosophy and Rhetoric* 1 (1968): 1–14.

Booth, Wayne C. *The Rhetoric of Fiction*. 2nd ed. Chicago: University of Chicago Press, 1983.

_____. *The Vocation of a Teacher: Rhetorical Occasions*. Chicago: University of Chicago Press, 1988.

Bouvy, E. "Saint Augustin. Les Énarrationes sur les psaumes," *Revue Augustinienne* 3 (1903): 418–36.

Bratcher, Robert and William Reyburn. *A Translator's Handbook on the Book of Psalms*. New York: United Bible Societies, 1991.

Briggs, Charles Augustus and Emilie Grace Briggs. *The Book of Psalms: Vol. 1*. ICC. Edinburgh: T&T Clark, 1906.

_____. *The Book of Psalms: Vol. 2*. ICC. Edinburgh: T&T Clark, 1907.

Brogen, T. V. F. "Rhetoric and Poetry." Pages 1045–52 in *The New Princeton Encyclopedia of Poetry and Poetics*. Edited by Alex Preminger and T. V. F. Brogen. New York: MJF Books, 1993.

Brooks, Cleanth. "The Language of Paradox." Pages 1–20 in *The Well Wrought Urn: Studies in the Structure of Poetry*. London: Dobson, 1947.

Brown, Jeannie. "Genre Criticism." Pages 111–50 in *Words & the Word: Explorations in Biblical Interpretation & Literary Theory*. Edited by David Firth and Jamie Grant. Downers Grove, IL: IVP Academic, 2008.

Brown, William P. *Seeing the Psalms: A Theology of Metaphor*. Louisville: Westminster John Knox, 2002.

_____. "The Psalms and 'I': The Dialogical Self and the Disappearing Psalmist." Pages 26–44 in *Diachronic and Synchronic: Reading the Psalms in Real Time*. Edited by W. H. Bellinger et al. Library Hebrew Bible/Old Testament Studies 488. New York: T&T Clark, 2007.

_____. "'Here Comes the Sun!' The Metaphorical Theology of Psalms 15–24." Pages 259–77 in *Composition of the Book of Psalms*. Edited by Erich Zenger. Leuven: Uitgeverij Peeters, 2010.

Brueggemann, Walter. "From Hurt to Joy, from Death to Life." *Interpretation* 28 (1974): 3–19.

_____. *The Message of the Psalms: A Theological Commentary*. Minneapolis: Ausburg, 1984.

_____. "The Psalms and the Life of Faith: A Suggested Typology of Function." *JSOT* 17 (1980): 3–32.

_____. *Israel's Praise: Doxology against Idolatry and Ideology*. Philadelphia: Fortress, 1988.

_____. *Abiding Astonishment: Psalms, Modernity, and the Making of History*. Louisville: Westminster, 1991.

_____. *The Psalms and the Life of Faith*. Edited by Patrick Miller. Minneapolis: Fortress, 1995.

Bultmann, C. *Die biblische Urgeschichte in der Aufklärung*. Tübingen: Mohr Siebeck, 1999.

Burke, Kenneth. *Language as Symbolic Action: Essays on Life, Literature, and Method*. Berkeley: University of California Press, 1968.

_____. "Antony in Behalf of the Play," Pages 103–114 in *Rhetorical Analyses of Literary Works*. Edited by Edward Corbett. London: Oxford University Press, 1969.

_____. *A Grammar of Motives*. Berkeley: University of California Press, 1969.

_____. *Rhetoric of Motives*. Berkeley: University of California Press, 1969.

_____. *Rhetoric of Religion: Studies in Logology*. Berkeley: University of California Press, 1970.

Burns, Robert. "Rhetoric and the Law." Pages 442–56 in *Companion to Rhetoric and Rhetorical Criticism*. Edited by Walter Jost and Wendy Olmsted. Oxford: Blackwell, 2004.

Buttenwieser, Moses. *The Psalms: Chronologically Treated with a New Translation*. Chicago: University of Chicago Press, 1938.

Calvin, John. *Institutes of the Christian Religion*. Translated by F. L. Battles. Philadelphia: Westminster, 1960.

Carter, Michael. "*Stasis* and *Kairos*: Principles of Social Construction in Classical Rhetoric," *Rhetoric Review* 7 (1988): 97–11.

Castelli, Elizabeth and Stephen Moore et al., eds. *The Postmodern Bible*. New Haven:Yale University Press, 1995.

Ceresko, Anthony. "A Rhetorical Analysis of David's 'Boast' (1 Samuel 17:34–37): Some Reflections on Method." *Catholic Biblical Quarterly* 47 (1985): 58–74.

Cha, Kilnam. *Psalm 146–150: The Final Hallelujah Psalms as a Fivefold Doxology to the Hebrew Psalter*. Ph.D. Diss., Baylor University, 2006.

Charney, Davida. "Keeping the Faithful: Persuasive Strategies in Psalms 4 and 62." *JHebS* 12 (2012): 1–13.

_____. "Maintaining Innocence Before a Divine Hearer: Deliberative Rhetoric in Psalm 22, Psalm 17, and Psalm 7." *Biblical Interpretation* 21 (2013): 33–63.

_____. *Persuading God: Rhetorical Studies of First-Person Psalms*. Hebrew Bible Monographs 73. Sheffield: Sheffield Phoenix, 2015.

Cheyne, Thomas Kelly. *The Book of Psalms or the Praises of Israel: A New Translation with Commentary*. New York: Thomas Whittaker, 1895.

Childs, Brevard. "Psalm Titles and Midrashic Exegesis." *JSS* 16 (1971): 137–50.

_____. "Reflections on the Modern Study of the Psalms." Pages 377–88 in *Magnalia Dei: The Mighty Acts of God: Essays on the Bible and Archaeology: In Memoriam G. E. Wright*. Edited by F. M. Cross. Garden City: Doubleday, 1976.

_____. *Introduction to the Old Testament as Scripture.*

Philadelphia: Fortress, 1979.

Clark, Gordon R. *The Word Ḥesed in the Hebrew Bible*. JSOTSup 157. Sheffield: Sheffield, 1993.

Clements, Ronald. "Interpreting the Psalms." Pages 76–98 in *One Hundred Years of Old Testament Interpretation*. Philadelphia: Westminster, 1976.

Clines, David J. A. "Psalm Research Since 1955: I. The Psalms and the Cult." *Tyndale Bulletin* 18 (1967): 103–26.

_____. "Psalm Research Since 1955: II. The Literary Genres." *Tyndale Bulletin* 20 (1969): 105–25.

_____. "Tree of Knowledge and the Law of Yahweh: Psalm 19." *VT* 24 (1974): 8–14.

_____. "A World Established on Water (Psalm 24): Reader-Response, Deconstruction and Bespoke Interpretation." Pages 79–90 in *New Literary Criticism and the Hebrew* Bible. Edited by David J. Clines & J. Cheryl Exum. JSOTSup 143. Sheffield: Sheffield, 1993.

Cook, John. *Time and the Biblical Hebrew Verb: The Expression of Tense, Aspect, and Modality in Biblical Hebrew*. Edited by Cynthia Miller-Naudé and Jacobus Naudé. Volume 7. *LSAWS*. Winona Lake, IN: Eisenbrauns, 2012.

Cook, Ryan. "Prayers that Form Us: Psalms and Rhetorical Criticism." *JSOT* 39 (2015): 451–67.

_____. "'They were Born There': The Nations in Psalmic Rhetoric." *HBT* 39 (2017): 16–30.

Corbett, Edward P.J. *Rhetorical Analyses of Literary Works*. New York: Oxford University Press, 1969.

_____. "The Rhetoric of the Open Hand and the Rhetoric of the Closed Fist." *College Composition and Communication* 20 (1969): 288–96.

Coetzee, Johan. "Politeness Strategies in the So Called 'Enemy Psalms': An Inquiry into Israelite Prayer Rhetoric." Pages 209–36 in *Rhetorical Criticism and the Bible*. Edited by Stanley Porter & Dennis Stamps. JSNTSup 195. Sheffield: Continuum, 2002.

Craigie, Peter. *Psalms 1–50*. Word Biblical Commentary 19. Waco, TX: Word, 1983.

Craven, Toni. *Artistry and Faith in the Book of Judith*. Chico, CA: Scholars Press, 1983.

Creach, Jerome. *Yahweh as Refuge and the Editing of the Hebrew Psalter*. LHBOTS 217. Sheffield: Sheffield, 1996.

Croft, Steven. *The Identity of the Individual in the Psalms*. JSOTSup 44. Sheffield: Sheffield Academic, 1987.

Cross, Frank Moore. *Canaanite Myth and Hebrew Epic: Essays in the History of the Religion of Israel*. Cambridge: Harvard University Press, 1973.

_____. *From Epic to Canon: History and Literature in Ancient Israel*. Baltimore: Johns Hopkins University Press, 1998.

Dahood, Mitchell. *Psalms I: 1–50*. AB 16. New Haven: Yale University Press, 1965.

_____. *Psalms III: 101–150*. AB 17A. New Haven: Yale University Press, 1970.

Davison, W. T. *The Praises of Israel: An Introduction to the Study of Psalms*. London: Charles H. Kelly, 1893.

Day, Dennis G. "Persuasion and the Concept of Identification." *Quarterly Journal of Speech* 46 (1960): 270–73.

deClaissé-Walford, Nancy. *Reading from the Beginning: The Shaping of the Hebrew Psalter*. Macon, GA: Mercer University Press, 1997.

Deissler, Alfons. "Zur Datierung und Situierung der 'Kosmischen Hymnen' Pss 8, 19, 29." Pages 47–58 in *Lex tua veritas; Festschrift für Hubert Junker zu Vollendung des siebzigsten Lebensjahres am 8 August 1961*. Trier: Paulinus-Verlag, 1961.

Delitzsch, Franz. *Biblischer Commentar über den Psalter*. 2 vols. Leipzig: Döbffling and Franke, 1859–1869.

_____. *Biblical Commentary on the Psalms*. Translated by David Eaton. 3 vols. New York: Funk and Wagnalls, 1883–1885.

Dion, Paul-Eugène. "Psalm 103: A Meditation on the 'Ways' of the Lord." *Église et théologie* 21 (1990): 13–31.

Donald, Trevor. "The Semantic Field of" Folly" in Proverbs, Job, Psalms, and Ecclesiastes." *VT* 13 (1963): 285–92.

Dowden, Ken. "Rhetoric and Religion." Pages 320–35 in *A Compantion to Greek Rhetoric*. Edited by Ian Worthington. Oxford: Blackwell, 2007.

Dozeman, Thomas B. "Inner-Biblical Interpretation of Yahweh's Gracious and Compassionate Character." *JBL* 108 (1989): 207–23.

_____. "Old Testament Rhetorical Criticism." Pages 712–15 in *ABD*, vol. 5. Edited by D. N. Freedman et al. New York: Doubleday, 1992.

Driver, Samuel. *An Introduction to the Literature of the Old Testament*. New York: Charles Scribner's Sons, 1892.

Durlesser, James. "A Rhetorical Critical Study of Psalms 19, 42, and 43." *Studia Biblica et Theologica* 10 (1980): 179–97.

Duhm, Bernhard. *Die Psalmen*. Kurzer Hand-Commentar zum Alten Testament 14. Freiburg: J. C. B. Mohr, 1899.

Eagleton, Terry. *How to Read a Poem*. Oxford: Blackwell, 2007.

Earwood, Greg C. "Psalm 46." *RevExp* 86 (1989): 79–86.

Eaton, John H. *Psalms of the Way and the Kingdom: A Conference with the Commentators*. JSOTSup 199. Sheffield: Sheffield Academic, 1995.

_____. *The Psalms: A Historical and Spiritual Commentary*. New York: T&T Clark, 2003.

Eco, Umberto. *The Open Work*. Translated by A. Cancogni. London: Hutchinson Radius, 1989.

_____. *The Limits of Interpretation*. Bloomington: Indiana University Press, 1990.

_____. *Interpretation and Overinterpretation*. Edited by S. Collini. Cambridge: Cambridge University Press, 1992.

Eliade, Mircea. *The Sacred and the Profane: The Nature of Religion*. New York: Harper & Row, 1961.

Eliot, T. S. "The Social Function of Poetry." Pages 3–16 in *On Poetry and Poets*. London: Faber and Faber, 1962.

Emerton, John A. "How does the Lord Regard the Death of His Saints in Psalm 116:15." *JTS* 34 (1983): 146–56.

Enoch, Jessica and Dana Anderson. *Burke in the Archives: Using the Past to Transform the Future of Burkean Studies.* Studies in Rhetoric/Communication. Columbia: University of South Carolina Press, 2013.

Evans, Donald. *The Logic of Self-Involvement: A Philosophical Study of Everyday Language with Special Reference to the Christian Use of Language about God as Creator.* London: SCM Press, 1963.

Ewald, Heinrich. *Die Dichter des Alten Bundes.* 2 vols. Göttingen: Vandenhoeck & Ruprecht, 1835–1839.

_____. *Commentary on the Psalms.* Translated by E. Johnson. 2 vols. London: Williams and Norgate, 1880.

Fahnestock, Jeanne. *Rhetorical Style: The Uses of Language in Persuasion.* Oxford: Oxford University Press, 2011.

Feininger, Bernd. "A Decade of German Psalm-Criticism." *JSOT* 20 (1981): 91–103.

Fishbane, Michael A. *Text and Texture: Close Readings of Selected Biblical Texts.* New York: Schocken, 1979.

_____. *Biblical Interpretation in Ancient Israel.* Oxford: Oxford University Press, 1985.

Fisch, Harold. *Poetry with a Purpose: Biblical Poetics and Interpretation.* Bloomington: Indiana University Press, 1988.

Fish, Stanley. *Is there a Text in this Class? The Authority of Interpretive Communities.* Cambridge: Harvard University Press, 1982.

_____. *Surprised by Sin: The Reader in "Paradise Lost."* 2nd ed. Cambridge: Harvard University Press, 2003.

Fokkelman, J. P. "Psalm 103: Design, Boundaries, and Mergers." Pages 109–118 in *Psalms and Prayers*, OtSt 55. Edited by Bob Becking and Eric Peels. Leiden: Brill, 2007.

_____. *The Psalms in Form: The Hebrew Psalter in its Poetic Shape.* Leiden: Brill, 2002.

_____. *Major Poems of the Hebrew Bible: At the Interface of Hermeneutics and Structural Analysis.* SSN 41. Assen: Uitgeverij Van Gorcum, 2000.

_____. *Major Poems of the Hebrew Bible: At the Interface of Prosody and Structural Analysis. Volume 3: The Remaining 65 Psalms.* SSN 47. Assen: Van Gorcum, 2003.

Fokkelman, J. P. and Gary A. Rendsburg. "NGDH NH LKL 'MW (Psalm CXVI 14B, 18B)." *VT* 53 (2003): 328–36.

Folger, Arie. "Understanding Psalm 46." *JBQ* 41 (2013): 35–43.

Fontaine, Carole and Athalya Brenner, eds. *A Feminist Companion to Wisdom and Psalms.* Feminist Companion to the Bible 2. New York: T&T Clark, 1998.

Foster, Robert L. "*Topoi* of Praise in the Call to Praise Psalms: Toward a *Theo*logy of the Book of Psalms." Pages 75–88 in *My Words are Lovely: Studies in the Rhetoric of the Psalms,* LHBOTS 467. Edited by Robert Foster and David M. Howard, Jr. New York: T&T Clark, 2008.

Fox, Michael. "The Rhetoric of Ezekiel's Vision of the Valley of the Bones." *HUCA* 51 (1980): 1–15.

Franz, Matthias. *Der barmherzige und gnädige Gott: Die Gnadenrede vom Sinai (Exodus 34, 6–7) und ihre Parallelen im Alten Testament und seiner Umwelt.* Volume 20. Stuttgart: Kohlhammer, 2003.

Garrett, Mary. "Classical Chinese Conceptions of Argumentation and Persuasion." *Argumentation and Advocacy* 29 (1993): 105–15.

Gerstenberger, Erhard. "Literatur zu den Psalmen." *VF* 17 (1972): 82–99.

_____. "Psalms." Pages 179–233 in *Old Testament Form Criticism.* Trinity University Monograph Series in Religion 2. Edited by J. H. Hayes. San Antonio: Trinity University Press, 1974.

_____. *Der bittende Mensch: Bittritual und Klagelied des Einzelnen im Alten Testament.* WMANT 51. Neukirchen-Vluyn: Neukirchener Verlag, 1980.

_____. "The Lyrical Literature." Pages 409–44 in *The Hebrew Bible and Its Modern Interpreters.* Edited by D. A. Knight and G. M. Tucker. Chico, CA: Scholars Press, 1985.

_____. *Psalms: Part 1: With an Introduction to Cultic Poetry.* FOTL 14. Grand Rapids: Eerdmans 1988.

_____. *Psalms: Part 2 and Lamentations.* Forms of Old Testament Literature 15. Grand Rapids: Eerdmans, 2001.

Gill, Sam. "Prayer." Pages 7367–72 in *Encyclopedia of Religion.* Edited by Lindsay Jones. 11 vols. New York: MacMillan, 2004

Gillingham, Susan. *Psalms through the Centuries.* Blackwell Bible Commentaries. Oxford: Blackwell, 2008.

Girard, M. *Les psaumes redécouverts: De la structure au sens.* 3 vols. Quebec: Belarmin, 1994–1996.

Gitay, Yehoshua. *Prophecy and Persuasion: A Study of Isaiah 40–48.* Bonn: Linguistica Biblica, 1981.

_____. "Rhetorical Criticism." Pages 135–52 in *To Each Its Own Meaning: An Introduction to Biblical Criticisms and Their Application.* Edited by Steven L. McKenzie and Stephen R. Haynes. Louisville: Westminster/John Knox, 1993.

Glass, Jonathan T. "Some Observations on Psalm 19." Pages 147–59 in *Listening Heart: Essays in Wisdom and the Psalms in Honour of Roland E. Murphy.* Edited by Kenneth Hoglund. JSOTSup 58. Sheffield: Sheffield, 1987.

Goulder, Michael. *The Psalms of the Sons of Korah.* JSOTSup 20. Sheffield: Sheffield, 1982.

Goldingay, John. "The Dynamic Cycle of Praise and Prayer in the Psalms." *JSOT* 6 (1981): 85–90.

_____. *Psalms: Volume 1: Psalms 1–41.* Edited by Tremper Longman. BCOTWP. Grand Rapids: Baker, 2006.

_____. *Psalms: Volume 3: Psalms 90–150.* Edited by Tremper Longman. BCOTWP. Grand Rapids: Baker Academic, 2008.

Grabenhorst, Thomas Kyrill. *Das argumentum a fortiori.* Schweiz: Lang, 1990.

Grant, Jaime. "Poetics." Pages 187–225 in *Words & the Word: Explorations in Biblical Interpretation & Literary Theory.* Edited by David Firth and Jamie Grant. Downers Grove, IL: IVP, 2008.

Grassi, Ernesto. *Rhetoric as Philosophy: The Humanist Tradition.* University Park: Pennsylvania State University Press, 1980.

Gregory, Bradley C. "The Legal Background of the Metaphor for Forgiveness in Psalm CIII 12." *VT* 56 (2006): 549–51.

Gunkel, Hermann. "Psalm 46: An Interpretation." *The Biblical World* 21 (1903): 28–31.

_____. *Ausgewahlte Psalmen: Ubersetzt und Erklart.* 4th ed. Göttingen: Vandenhoeck & Ruprecht, 1917.

_____. "Psalmen." Pages 1927–49 in *Die Religion in Geschichte und Gegenwart: Handwörterbuch in gemeinverständlicher Darstellung.* Vol. 4. Edited by Freidrich Schiele und Leopold Richarnad. Tübingen: J. C. B. Mohr, 1913.

Gunkel, Hermann. *Die Religion in Geschicht und Gegenwart.* Vol. 1. Tübingen: Mohr, 1913.

_____. *The Psalms: A Form-Critical Introduction.* Translated by Thomas Homer. Philadelphia: Fortress, 1967.

Gunkel, Hermann and Joachim Begrich, *Einleitung in die Psalmen: Die Gattungen der religiösen Lyrik Israels.* Göttingen: Vandenhoeck & Ruprecht, 1933.

_____. *Introduction to the Psalms: The Genres of the Religious Lyric of Israel.* Translated by James Nogalski. Macon, GA: Mercer University Press, 1998.

Haller, M. "Ein Jahrzehnt Psalmenforschung." *Theologische Rundschau* 1 (1929): 377–402.

Harding, T. Swann. "Science at the Tower of Babel." *Philosophy of Science* 5 (1938): 338–53.

Harrelson, Walter. "Psalm 19: A Meditation on God's Glory in the Heavens and in God's Law." Pages 141–47 in *Worship and the Hebrew Bible: Essays in Honour of John T. Willis.* Edited by M. Patrick Graham. JSOTSup 284. Sheffield: Sheffield, 1999.

Harrod, R. F. *Foundations of Inductive Logic.* London: Macmillan, 1956.

Hehn, J. *Siebenzahl und Sabbat bei den Babyloniern und im Alten Testament: Eine religionsgschichtliche Studie.* LSS. Leipzig: J. C. Hinrichs, 1907.

Heidegger, Martin. "The Origin of the Work of Art." Pages 15–86 in *Poetry, Language, Thought.* Translated by Albert Hofstadter. New York: HarperPerennial, 1971.

Hengstenberg, E. W. *Commentar über die Psalmen.* 3 vols. Berlin: Ludwig Oehmigke, 1842–1849.

Herrick, James. *The History and Theory of Rhetoric*. 4th ed. Boston: Pearson, 2009.

Hirsch, Jr., E. D. *Validity in Interpretation*. New Haven: Yale University Press, 1967.

Holladay, William. *The Psalms through Three Thousand Years: Prayerbook of a Cloud of Witnesses*. Minneapolis: Fortress, 1993.

Holland, Virginia. "Rhetorical Criticism: A Burkeian Method." *Quarterly Journal of Speech* 39 (1953): 444–50.

Holyoak, Keith and Hee Seung Lee "Absence Makes the Thought Grow Stronger: Reducing Structural Overlap Can Increase Inductive Strength." Pages 297–302 in *Proceedings of the Thirtieth Annual Conference of the Cognitive Science Society*. Edited by V. B. Love Sloutsky, and K. McRae. Austin: Cognitive Science Society, 2008.

Hossfeld, Frank-Lothar and Erich Zenger. *Psalms 2: A Commentary on Psalms 51–100*. Hermeneia. Translated by Linda Maloney. Minneapolis: Fortress 2005.

_____. *Psalms 3: A Commentary on Psalms 101–150*. Hermeneia. Translated by Linda Maloney. Minneapolis: Fortress, 2011.

Howard, Jr. David M. *The Structure of Psalms 93–100*. Winona Lake, IN: Eisenbrauns, 1997.

_____. "Rhetorical Criticism in Old Testament Studies." *BBR* 4 (1994): 87–104.

_____. "Recent Trends in Psalm Study." Pages 329–68 in *The Face of Old Testament Studies: A Survey of Contemporary Approaches*. Edited by David W. Baker and Bill T. Arnold. Grand Rapids: Baker, 1999.

_____. "Psalm 88 and the Rhetoric of Lament." Pages 132–46 in *My Words are Lovely: Studies in the Rhetoric of the Psalms*. Edited by Robert Foster and David M. Howard, Jr. LHBOTS 467. New York: T&T Clark, 2008.

Humbert, Paul. "La relation de Genèse 1 et du Psaume 104 avec la liturgie du Nouvel-An israélite," Pages 78–80 in *Opuscules d'un hébraïsant*. Edited by Paul Humbert. Neuchâtel: Secrétariat de l'Universit, 1958.

Jacobson, Rolf. "The Altar of Certitude": Reflections on the 'Setting' and Rhetorical Interpretation of the Psalms." Pages 3–18 in *My Words are Lovely: Studies in the Rhetoric of the Psalms*. Edited by Robert Foster and David M. Howard, Jr. LHBOTS 467. New York: T&T Clark, 2008.

_____, ed. *Soundings in the Theology of Psalms: Perspectives and Methods in Contemporary Scholarship*. Minneapolis: Fortress, 2010.

Jacobsen, Thorkild. *The Treasures of Darkness: A History of Mesopotamian Religion*. New Haven: Yale University Press, 1976.

Jackson, J. J. and M. Kessler, eds. *Rhetorical Criticism: Essays in Honor of James Muilenburg*. Pittsburgh: Pickwick, 1974.

Jakobson, Roman. *Language in Literature*. London: Belknap, 1987.

Janowski, Bernd. "Dankbarkeit: Ein anthropologischer Grundbegriff im Spiegel der toda Psalmen." Pages 91–136 in *Ritual und Poesie: Formen und Orte religiöser Dichtung im Alten Orient, im Judentum und im Christentum*. Edited by Erich Zenger. Herders biblische Studien 36. Freiburg: Herder, 2003.

Jensen, Vernon. "Rhetorical Emphasis of Taoism." *Rhetorica* 5 (1987): 219–29.

Jobling, David. "Deconstruction and the Political Analysis of Biblical Texts: A Jamesonian Reading of Psalm 72." *Semeia* 59 (1992): 95–127.

Johnson, A. R. "The Role of the King in the Jerusalem Cultus." Pages 71–111 in *The Labyrinth: Further Studies in the Relation between Myth and Ritual in the Ancient World*. Edited by S. H. Hooke. New York: Macmillan, 1935.

_____. "The Psalms." Pages 162–209 in *The Old Testament and Modern Study*. Edited by H. H. Rowley (Oxford: Oxford, 1951).

Kapelrud, Arvid. "Number Seven in Ugaritic Texts." *VT* 18 (1968): 494–99.

_____. "Scandinavian Research in the Psalms after Mowinckel." *Annual of the Swedish Theological Institute* 4 (1965): 148–62.

Keel, Othmar. *The Symbolism of the Biblical World: Ancient Near Eastern Iconography and the Book of Psalms*. Translated by Timothy Hallett. Winona Lake, IN: Eisenbrauns, 1997.

Kelly, Sidney. "Psalm 46: A Study in Imagery." *JBL* 89 (1970): 305–12.

Kennedy, George. *New Testament Interpretation Through Rhetorical Criticism*. Chapel Hill: University of North Carolina Press, 1984.

_____. *Comparative Rhetoric: An Historical and Cross-Cultural Introduction*. Oxford: Oxford University Press, 1998.

Kinneavy, James, Stephen Paul Witte, Neil Nakadate, and Roger Cherry. *A Rhetoric of Doing: Essays on Written Discourse in Honor of James L. Kinneavy*. Carbondale: Southern Illinois University Press, 1992.

Kern, Phillip. *Rhetoric and Galatians: Assessing an Approach to Paul's Epistle*. Society for New Testament Studies Monograph Series 101. Cambridge: Cambridge University Press, 1998.

Kim, Yeol and Herrie van Rooy. "Reading Psalm 78 Multidimensionally: The Dimension of the Reader." *Scriptura* 88 (2005): 101–17.

Kirkpatrick, Alexander F. *The Book of Psalms*. Cambridge: Cambridge University Press, 1902.

Knierim, Rolf P. "On the Theology of Psalm 19." Pages 439–58 in *Ernten, was man sät*. Neukirchen-Vluyn: Neukirchener Verlag, 1991.

Knobnya, Svetlana. "God the Father in the Old Testament." *EuroJTh* 20 (2011): 139–48.

Kraus, Hans-Joachim. *Psalms 1–59: A Continental Commentary*. Translated by Hilton Oswald. Minneapolis: Fortress, 1988.

_____. *Psalms 60–150: A Continental Commentary*. Translated by Hilton Oswald. Minneapolis: Fortress, 1993.

Kugel, James L. *The Idea of Biblical Poetry: Parallelism and Its History*. Baltimore: Johns Hopkins University Press, 1998.

Kuntz, Kenneth. "Psalm 18: A Rhetorical Critical Analysis." *JSOT* 26 (1983): 3–31.

_____. "King Triumphant: A Rhetorical Study of Psalms 20–21." *Harvard Annual Review* 10 (1987): 157–76.

Lanham, Richard A. *A Handlist of Rhetorical Terms.* Berkeley: University of California Press, 1991.

Lenzi, Alan ed. *Reading Akkadian Prayers and Hymns: An Introduction.* ANEM 3. Atlanta: Scholars Press, 2011.

Levenson, Jon D. "The Temple and the World." *JR* 64 (1984): 275–98.

_____. *Creation and the Persistence of Evil: The Jewish Drama of Divine Omnipotence.* San Francisco: Harper & Row, 1988.

Levine, Herbert. *Sing unto God a New Song: A Contemporary Reading of the Psalms.* Bloomington: Indiana University Press, 1995.

Lewis, C. S. *Reflections on the Psalms.* Orlando, FL: Harcourt, 1958.

Lipson, Carol and Roberta Binkley, eds. *Rhetoric Before and Beyond the Greeks.* Albany: State University of New York Press, 2004.

_____. *Ancient Non-Greek Rhetorics.* West Lafayette, IN: Parlor, 2009.

Lo, Alison. *Job 28 as Rhetoric: An Analysis of Job 28 in the Context of Job 22–31.* VTSup 97. Leiden: Brill, 2003.

Longinus. *On the Sublime.* Translated by W. H. Fyfe. LCL 23. Cambridge, Harvard University Press, 1995.

Lowth, Robert. *Lectures on the Sacred Poetry of the Hebrews.* Translated by G. Gregory. Andover: Crocker & Brewster, 1829.

Lu, Xing. *Rhetoric in Ancient China, Fifth to Third Century B.C.E.: A Comparison with Classical Greek Rhetoric.* Columbia: University of South Carolina Press, 1998.

Lundbom, Jack. *Jeremiah: A Study in Ancient Hebrew Rhetoric.* SBLDS 18. Missoula, MT: Scholars Press, 1975.

Matthews, Victor. *The Hebrew Propets and Their Social World: An Introduction.* 2nd ed. Grand Rapids: Baker Academic, 2012.

Mattlock, Michael. *Discovering the Traditions of Prose Prayers in Early Jewish Literature,* LSTS 81. New York: T&T Clark, 2012.

Mays, James Luther. "The Place of the Torah-Psalms in the Psalter." *JBL* 106 (1987): 3–12.

_____. *The Lord Reigns: A Theological Handbook to the Psalms.* Louisville: Westminster, 1994.

_____. "Past, Present, and Prospect in Psalms Study." Pages 147–56 in *Old Testament Interpretation: Past, Present, and Future: Essays in Honor of Gene M. Tucker*. Edited by James Luther Mays, David L. Petersen, and Kent Richards. Nashville: Abingdon, 1995.

McCann, J. Clinton. *Psalms*. Vol. 4, *New Interpreter's Bible*. Nashville: Abingdon, 1996.

_____. *A Theological Introduction to the Book of Psalms: The Psalms as Torah*. Nashville: Abingdon 1993.

McFall, Leslie. *The Enigma of the Hebrew Verbal System*. Historic Texts and Interpreters in Biblical Scholarship 2. Sheffield: Almond, 1982.

McKeon, Richard. *Rhetoric: Essays in Invention and Discovery*. Edited by Mark Backman. Woodbridge, CT: Ox Bow, 1987.

Meynet, Roland. *Rhetorical Analysis: An Introduction to Biblical Rhetoric*. Library of Hebrew Bible/Old Testament Studies 256. Sheffield: Sheffield Academic, 1998.

Milgrom, Jacob. "Cultic שגגה and Its Influence in Psalms and Job." *JQR* 58 (1967): 115–25.

Mill, John Stuart. "What is Poetry?" Pages 56–72 in *John Stuart Mill: Literary Essays*. Edited by Edward Alexander. Indianapolis: Bobbs-Merrill, 1967.

Millard, Matthias. *Die Komposition des Psalters: Ein formgeschichtlicher Anstaz*. FAT 9. Tübingen: Mohr, 1994.

Miller, Patrick. "Prayer as Persuasion: The Rhetoric and Intention of Prayer." *Word & World* 4 (1993): 356–62.

_____. "Kingship, Torah Obedience, and Prayer: The Theology of Psalms 15–24." Pages 127–42 in *Neue Wege der Psalmenforschung: Für Walter Beyerlin*. Edited by Erich Zenger. Freiburg: Herder, 1994.

_____. *They Cried to the Lord: The Form and Theology of Biblical Prayer*. Minneapolis: Fortress, 1994.

Mitchell, M. *Analogy-Making as Perception*. Cambridge: Bradford, 1993.

Möller, Karl. *Prophet in Debate: The Rhetoric of Persuasion in the Book of Amos*. JSOTSup 372. Sheffield: Sheffield, 2003.

_____. "Reading, Singing and Praying the Law: An Exploration of the Performative, Self-Involving, Commissive Language of Psalm 101." Pages 111–37 in *Reading the Law: Studies in Honour of Gordon J. Wenham*. Edited by J. G. McConville and Karl Möller. LHBOTS 461. London: T&T Clark, 2007.

Montgomery, J. A. "Recent Developments in the Study of the Psalms." *Anglican Theological Review* 16 (1934): 185–98.

Morgenstern, Julian. "Psalms 8 and 19a." *HUCA* 19 (1946): 491–523.

Mowinckel, Sigmund. *Psalmenstudien*. 4 vols. Skrifter utgitt av Det Norske Videnskaps Akademi i Oslo. Kristiania: Dybwad, 1921–1924.

_____. *Offersang og sangoffer*. Oslo: Aschehoug, 1951.

_____. *The Psalms in Israel's Worship*. Translated by Dafydd R. Ap-Thomas. 2 vols. New York: Blackwell, 1967.

_____. "Psalm Criticism between 1900 and 1935 (Ugarit and Psalm Exegesis)." *VT* 5 (1955): 13–33.

Muffs, Y. *Studies in the Aramaic Legal Papyri from Elephantine*. Leiden: Brill, 1969.

Muilenburg, James. "Form Criticism and Beyond." *JBL* 88 (1969): 1–18.

Murphy, James J., et al. *A Synoptic History of Classical Rhetoric*. 3rd ed. New York: Routledge, 2003.

Murphy, James. "The Four Faces of Rhetoric: A Progress Report." *College Composition and Communication* 17 (1966): 55–59.

Nasuti, Harry. *Defining the Sacred Songs: Genre, Tradition and the Post-Critical Interpretation of the Psalms*. JSOTSup 218. Sheffield: Sheffield, 1999.

_____. "The Sacramental Function of the Psalms in Contemporary Scholarship and Liturgical Practice." Pages 78–98 in *Psalms and Practice: Worship, Virtue, and Authority*. Edited by Stephen Reid. Collegeville, MN: Liturgical Press, 2001.

Neihr, H. "Host of Heaven," Pages 428–30 in *Dictionary of Deities and Demons*. Edited by Karel Van der Toorn and Bob Becking. Leiden: Brill, 1999.

Nel, Philip. "Psalm 19: The Unbearable Lightness of Perfection." *JNSL* 30 (2004): 103–17.

Nielsen, Kirsten. "The Variety of Metaphors about God in the Psalter: Deconstruction and Reconstruction?" *SJOT* 16 (2002): 151–59.

O'Connor, Michael. *Hebrew Verse Structure.* 2nd ed. Winona Lake, IN: Eisenbrauns, 1997.

Ogden, Graham. "Psalm 60: Its Rhetoric, Form, and Function." *JSOT* 31 (1985): 83–94.

O'Kennedy, D. F. "The Relationship between Justice and Forgiveness in Psalm 103." *Scriptura* (1998): 109–21.

Olbricht, T.H. "Briggs, Charles." Pages 219–23 in *Dictionary of Major Biblical Interpreters.* Edited by Donald McKim. Downers Grove, IL: IVP Academic, 2007.

Pardee, Dennis. "The Preposition in Ugaritic." *UF* 8 (1976): 215–322.

Parker, Simon B. and Mark S. Smith. *Ugaritic Narrative Poetry.* Atlanta: Scholars Press, 1997.

Patrick, Dale. *The Rhetoric of Revelation in the Bible.* Overtures to Biblical Theology. Minneapolis: Fortress, 1999.

Petersen, David and Kent Richards. *Interpreting Hebrew Poetry.* Minneapolis: Fortress, 1992.

Perelman, Chaim and William Kluback. *The New Rhetoric and the Humanities: Essays on Rhetoric and Its Applications.* London: D. Reidel 1979.

Perelman, Chaim and Lucie Olbrechts-Tyteca. *The New Rhetoric: A Treatise on Argumentation.* Translated by John Wilkinson. Notre Dame: University of Notre Dame Press, 1969.

Perowne, J. J. S. *The Book of Psalms.* 7th ed. 2 vols. Andover: Draper, 1890.

Phillips, Peter. "Rhetoric." Pages 226–65 in *Words & the Word: Explorations in Biblical Interpretation and Literary Theory.* Edited by David Firth and Jaime Grant. Downers Grove, IL: IVP Academic, 2009.

Pickut, William D. "Additional Observations Relating to the Legal Significance of Psalm CIII 12." *VT* 58 (2008): 550–56.

Plato, *Lysis. Symposium. Gorgias.* Translated by W. M. Lamb. LCL 166. Cambridge: Harvard University Press, 1925.

Pleins, John. *The Psalms: Songs of Tragedy, Hope, and Justice.* Bible and Liberation. Maryknoll, NY: Orbis, 1993.

Plett, Heinrich. *Literary Rhetoric: Concepts-Structure-Analyses.* International Studies in the History of Rhetoric 2. Leiden: Brill, 2010.

Rahlfs, A. *'Ani und 'Anau in den Psalmen.* Göttingen: Vandenhoeck & Ruprecht, 1892.

Rice, Gene. "An Exposition of Psalm 103." *JRT* 39 (1982): 55–61.

Richards, I. A. *The Philosophy of Rhetoric.* Oxford: Oxford University Press, 1965.

Ricœr, Paul. *The Rule of Metaphor: Multi-disciplinary Studies of the Creation of Meaning in Language.* Toronto: University of Toronto Press, 1977.

_____. "Naming God." Pages 166–81 in *Rhetorical Invention and Religious Inquiry.* Edited by Walter Jost and Wendy Olmstead. New Haven: Yale University Press, 2000.

Roberts, J. J. M. "The Davidic Origin of the Zion Tradition." *JBL* 92 (1973): 329–44.

_____. "Mowinckel's Enthronement Festival: A Review." Pages 97–115 in *The Book of Psalms: Composition and Reception.* Edited by Peter Flint & Patrick Miller. VTSup 99. Leiden: Brill, 2005.

Robertson, David. *Linguistic Evidence in Dating Early Hebrew Poetry.* SBLDS 3. Missoula: Scholars Press, 1972.

Rogerson, John. *Old Testament Criticism in the Nineteenth Century: England and Germany.* Minneapolis: Fortress, 1984.

_____. "Lowth, Robert." Pages 679–82 in *Dictionary of Major Biblical Interpreters.* Edited by Donald McKim. Downers Grove, IL: IVP Academic, 2007.

Rohland, Edzard. *Die Bedeutung der Erwählungstraditionen Israels für die Eschatologie der alttestamentlichen Propheten.* ThD. diss., Ruprecht-Karls-Universität Heidelberg, 1956.

Ross, Allen. *A Commentary on the Psalms: Vol. 1.* Grand Rapids: Kregel, 2011.

Russell, Donald and Nigel Wilson. *Menander Rhetor*. Oxford: Clarendon, 1981.

Saebø, Magne, ed. *Hebrew Bible/Old Testament: The History of Its Interpretation: Volume II: From the Renaissance to the Enlightenment*. Göttingen: Vandenhoeck & Ruprecht, 2008.

_____, ed. *Hebrew Bible/Old Testament: The History of Its Interpretation: Volume I: From the Beginning to the Middle Ages. Part II: The Middle Ages*. Göttingen: Vandenhoeck & Ruprecht, 2000.

_____, ed. *Hebrew Bible/Old Testament: The History of Its Interpretation: Volume I: From the Beginning to the Middle Ages. Part I: Antiquity*. Göttingen: Vandenhoeck & Ruprecht, 1996.

Sakenfeld, Katharine Doob. *The Meaning of Hesed in the Hebrew Bible: A New Inquiry*. HSM 17. Atlanta: Scholars Press, 1978.

Sarna, Nahum M. *Songs of the Heart: An Introduction to the Book of Psalms*. New York: Schocken, 1993.

Scharbert, Josef. "Formgeschichte und Exegese von Ex 34:6f und seiner Parallelen." *Biblica* 38 (1957): 130–50.

Schökel, L. Alonso. *A Manual of Hebrew Poetics*. SubBi 11. Rome: Pontifical Biblical Institute, 1988.

Schottroff, Luise and Marie-Theres Wacker, eds. *Feminist Biblical Intrepretation: A Compendium of Critical Commentary on the Books of the Bible and Related Literature*. Grand Rapids: Eerdmans, 2012.

Sloan, Thomas. "Rhetorical Analysis of John Donne's 'The Prohibition.'" Pages 3–15 in *Rhetorical Analysis of Literary Works*. Edited by Edward Corbett. London: Oxford University Press, 1969.

Sloane, Thomas, ed. *Encyclopedia of Rhetoric*. Oxford: Oxford University Press, 2001.

Slomkowski, P. *Aristotle's Topics*. Edited by J. Mansfeld et al. PhA 74. Leiden: Brill, 1997.

Smend, Rudolf. "Über das Ich der Psalmen." *ZAW* 18 (1888): 49–147

Smith, Arthur Y. "Kenneth Burke's Concept of Identification in the Perception and Evocation of Literature." *Communicator* 7 (1977): 69–76.

Smith, Kevin Gary and Bill Domeris. "A Brief History of Psalms Studies." *Conspectus* 6 (2008): 97–119.

Smith, Mark S. "Setting and Rhetoric in Psalm 23." *JSOT* 41 (1988): 61–66.

Spieckermann, Hermann. "Barmherzig und gnädig ist der Herr." *ZAW* 102 (1990): 1–18.

_____. "Lieben und Glauben: Beobachtungen in Psalm 116." Pages 266–75 in *Meilenstein: Festgabe für Herbert Donner zum 16. Februar 1995*. Edited by Manfred Weippert and Stefan Timm. Weisbaden: Harrassowitz, 1995.

Stamm, J. J. "Ein Vierteljahrhundert Psalmenforschung." *Theologische Rundschau* 26 (1955): 1–68.

Stek, John H. "Psalm 103: Its Thematic Architecture." Pages 23–38 in *Text and Community*. Sheffield: Sheffield 2007.

Stevenson, C. L. "On 'What is a Poem?'" *Philosophical Review* 66 (1957): 329–62.

Stratton, Beverly. *Out of Eden: Reading, Rhetoric, and Ideology in Genesis 2–3*. JSOTSup 208. Sheffield: Sheffield Academic, 1995.

Sutton, Jane. "Kairos" Pages 412–15 in *Encyclopedia of Rhetoric*. Edited by Thomas Sloane. Oxford: Oxford University Press, 2001.

Sustein, C. "On Analogical Reasoning." *Harvard Law Review* 106 (1993): 741–91.

Tanner, Beth LaNeel. *The Book of Psalms through the Lens of Intertexuality*. StBibLit 26. New York: Lang, 2001.

Terrien, Samuel. *The Psalms: Strophic Structure and Theological Commentary*. Grand Rapids: Eerdmans 2003.

Thagard, C. Eliasmith and P. "Integrating Structure and Meaning: A Distributed Model of Analogical Mapping." *Cognitive Science* 25 (2001): 245–86.

Thiselton, Anthony. *New Horizons in Hermeneutics: The Theory and Practice of Transforming Biblical Reading*. Grand Rapids: Zondervan, 1992.

Thom, Johan Carl. "Justice in the Sermon on the Mount: An Aristotelian Reading." *NovT* 51 (2009): 314–38.

Too, You Lee. "Epideictic Genre." Pages 251–57 in *Encyclopedia of Rhetoric*. Edited by T. Sloane. Oxford: Oxford University Press, 2001.

Trible, Phyllis. *Rhetorical Criticism: Context, Method, and the Book of Jonah*. Minneapolis: Fortress, 1994.

Trublet, Jacques. "Approche canonique des Psaumes du Hallel." Pages 339–76 in *The Composition of the Book of Psalms*. Edited by Eric Zenger. BETL 238. Leuven: Peeters, 2010.

Tull, Patricia. "Rhetorical Criticism and Intertextuality," Pages 156–82 in *To Each Its Own Meaning: An Introduction to Biblical Criticisms and Their Application*. Edited by Steven McKenzie and Stephen Haynes. Louisville: Westminster, 1999.

Van der Lugt, Pieter. *Cantos and Strophes in Biblical Hebrew Poetry: with Special Reference to the First Book of the Psalter*. Edited by Bob Becking. *OtSt* 53. Leiden: Brill, 2006.

_____. *Cantos and Strophes in Biblical Hebrew Poetry II: Psalms 42–89*. Edited by Bob Becking. *OtSt* 57. Leiden: Brill, 2010.

Van der Toorn, Karel. *Family Religion in babylonia, Syria, and Israel: Continuity and Change in the Forms of Religious Life*. Studies in the History and Culture of the Ancient Near East 7. (Leiden: Brill, 1996).

_____. *Scribal Culture and the Making of the Hebrew Bible*. Cambridge: Harvard University Press, 2007.

VanGemeren, Willem and Jason Stanghelle. "A Critical-Realistic Reading of the Psalm Titles," Pages 281–301 in *Do Historical Matters Matter to Faith? A Critical Appraisal of Modern and Post-Modern Approaches to Scripture*. Edited by James Hoffmeier et al. Wheaton, IL: Crossway, 2012.

VanGemeren, Willem. "Psalms." Pages 1–882 in *Expositor's Bible Commentary*. Edited by Frank Gaebelein. Grand Rapids: Zondervan, 1991.

Vanoni, G. *"Du bist doch unser Vater" (Jes 63, 16): Zur Gottesvorstellung des Ersten Testaments*. Stuttgart: Katholisches Bibelwerk, 1995.

Vatz, Richard. "The Myth of the Rhetorical Situation." *Philosophy and Rhetoric* 6 (1973): 154–61.

Vesco, Jean-Luc. *Le Psautier de David: Traduit et Commenté.* 2 vols. Paris: Cerf, 2006.

Vickers, Brian. *In Defense of Rhetoric.* Oxford: Clarendon, 1989.

Wagner, Andreas. *Beten und Bekennen: Über Psalmen.* Newkirchen-Vluyn: Neukirchener Verlag, 2008.

Wagner, J. Ross. "From the Heavens to the Heart: The Dynamics of Psalm 19 as Prayer." *CBQ* 61 (1999): 245–61.

Walker, Jeffrey. "Aristotle's Lyric: Re-Imagining the Rhetoric of Epideictic Song." *College English* 51 (1989): 5–28.

Waltke, Bruce and James Houston. *The Psalms as Christian Worship: A Historical Commentary.* Grand Rapids: Eerdmans, 2010.

Walton, John. *Ancient Near Eastern Thought and the Old Testament: Introducing the Conceptual World of the Hebrew Bible.* Grand Rapids: Baker Academic, 2006.

_____. "Retribution." Pages 647–55 in *Dictionary of the Old Testament: Wisdom, Poetry and Writings.* Edited by Tremper Longman and Peter Enns. Downers Grove: IVP Academic, 2008.

_____. *Genesis 1 as Ancient Cosmology.* Winona Lake, IN: Eisenbrauns, 2011.

Warren, Andy. "Modality, Reference and Speech Acts in the Psalms." *Tyndale Bulletin* 53 (2002): 149–52.

Watson, Duane and Alan Hauser. *Rhetorical Criticism of the Bible: A Comprehensive Bibliography with Notes on History and Method.* Leiden: Brill, 1994.

Weiser, Artur. *The Psalms: A Commentary.* OTL. Translated by Herbert Hartwell. Philadelphia: Westminster, 1962.

Wellhausen, Julius. *The Book of Psalms.* Polychrome Bible. Translated by H. H. Furness et al. London: Clarke, 1898.

Wells, Bruce. "Law and Practice," Pages 183–95 in *A Companion to the Ancient Near East.* Edited by Daniel Snell. Oxford: Blackwell, 2005.

Wendland, Ernst ed. *Discourse Perspectives on Hebrew Poetry in the Scriptures.* United Bible Society 7. New York: United Bible Society, 1994.

Wenham, Gordon. "Reflections on Singing the Ethos of God." *Euro-JTh* 18 (2009): 115–24.

Wenham, Gordon. *Psalms as Torah: Reading Biblical Song Ethically.* Grand Rapids: Baker Academic, 2012.

Westermann, Claus. *Lob und Klage in den Psalmen.* Göttingen: Vandenhoeck & Ruprecht, 1977.

_____. *Praise and Lament in the Psalms.* Translated by Keith Crim. Atlanta: John Knox, 1981.

_____. *Elements of Old Testament Theology.* Translated by Douglas Scott. Atlanta: John Knox 1982.

_____. *Prophetic Oracles of Salvation in the Old Testament.* Translated by Keith Crim. Louisville: Westminster, 1991.

Wette, W. M. L. de. *Beiträge zur Einleitung in das Alte Testament.* 2 vols. Halle: Schimmelpfennig, 1806–1807.

_____. *Commentar über die Psalmen.* Heidelberg: J.C.B. Mohr, 1811, 1823, 1829.

Whately, Richard. *Elements of Rhetoric.* London: Longmans, 1867.

Whitley, Charles Francis. "The Semantic Range of Chesed." *Biblica* 62 (1981): 519–26.

Whybray, Norman. *Reading the Psalms as a Book.* JSOTSup 222. Sheffield: Sheffield Academic Press, 1996.

Wieringen, A. "Psalm 122: Syntax and the Position of the I-Figure and the Text-Immanent Reader." Pages 745–54 in *Composition of the Book of Psalms.* Edited by Erich Zenger. BETL 238. Leuven: Paris, 2010.

Willis, Timothy M. "'So Great is His Steadfast Love': A Rhetorical Analysis of Psalm 103." *Biblica* 72 (1991): 525–37.

Wilson, Gerald. *The Editing of the Hebrew Psalter.* SBLDS 76. Chico, CA: Scholars Press, 1985.

_____. *Psalms, Volume 1.* New International Version Application Commentary. Grand Rapids: Zondervan, 2002.

Wolterstorff, Nicholas. *Art in Action: Toward a Christian Aesthetic.* Grand Rapids: Eerdmans, 1980.

Wuellner, Wilhelm. "Where is Rhetorical Criticism Taking Us?" *CBQ* 49 (1987): 448–63.

Wylie, A. "An Analogy by Any Other Name is Just as Analogical." *Journal of Anthropological Archaeology* 1 (1982): 382–401.

Zakovitch, Yair. "The Interpretive Significance of the Sequence of Psalms 111–112.113–118.119." Pages 215–27 in *Composition of the Book of Psalms.* Edited by Eric Zenger. Leuven: Peeters, 2010.

Zenger, Erich. "The Composition and Theology of the Fifth Book of Psalms, Psalms 107–45." *JSOT* 80 (1998): 77–102.

_____. "Der Psalter als Buch: Beobachtungen zu seiner Enstehung, Komposition und Funktion." Pages 1–57 in *Psalter in Judentum und Christentum.* Edited by E. Zenger. Herders biblische Studien 18. Freiburg im Breisgau: Herder, 1998.

Zulick, Margaret. "The Active Force of Hearing: The Ancient Hebrew Language of Persuasion." *Rhetorica* 10 (1992): 367–80.

_____. "The Agon of Jeremiah: On the Dialogic Invention of Prophetic Ethos." *Quarterly Journal of Speech* 78 (1992): 125–48.

Zyl, Van. "Psalm 19." Pages 146–7 in *Studia biblica et semitica: Festschrift Theodoro Christiano Vriezen.* Edited by W. C. Van Unnik and A. S. Van Der Woude. Wangeningen: Veenman, 1966.

Scripture Index

EXTRABIBLICAL SOURCES

Subject Index

Author Index

www.ingramcontent.com/pod-product-compliance
Lightning Source LLC
Chambersburg PA
CBHW062046080426
42734CB00012B/2567